The BIG BOOK of Baritone Ukulele Chords

An In-Depth Exploration of D-G-B-E Tuning

HARVEY REID

York, Maine USA

ISBN: 978-1-63029-047-4

PO Box 815 York Maine 03909 USA

www.woodpecker.com

CONTENTS

About This Book

This book grew out of my lifelong fascination with plucked-string fingerboards, and follows a series of extensive chord books in guitar tunings, as well as banjo and mandolin chord books. I have been a professional acoustic musician my entire adult life, and now after almost 50 years of playing stringed instruments, I find myself probing deeper than ever into the mysteries of what make different chords and voicings on behave the way they do on a fingerboard.

Players of the baritone uke seem to use standard tuning almost exclusively, though like any stringed instrument, ukes are sometimes tuned to open chords for beginners and children to have a more successful experience. **In the last section of this book I offer two ground-breaking new ways to play simpler chord fingerings by using partial capos.** I have also published *Baritone Ukulele Simplified*, an entire book of simplified chords on the baritone uke that explores 8 different fretboard environments, including new tunings, partial capos and combinations of the two ideas.

The idea of this book was to provide an accurate, readable and complete library of left-hand fingerings for the instrument in its typical tuning: D-G-B-E. Instead of showing you the easiest or my favorite versions of the various chords, I'm giving you essentially all the reasonable choices, and you can decide which to use. I have become increasingly fascinated with how many total possibilities there are, and how much diversity and complexity can come from even something like a simple major or minor chord, with just three notes occupying the musical landscape. I have also become increasingly intrigued with the decisions, strategies and possibilities that arise from the trying to play a certain group of notes on a fingerboard. Trying to determine which ones were both playable and musical has become a pastime for me, and it really brings the fretboard logic of an instrument into focus.

Because the baritone uke is so often used as a solo instrument, and is not something you see played much in jazz ensembles, I have chosen to include only chords that sound good on their own. In a band, you could play chords that had no root notes, and expect that a guitar or bass (or both) would provide the roots.

I have reached the conclusion that the set of possibilities generated by one stringed instrument in one tuning are enough to occupy our entire mental capacity, and no matter how much I feel like I know where things lie on the fretboard, I am surprised at what I find when I keep digging deeper. Seeing the chord forms laid out on the entire fingerboard the way I show them in this book, you can absorb what is going on visually, in a vital way that is missing when the chords are depicted in the typical way, with only a few frets showing and a numeral to indicate what fret the fingerings occur. Just scanning the book is even quite informative, and you immediately start to get a sense of how the tuning works and how the musical structures map themselves spatially onto it.

Ukuleles and Music Education

When drawn into discussions of what is wrong with music education these days I have always brought up the facts that 1) you aren't allowed to sing and play your instrument at the same time at a music conservatory and 2) you can't major in banjo in college. Ukulele, mandolin and banjo are not an ephemeral trend; they are here to stay. Why can't they find a place in the list of "respectable" instruments that one can devote meaningful time and energy to learning? How long did it take the guitar to find a place in music conservatories? There is nothing inherent about an instrument itself that invites this "lower class" image– all the prejudice and lack of respect come entirely from the way it is perceived.

Essentially all uke players today are self-taught, or they rely on folk-knowledge learning, family, friends, local teachers, books, videos or the internet. The internet is now the village square where we learn from peers and anyone who is willing to share. The point of this book is to offer an in-depth and somewhat scholarly contribution to the pile of mostly "not-in-depth" and "un-scholarly" books, and to provide something of value you can't get from a YouTube video. It would not be reasonable to demonstrate 2000 ukulele chords on a video, since no one would be able to remember them or find particular ones again. The web sites I have visited that claim to show or build chord fingerings seem to be made by computer programmers rather than musicians, and they are all lacking in various important ways.

The amount of information embedded in a musical instrument fingerboard is essentially more than any human brain can retain, which is why I decided to put it in a book like this. The information here is even a bit overwhelming for a smartphone, though I intend to make a digital version of this book so you'll be able to take it with you everywhere you take your instrument. It should work reasonably well on an iPad or graphics-intensive tablet device, though it's easy to get lost in a pile of thousands of chords on a tiny screen.

About Chord Voicings

Players who cannot sight-read are not usually encouraged to try to understand how the notes that make up each chord construct the various voicings, and from my years of studying guitar tunings I have learned that this subject is subtle, valuable and much deeper than it seems at a glance. The tools and terminology of music theory are rooted in piano, choral and orchestral music, and though the plucked-string market is vastly larger than the classical or orchestral ones, there still is no standardized language or approach for determining how musical ideas apply to these instruments.

The ukulele has a much shorter scale length than the guitar, so there are a lot of new chord voicings available that span more than 5 frets on the fingerboard.

The first ones you'll see are #23, 25 and #34, which is a very appealing way to play A7. You can drop the note on the high string down another fret and you'll get #105 which is a memorable A6. #134 is an example of a new kind of voicing (Aadd11) that the short scale allows. When arpeggiated these chords have a striking sound.

When you look at a piano keyboard, for example, it makes total sense to see that a major chord has 3 notes, and that those notes are separated by a certain pattern of "distance" that is represented by keys of a fixed width. Flat the middle of the 3 notes and you get a minor chord. Sharp the 5th to augment the chord. Music theory books generally teach chord theory in terms of *intervals*, which means just two notes. Major chords are usually defined in a theory textbook as "an interval of a *major 3rd* (4 half-steps) followed by an interval of a *minor 3rd* (3 half-steps)." This makes perfect sense on a piano: you can start on any key on the piano, add the pitch that is 4 positions to the right, then the pitch that is 3 more positions higher, and you get a major chord every time.

On a violin, mandolin or bass, where the strings are tuned regularly, with the same musical distance between each string, you can still apply some of this kind of linear thinking to chordal ideas, even though the notes now occupy a 2-dimensional fingerboard and are not just all in a linear layout like a piano. The ukulele is almost tuned in 4ths (only one place has a spacing between strings of 4 frets not 5) but there is much less logical value in applying linear intervallic thinking.

Please relax about names of chords. There are no "official names" for chords, and people use different symbols and abbreviations, like dialects of language. You will often see a capital M7 for major 7th, an add2 or sus2 for what I call an add9, sus for sus4, add4 for add11, etc. A minus sign is often used for minor. I used *Adim* in this book for diminished because there is no convenient typographic symbol in my publishing software for A^0, with the superscript zero, a common symbol used for this chord.

"Enharmonic" Chords

Some chords have special names and other types don't. It's also not uncommon for the same group of notes to have more than one name. The most common example of this is that a minor 7th chord has the same notes as a 6th chord. (Am7= A C E G and C6= C E G A, for example.) Minor 9th chords are often the same notes as major 7th chords, and I have sometimes included both.

There are many oyther instances in music where the same group of notes can make different chords. Normally, the name of the chord would reflect how it is used in context, but in a chord book like this there is no context. An Aadd9 chord with no 3rd has the same notes (A-B-E) as an inversion of an Esus. Which is it? It's both, depending on how you use it:

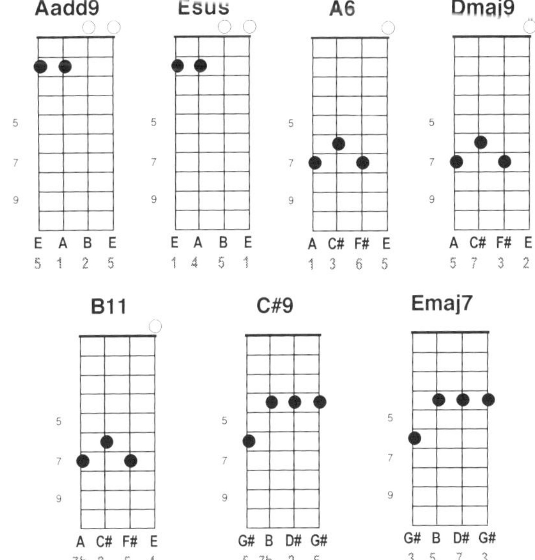

A complex issue underlies all chord books. As a guitar player, I am accustomed to generating the songs myself, and making the chord progressions work means that the chords need to be full-sounding, and they need to define the harmonic structure of the song. My guitar chord books are optimized for solo guitarists and "troubadour-style" players, rather than orchestra or band members. Higher pitched instruments like mandolin or banjo generally don't have the job of defining the harmonic movement of the music and rarely perform solo, so what they play does not require root bass notes at all. The baritone ukulele is very often used alone, so the chords included here reflect that reality.

Terminology

The terminology of music theory behaves like any language, and there are dialects and slang terms that constantly change, and that vary regionally and in different social groups. I may use terms that are not the ones you may be used to, but hopefully you can make the necessary "translations." Guitarists are used to the term "9th" chord, though you'll notice that I use the numeral 2 in the chord diagram, which is the same musical note name as the 9th. Technically, there is somewhere a "root" or lowest numeral 1 against which the other tones are "measured," and adding the 2nd scale tone an octave higher than the 2nd would become the 9th, since the 8th scale degree is the octave. In common language, musicians commonly call them 9th chords, even if the musical 2nd scale pitch is in any octave, and we don't hear musicians talk at all about 16ths or 23rds. The "street language" of chords seems to allows 9ths, 11ths and 13ths, but nothing higher than that.

Likewise, I use the term *add9* to mean that a 2nd scale tone has been added to a 1-3-5 major chord, when others might call it an *add2* or even a *sus2*. There is no logical reason why you couldn't call a chord an *add16* but I have never seen it done. Likewise, I use "sus" just for the 3rd being replaced with the 4th, and I use *add11* to mean that there are both a musical 3rd and a 4th in the chord, and not to mean that the 4th is being added an octave higher. It would make sense to call that an *add4*, but I didn't.

Missing Tones

There isn't a terminology to indicate that a tone is absent from a chord, and a whole set of "thorny issues" appears. It's tough enough on a 6-string guitar to deal with the missing tones in extended chords like 11ths or 13ths, and the ukulele, with even fewer strings makes the problem harder. Two of these Gadd9 chords have no 3rd:

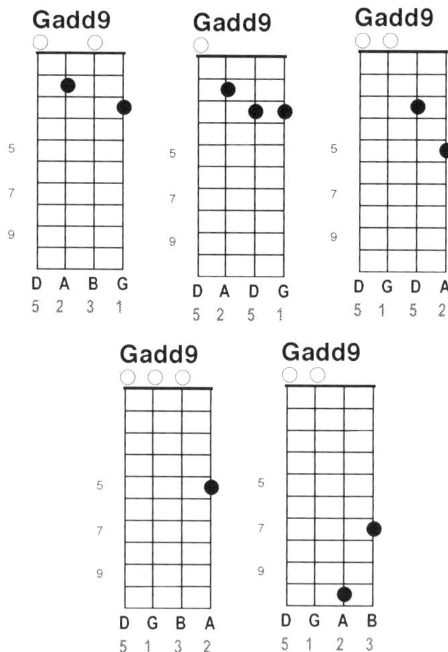

These G9 chords have various missing tones, since the "full" G9 (1-3-5-7b-2) cannot be played: G-B-D-F-A:

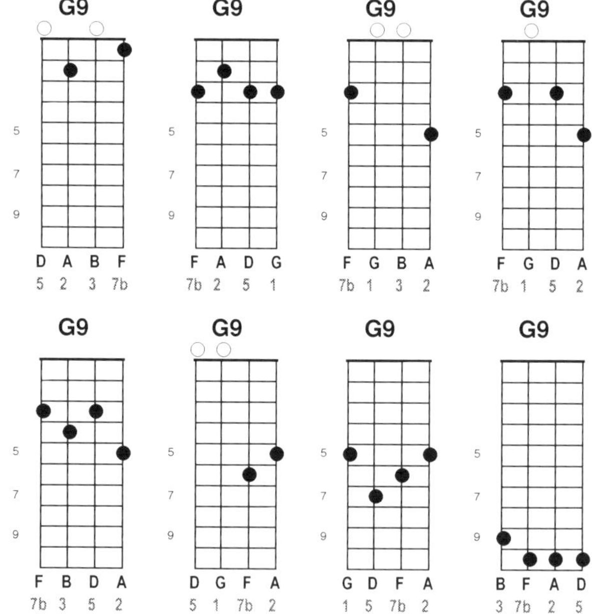

What's In This Book

Even if you just want to play tablature arrangements of instrumental music on the uke, the left-hand positions as shown in this book are really the starting point for understanding how the fingerboard works. A striking or appealing chord voicing in this book could easily be the starting point for a song accompaniment or an instrumental piece, and players of all levels commonly think in terms of putting their fingers in a particular place on the neck, thus creating a "chord shape." Even when we play single-note music, we usually don't just have one finger on the fingerboard at a time, and scales and melodies constantly thread themselves through chord shapes all across the fingerboard.

It's one thing to play a chord that "fits" in a band arrangement, but players often need the best possible chord with the fullest sound.
Chord books for fretted instruments tend to be incomplete and simplistic, and don't even hint at the depth and complexity of the fingerboard or all the musical options. There is a surprising amount of diversity in the voicings and fingerings of any kind of chord, including the simplest ones.

Why most chord books only show 3 or 4 voicings of every chord is a mystery. In any tuning, there are bound to be many more ways to play certain chords than others.

The whole fingerboard is shown for every chord, making it much easier to identify and use them.
You can visually see the "logic" of a chord as you scan all the ways to play it. You can't see this at all on 5-fret diagrams the way other chord books show them. I feel that it is well worth the ink and paper to show the whole fingerboard, to help you grasp the whole instrument and see what is happening.

Possibly the most important feature in this book is that the letter names and musical function of every note in every chord are shown. This is a valuable theory lesson, and allows you to see the voicing and structure of every chord. No other books I have found provide this.

All the chords in this book are playable, and they have all been carefully "hand-tested" and are not generated with software merely cranking out permutations of notes. Like dictionaries of words, choices had to be made about what to include and leave out. Some of them were too difficult, and for a few I rejected the sound. There is no substitute for taking time to try each chord fingering, and I have done that for you in this book.

Why do you even need different ways to play chords? One important reason is that musicians often like to keep as many strings ringing as possible for the fullest sound. As the melody of a song moves around or changes octaves, it often requires us to switch voicings of a chord to keep the song flowing as we support the melody with harmony and texture.

We also need both open and closed-position voicings of chords so we can either let open strings ring and resonate. If we want to play more staccato, bouncier rhythm changes, we usually use chords without open strings.

Another vital reason to know multiple voicings of a chord is that often a particular chord voicing has a sound that the others don't. So many classic songs have been built around the sound of a specific chord, and there are still chords out there that no one has made into a memorable part.

Muted-note duplicates. I decided to include more than one version of many chord shapes in this book where the only differences between them is a muted string, since most of the time the difference between them alters the fingering strategy. When you only have 4 strings, the difference between a muted or unmuted string can sometimes be critical, and I wanted to show when 3-string versions of the chords were complete voicings.

When you move a closed shape up the neck, it also makes sense that when it forms a C#root chord you would mute or fret the low D string, but when you move it a half step higher and it forms a D-root chord, you let the low string ring, because anybody would do that. Computer-generated chord lists often ignore situations like these. I generally include both versions here.

Modal and Suspended 4 Chords
Luckily, most fretted instrument players don't read music or adhere to music theory rules, and gladly accept certain types of chords, such as *modal* and *sus4* chords that are often absent from even encyclopedic jazz chord books.

Nearly all players make some use of the simple "modal" chord (that is technically not even a chord, since it has only 2 notes in it) that is just a root and a fifth with no third, commonly written with a numeral 5 as the suffix. Modal chords are musically powerful and widely used in fretted instrument music, and deserve a place in a chord book.

Jazz-oriented chord books generally omit the modal chord entirely as if it did not exist. I also included *add9* (sometimes called *add2* or *sus2*) chords, and gave a name to major "chords" that have no 5th, and you will see a C3 or G3 here, though they are not really fully-voiced chords.

The notes that make up any chord can be in different orders, and some notes may be repeated (doubled) or missing. The ways the notes combine and react with each other musically, due to their positions in the chord, are endlessly interesting and subtle.

Many chords in chord books are difficult or nearly impossible to finger. My rule was that I did not include a chord that I would not personally use in a song or instrumental piece. I have a good left hand, and if I can't play it, I left it out of this book. We can't just use computers to choose chords: humans have to make decisions, and I rejected a lot of chords that I thought were unreasonably hard to play. I sometimes wish I could have put some kind of a difficulty index into this book, since some chords are vastly harder than others. (This is of course subjective, and different players favor different kinds of left-hand shapes.)

I thought long and hard about barre chord symbols. All players don't make the same decisions about whether to use a barre or partial barre, and it is not that hard to find the fingering that is best for you.

Remember there are a lot of "gray areas" in naming and discussing chords. A group of notes can function as more than one chord, depending on which note is the root, and how it is used in the context of a song. You may not agree with my choices, and you may find the same chord shape with more than one name in this book. This is a big part of the reason I did the work to include the note names of every chord.

Diminished and augmented chords take up a lot of space. They have many voicings and also have multiple names. They have a lot of useful and nearly equivalent inversions, so they take up a lot of room in a book like this, though most players don't use them often. They are musically important, so they were included.

The chords in this book are playable. They have all been "hand-tested" and are not generated with software merely cranking out permutations of notes.

Every chord has 3 or 4 strings sounding. Both open-string and barre chord forms are included.

All the chords in this book will also work for the tenor guitar or tenor banjo, as long as they have the same D-G-B-E tuning. Since the scale length of the uke is shorter, your hands will be able to stretch across many more frets than on a longer-scale instrument in the same tuning.

What's Not In This Book

Obviously, this kind of book is bound to have some errors and omissions, so the chords that I neglected to put in are not here. Hopefully they are few and not really important ones...

Left-hand finger numbers are not shown here because not everyone plays every chord the same way. The truth is, if you play a stringed instrument, you will constantly be learning new fingerings, so get used to always changing. You'll be a better musician if you can learn to use alternate fingerings whenever it makes sense, and not be "frozen" into using only certain fingerings.

There are no double sharps or double flats. There are valid musical reasons for using double accidentals, but there is physically no room for them in my chord diagrams, and they are confusing, so I vetoed them. This book is designed for people who don't have degrees in music theory. It's hard enough to tell people that the 4th fret of the 1st string is sometimes called G# and sometimes an Ab. To insist that an A note is sometimes a G## and sometimes a Bbb is being a little too rigorous. If you know enough music theory to be bothered by the lack of double accidentals then you should understand what is going on and not be bothered. The purpose of the book is to show you a lot of chords and choices for chord fingerings, and what notes are in them.

Here is how double flats occur: diminished chords are technically triads, with just 3 notes in them, but they are almost always played as four-note diminished 7th chords, with three minor 3rds stacked up instead of 2. The Cdim chords in every chord book in the world have an A (7th) note along with the C-Eb-Gb diminished triad. I have "illegally"called it an A, since "technically" it should be called a Bbb. Diminished chords are unique, and each one has 4 names, and the notes in them get renamed if you give the chord a different name. The key is A, which has the 6th note of F#, but the "rules" say the note in the chord has to be called a Gb. The Fdim chords here show a 6th scale degree= D note, which technically should be an Ebb, and therefore a 7bb and not a 6th.

This situation is an example of terminology and explanations that become more obscure as they try to be more clear. It happens in pronunciation and grammar also. To avoid ending sentences with prepositions, we end up saying things "correctly" like "*That is something up with which I shall not put.*"

A prominent web discussion on *Yahoo.com* said this to "explain" the apparent A note when someone asked why there is an A in a Cdim chord: "*The distance from C to B is a Major 7th. The distance from C to Bb is a minor 7th. The distance from C to Bbb is a diminished 7th. In no way is it a 6th. That would be from a C of some sort up to an A of some sort. There is a logic to our theoretical terminology. There are many things implied in the spelling of a chord, not the least of which is actual intonation. A and Bbb are NOT the same pitch. Another implication is one of voice leading. And there is the question as to what the root of the chord is. Spelled the proper way, the root is C. Spelled your way the root becomes A. Then it would be an A diminished 7th. (A C Eb Gb) Are you then going to insist that the Gb be respelled as an F#?? Oops -- then we have an F# diminished 7th -- F# A C Eb -*"

I am not sure this clarifies anything. Likewise a C# augmented (+) chord would have the notes C# E# G##, which if rigorously enforced, would indeed mean that we would have to tell troubadours to be ready to call an F# a Gb, and that they should also be ready to call a G an Abb or an F##. To us fretted instrument players, the G string is the G string, it's not the F## string sometimes. In this book, you'll see the C#+ chords incorrectly show an F and not an E#, and an A instead of the G##. Apologies.

Chord Substitutions

If you are looking for something to use for a C chord in a song the key of D, for example, you might decide that a Cadd9 or a C5 works best, and your ear is by far the best guide, and it depends on the song and the style of music. You'll want to try a lot of fingerings to find the best one for what you are playing. You can't really apply any rulebook of music theory to tell you what substitutions are "correct," nor does it make sense to put all the possible substitute C chords next to each other in this book. You won't be able to see from looking at this book that a particular Cadd9 chord sounds better than a straight C chord in a song you are playing. These things are matters of musical taste, and different musicians and

Even when we play single-note music, we usually don't just have one finger on the fingerboard at a time, and scales and melodies constantly thread themselves through chord shapes all across the fingerboard.

listeners will undoubtedly have different opinions about what sounds good and what doesn't. It's not clear that there is any effective way to portray that kind of musical thinking in a book, and though it is a vital part of playing the instrument, it is not found here.

I left out a lot of chord types that are associated only with jazz. For example, the book would have been nearly twice as long if I had included these: *b5, augmented 7th, augmented 9th, 7 flat5, 9 flat5, 9#11, 7#9, 7 b9, 13b9, 13b5, minor 7 flat5, b7b9, minor 9 flat5, minor major 9th, b13b9, 13b5b9, 13b5b9, 11b9.* There are a few scattered extended chords that I liked and have included. Most fretted instrument chord books are based on older books written during the era when tenor banjo and ukulele were common in jazz, and they generally ignore open string voicings.

With a 4-stringed instrument that is commonly used by itself, without a bass player or guitarist to provide the chord roots, there are very few opportunities to explore extended chords. If an 11th or 13th chord has the 7th or 9th on the lower strings, our ears may not hear the root. It's impossible to make any rules or generalizations, and our ears are the best guide as to when a chord works" and when it doesn't. (Actually, to my ears, inversions of 9th chords that don't have a low root sound better and are more usable than other extended chords.)

There is nothing in the chord-naming systems to indicate if notes are doubled (repeated) or omitted. An 11th chord may or may not have a 7th or 9th in it, for example, and though technically something like a 6th chord is an "extension" of a major chord, and should have 1-3-5-6 scale notes, you may find voicings that are missing the 3rd or 5th. This is part of the way stringed instruments work, and part of what gives each voicing its own sound. The only way to know what is going on inside each chord is to listen carefully and to study the letters and numbers for every chord. (On a 4-string instrument like ukulele, there is not much doubling going on. That's more of a guitar and piano issue.)

A modal 7th chord, which has no 3rd, and has just the 1-5-7b notes, is important in blues but has no common name. It is generally just put in the pile with the other 7th chords, even though it has a little different sound. You'll have to study the small scale degree numbers under the chords to find these. (To my ears, Big Joe Williams' classic song "*Baby Please Don't Go*" doesn't sound right to me unless you use one.) Similarly, an augmented chord with no 3rd is just 1 and 5# notes. If you don't call it an augmented chord, then it really has no name other than perhaps "sharp 5." It's not really just an interval when there are 4 pairs of strings ringing.

This book doesn't use the open circle symbol to show an optional fingering. It's a common and useful thing to do, but it interferes with the way the letter names and the scale degrees of every note are shown under each chord in this book. (You can't really show the note names and scale degrees for the optional fingerings.) A chord diagram with several open circles is more of a puzzle than a chord, and it is not simple to extract the usable fingerings.

To illustrate how to play D chords, you could also just show the whole fingerboard of D-F#-A notes, which is also what a skilled player "sees" on the fingerboard to represent a D chord:

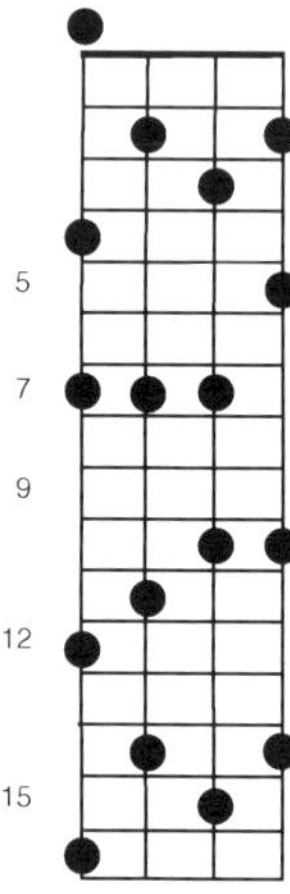

All possible D chords are encoded here, but the diagram doesn't really answer the question of how you play a D chord. This the kind of information that computer-generated chord charts and apps give you, but I don't think there is any substitute for a human editor who makes decisions about what chords don't sound good or are too hard to finger. It takes quite a bit of effort to take apart a diagram like this into the chords you can use. And it takes even more to actually know them and be able to use them in a song.

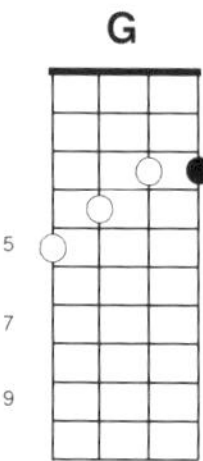

This G chord shown with open circles actually parses to 7 other G chords that are distinct left-hand shapes.

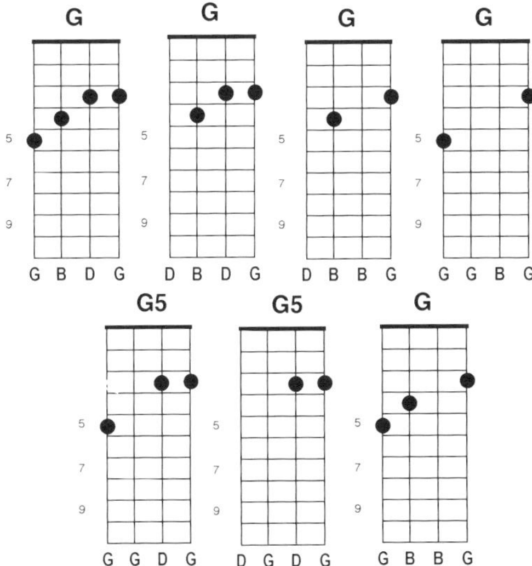

Arpeggiated Chords

The Italian word *arpeggio* literally means "broken chord" and the choice of whether the notes in a chord are played all at once or in staggered time can make a world of difference in the sound of the chord.

Before you decide that a chord in this book is "no good," make sure you play it forward and backwards in arpeggio, and also in a strummed form. Many chords really come to life when they are arpeggiated.

Chords in Context

This chord sounds like a G6 or Em chord when you play it by itself, but if you play is after this inversion of a C major chord, you can hear it as a Cmaj7 chord:

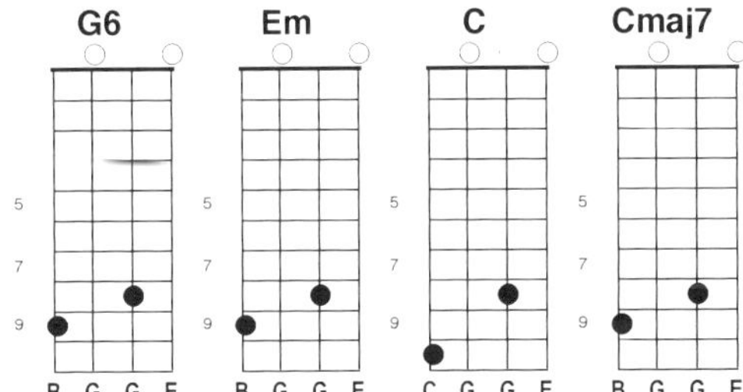

How Many Chords is Best?

Many readers who are opening this book are beginners and intermediate players, and the question arises as to whether it is better to include more or fewer chords, or perhaps to draw some lines in terms of difficulty or complexity.

If you have a lot of chords, you inevitably include "not-so-great" voicings and very difficult fingerings along with the easier and good-sounding chords. Is it perhaps better to just have the most vital and most common chords? In the spirit of "do-it-yourself," I decided to include a lot of choices of ways to play more common chords, and to not include more "obscure" types of chords. I don't think it hurts anyone to have a chord book with a lot of choices, any more than it hurts to have a dictionary with words in it than most of us will never really use.

There are issues of what is hard or easy, and also what is common or useful. If you like dissonant music, then what is a useful chord to you is not the same as it would be for someone who had more mainstream tastes and who liked consonance. Our tastes change as we get older also, and as we have life experiences. I had to make a lot of tough decisions about what chords to include, and I might have put in a chord on a day when I was feeling generous, and I may have tossed some out on other days when I was feeling differently.

A chord book is somewhat of an artistic statement, and reflects the personality as well as the musical tastes and skills of the author. I hope you like this one. I really had a lot of fun making it, and it really stirred up in me a constant and ever-deepening sense of awe at all the things a we can do with our strings, fingers and a thumb or two.

In this digital world, with an endless torrent of new gadgets, software, and new interfaces, there is something profoundly satisfying about focusing entirely on a centuries-old thing like a fingerboard.

Have fun exploring...

About the Diagrams in This Book

The chord diagrams in this book go up to fret 16. This is more than most of us need, but it does help to see each chord in context on the fingerboard chart.

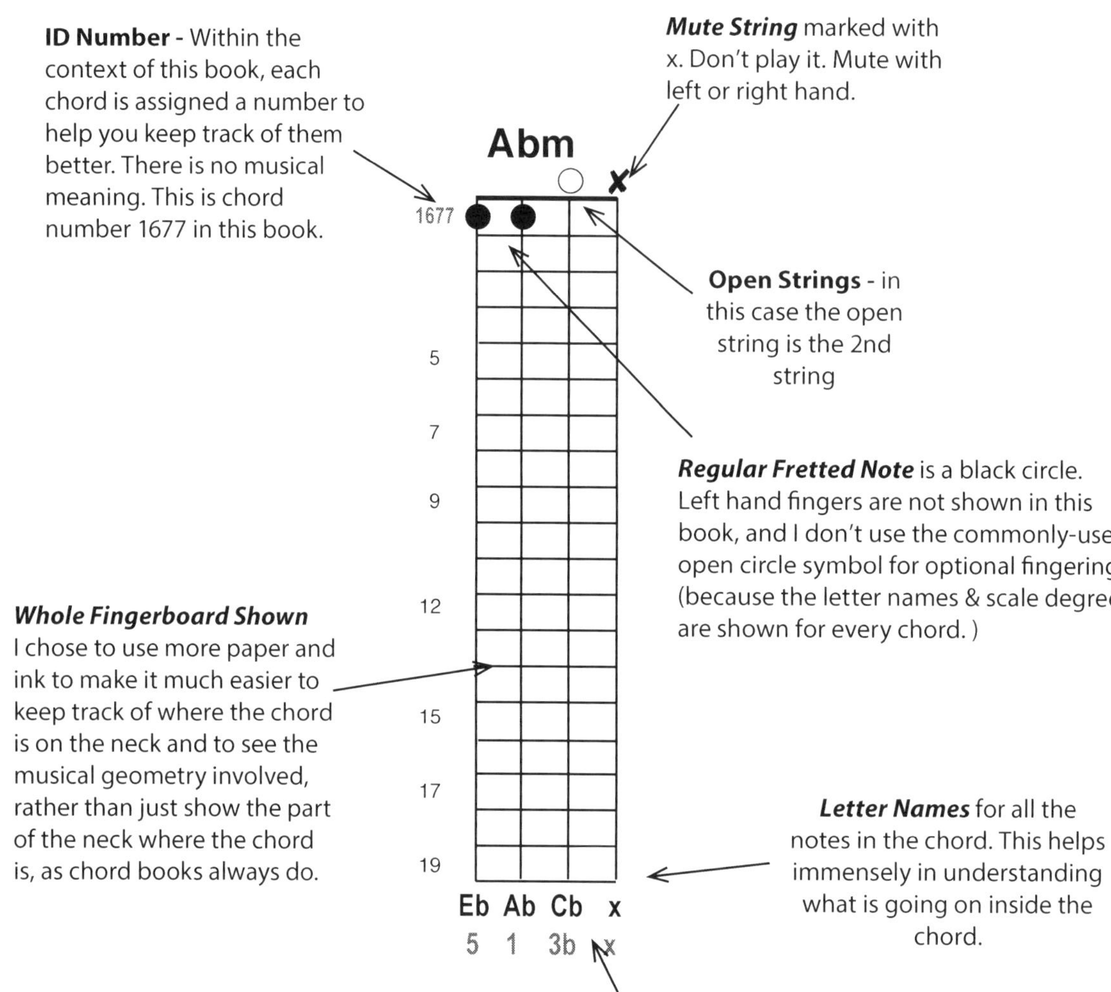

Scale Degrees of each note-- showing you the inversions, *"spelling"* and *voicing* of each chord. A big part of what gives each chord its musical identity is determined by which numbers are present. The order in which they appear, and which of them are absent or *doubled* (repeated) is also a vital factor. There are many voicings of any chord, and only a limited number of them are available.

In this example, A^b is the root or 1, the flat 3rd of an A^b scale is C^b and the 5th is Eb. These numbers show you the structure and help you analyze and understand the sound of each chord.

Sorting The chords in this book are sorted by root note first, and then by chord type, fret position and number of fingers in the chord. A 3-finger chord that starts at fret 4 will appear before a 3 finger barre chord at that same fret position. In a few instances I have moved a very common voicing to the front. Instead of trying to sort chord types by complexity, I put them in order of how often we use them. This is both helpful and frustrating, since it's hard to know if a minor 6th is more useful than a major 9th.

Standard Baritone Ukulele Tuning

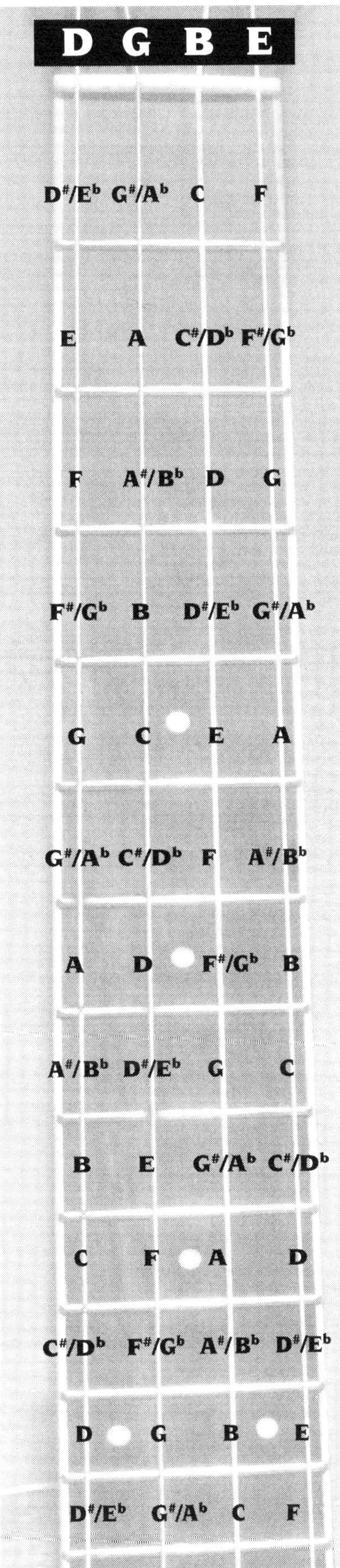

Baritone Ukulele Chords

TUNING: D G B E

A

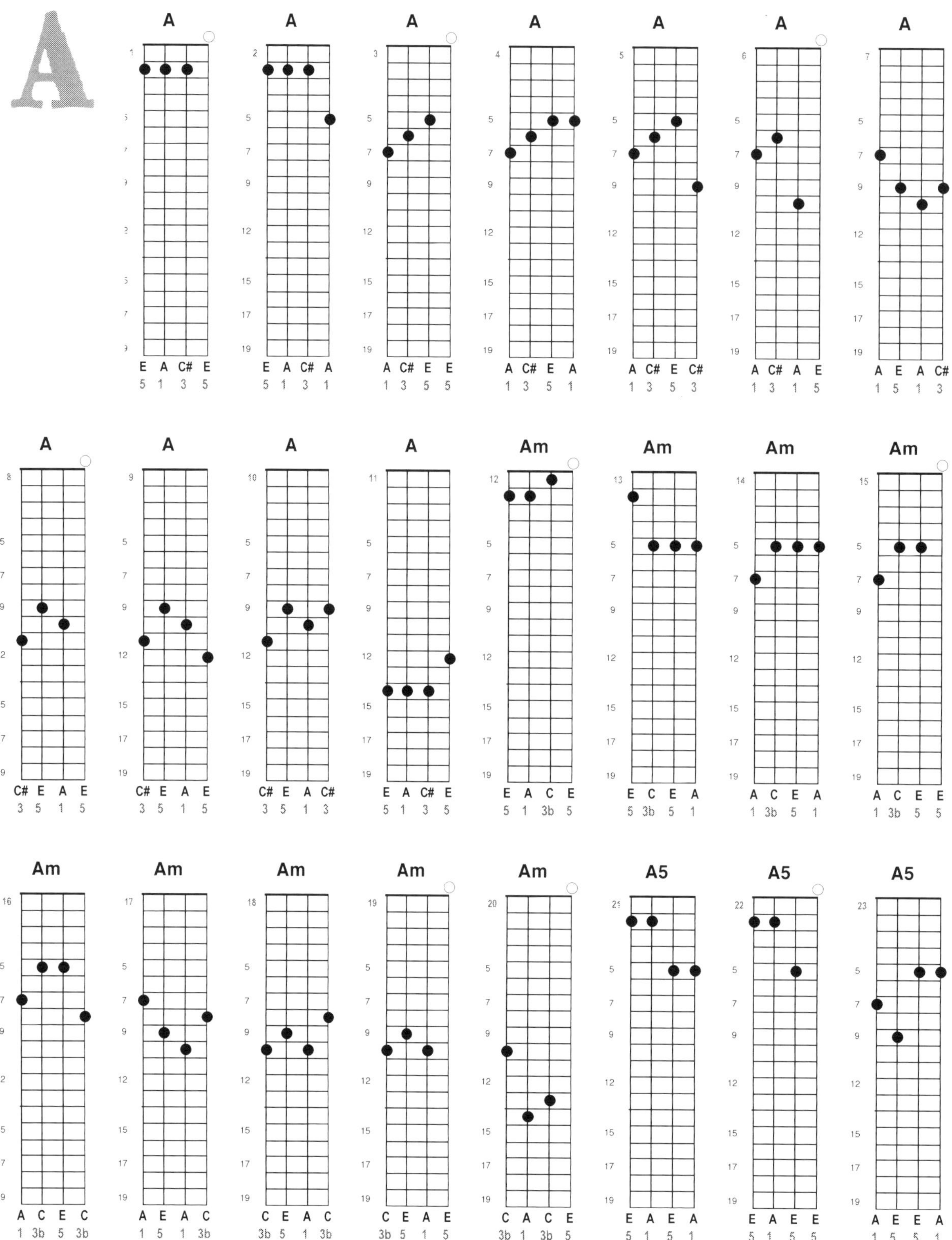

TUNING: D G B E

A5
A E A E
1 5 1 5
A5
A E A E
1 5 1 5
A5
E A A E
5 1 1 5
A7
G A C# E
7b 1 3 5
A7
E G C# E
5 7b 3 5
A7
E A C# G
5 1 3 7b
A7
E G C# A
5 7b 3 1
A7
E G C# G
5 7b 3 7b
A7
G A C# A
7b 1 3 1
A7
G C# E G
7b 3 5 7b
A7
A C# E G
1 3 5 7b
A7
G C# E A
7b 3 5 1
A7
A G E E
1 7b 5 5
A7
G C# G A
7b 3 7b 1
A7
G C# G E
7b 3 7b 5
A7
A G E A
1 7b 5 1
A7
G C# E E
7b 3 5 5
A7
A C# G A
1 3 7b 1
A7
A C# G E
1 3 7b 5
A7
A C# G C#
1 3 7b 3
A7
A G A E
1 7b 1 5
A7
A E G E
1 5 7b 5
A7
A E G C#
1 5 7b 3
A7
C# G G E
3 7b 7b 5

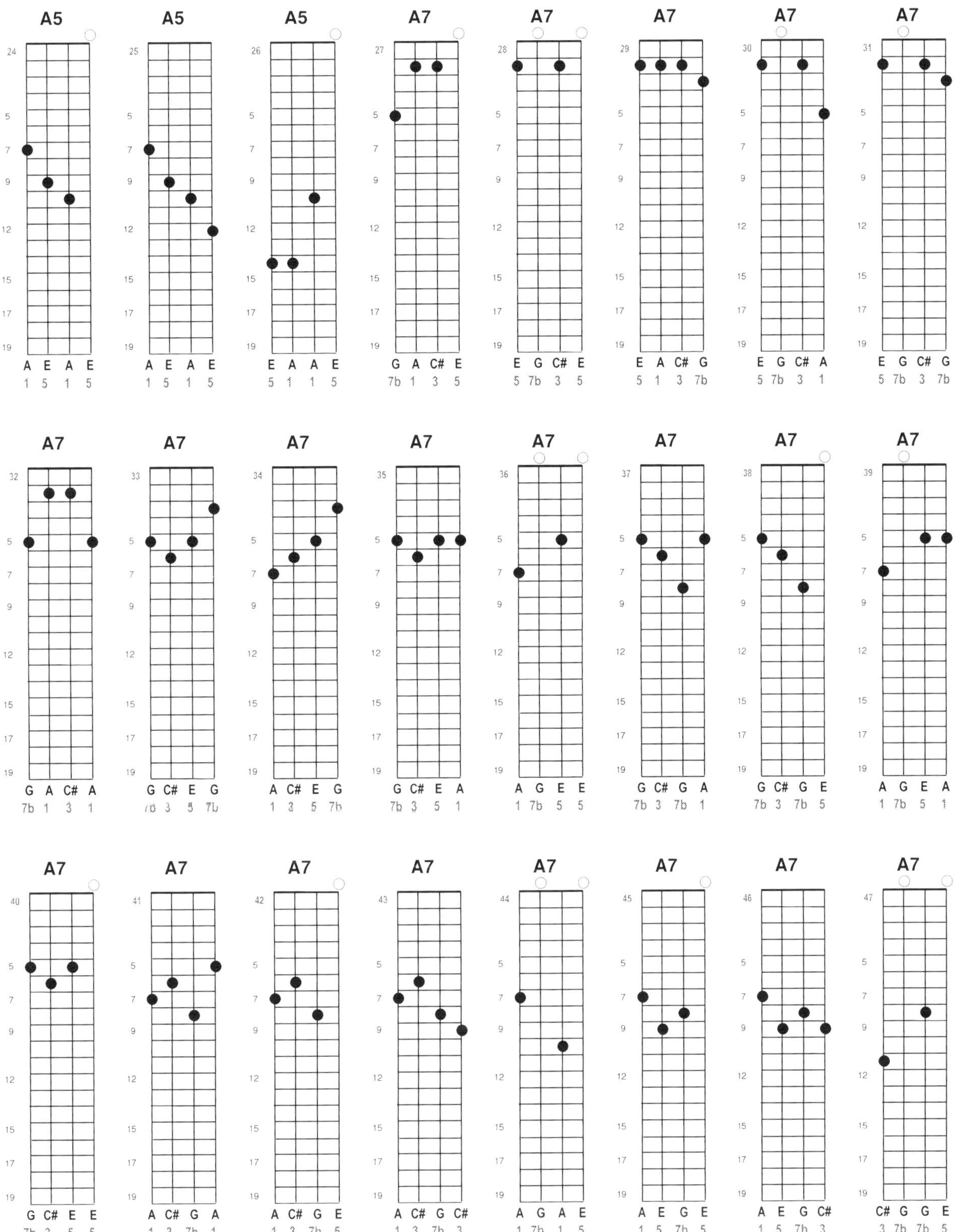

TUNING: D G B E

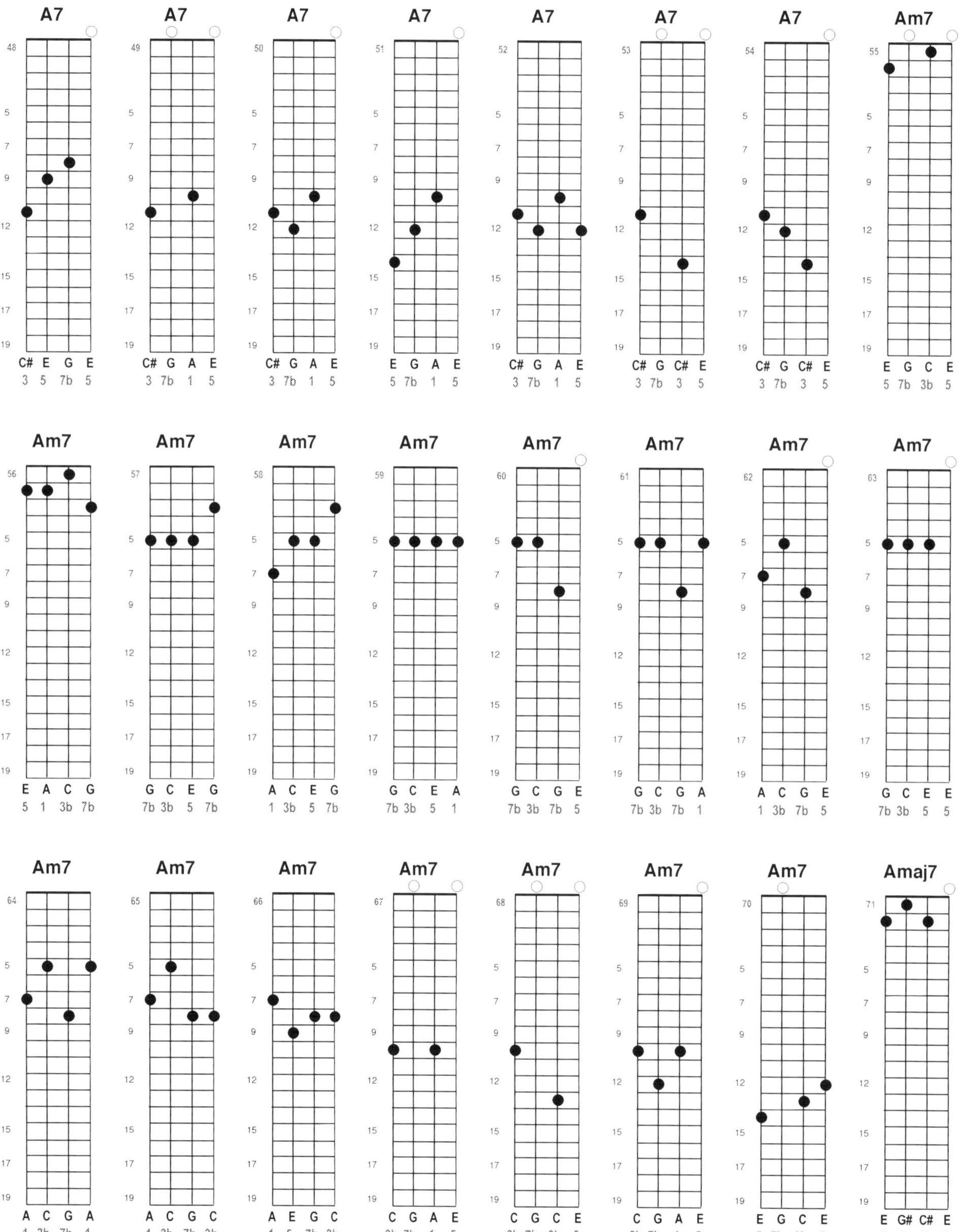

A7
48
C# E G E
3 5 7b 5
A7
49
C# G A E
3 7b 1 5
A7
50
C# G A E
3 7b 1 5
A7
51
E G A E
5 7b 1 5
A7
52
C# G A E
3 7b 1 5
A7
53
C# G C# E
3 7b 3 5
A7
54
C# G C# E
3 7b 3 5
Am7
55
E G C E
5 7b 3b 5
Am7
56
E A C G
5 1 3b 7b
Am7
57
G C E G
7b 3b 5 7b
Am7
58
A C E G
1 3b 5 7b
Am7
59
G C E A
7b 3b 5 1
Am7
60
G C G E
7b 3b 7b 5
Am7
61
G C G A
7b 3b 7b 1
Am7
62
A C G E
1 3b 7b 5
Am7
63
G C E E
7b 3b 5 5
Am7
64
A C G A
1 3b 7b 1
Am7
65
A C G C
1 3b 7b 3b
Am7
66
A E G C
1 5 7b 3b
Am7
67
C G A E
3b 7b 1 5
Am7
68
C G C E
3b 7b 3b 5
Am7
69
C G A E
3b 7b 1 5
Am7
70
E G C E
5 7b 3b 5
Amaj7
71
E G# C# E
5 7 3 5

TUNING: D G B E

Amaj7
72
E A C# G#
5 1 3 7
Amaj7
73
A C# E G#
1 3 5 7
Amaj7
74
G# C# E A
7 3 5 1
Amaj7
75
A C# G# A
1 3 7 1
Amaj7
76
G# C# G# E
7 3 7 5
Amaj7
77
G# C# G# C#
7 3 7 3
Amaj7
78
A C# G# C#
1 3 7 3
Amaj7
79
A C# G# E
1 3 7 5
Amaj7
80
C# G# A E
3 7 1 5
Amaj7
81
C# G# C# E
3 7 3 5
Amaj7
82
C# G# C# E
3 7 3 5
Asus
83
D A D E
4 1 4 5
Asus
84
E A D A
5 1 4 1
Asus
85
E A D E
5 1 4 5
Asus
86
A D E E
1 4 5 5
Asus
87
A D E A
1 4 5 1
Asus
88
A D A E
1 4 1 5
Asus
89
A E A D
1 5 1 4
A7sus
90
E G D E
5 7b 4 5
A7sus
91
E A D G
5 1 4 7b
A7sus
92
G A D E
7b 1 4 5
A7sus
93
E G D A
5 7b 4 1
A7sus
94
D A D G
4 1 4 7b
A7sus
95
A D E G
1 4 5 7b

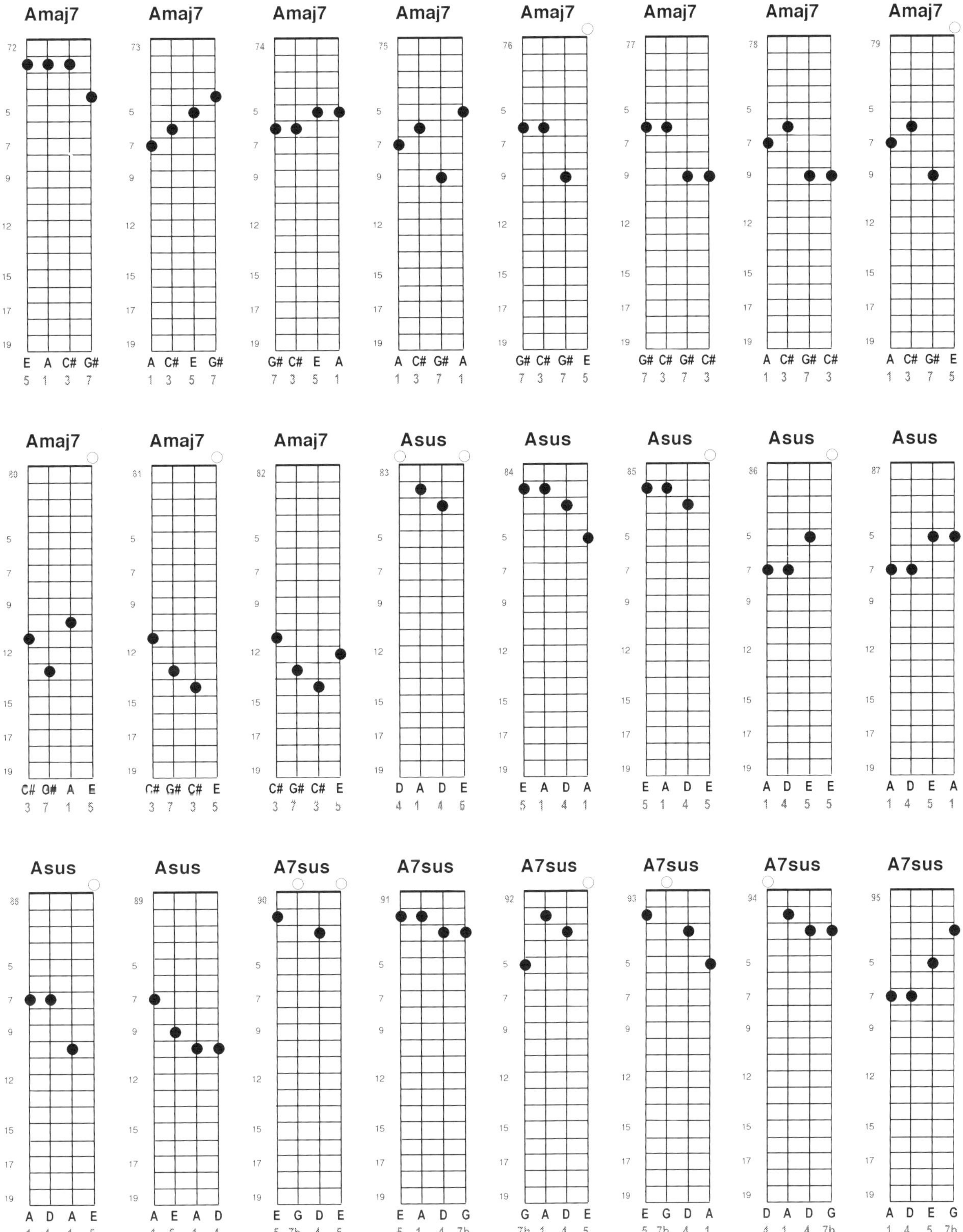

TUNING: D G B E

A7sus
96
G D E A
7b 4 5 1
A7sus
97
A D G E
1 4 7b 5
A7sus
98
A E G D
1 5 7b 4
A7sus
99
D G A E
4 7b 1 5
A7sus
100
D G A E
4 7b 1 5
A7sus
101
D G A D
4 7b 1 4
A6
102
E A C# F#
5 1 3 6
A6
103
F# A E A
6 1 5 1
A6
104
F# A E F#
6 1 5 6
A6
105
A C# E F#
1 3 5 6
A6
106
F# C# F# A
6 3 6 1
A6
107
F# C# E A
6 3 5 1
A6
108
A C# F# A
1 3 6 1
A6
109
A E F# A
1 5 6 1
A6
110
A C# F# E
1 3 6 5
A6
111
A F# A E
1 6 1 5
A6
112
A E F# E
1 5 6 5
A6
113
C# E F# E
3 5 6 5
A6
114
A E F# C#
1 5 6 3
A6
115
C# F# A C#
3 6 1 3
A6
116
C# F# A E
3 6 1 5
A6
117
C# F# C# E
3 6 3 5
A6
118
E F# C# E
5 6 3 5
A6
119
E F# C# F#
5 6 3 6

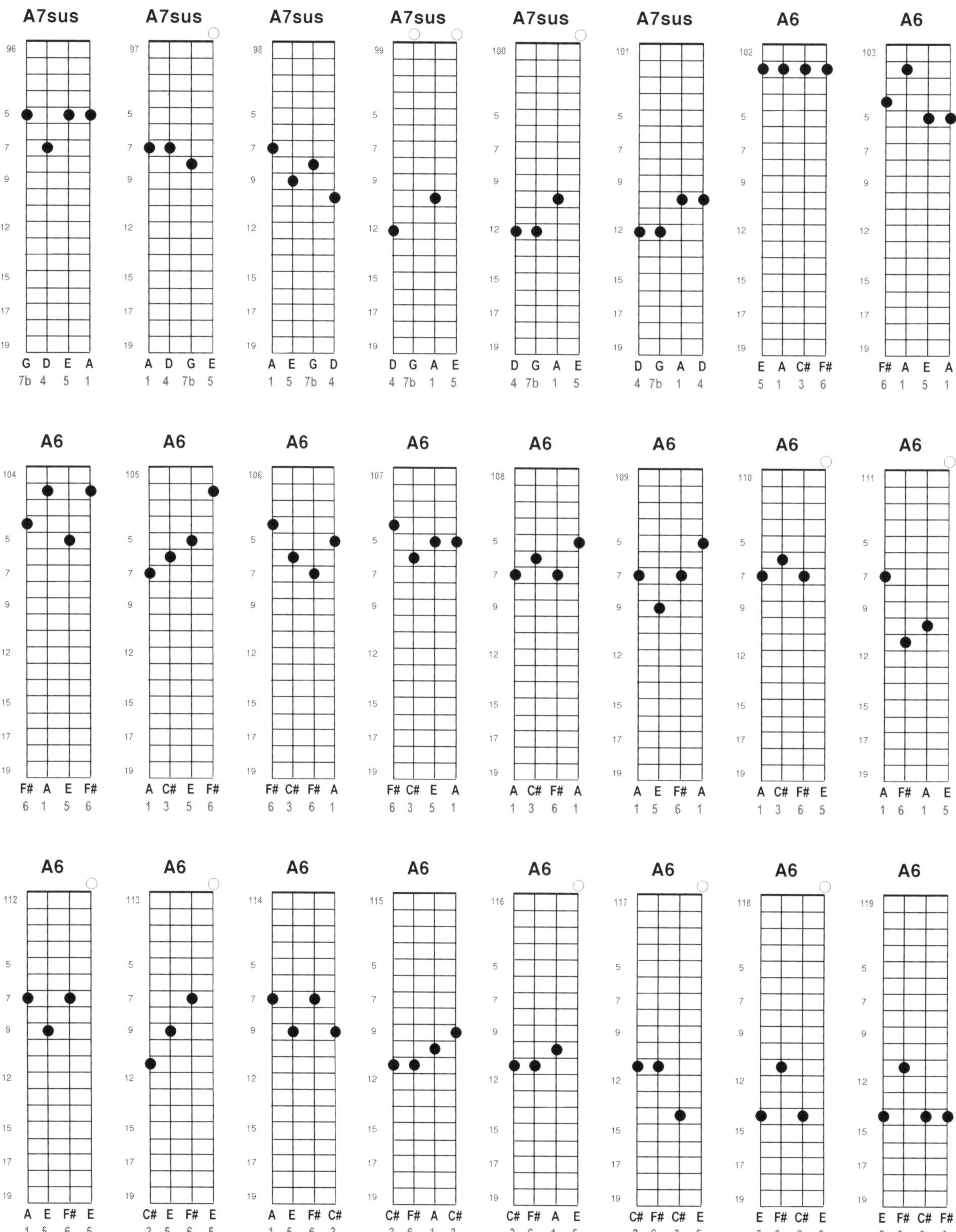

TUNING: D G B E

Aadd9 120 E A B E 5 1 2 5
Aadd9 121 E C# B E 5 3 2 5
Aadd9 122 E B C# E 5 2 3 5
Aadd9 123 A C# B A 1 3 2 1
Aadd9 124 B C# E E 2 3 5 5
Aadd9 125 B C# E A 2 3 5 1
Aadd9 126 A C# E B 1 3 5 2
Aadd9 127 A C# B E 1 3 2 5
Aadd9 128 A C# B C# 1 3 2 3
Aadd9 129 A E B E 1 5 2 5
Aadd9 130 A E A B 1 5 1 2
Aadd9 131 C# E A B 3 5 1 2
Aadd9 132 C# A B E 3 1 2 5
Aadd9 133 C# A B E 3 1 2 5
Aadd11 134 A C# D E 1 3 4 5
Aadd11 135 A C# A D 1 3 1 4
Aadd11 136 C# E A D 3 5 1 4
A9 137 G A B E 7b 1 2 5
A9 138 E A B G 5 1 2 7b
A9 139 G B C# E 7b 2 3 5
A9 140 G B C# A 7b 2 3 1
A9 141 E B C# G 5 2 3 7b
A9 142 E B E G 5 2 5 7b
A9 143 A C# B G 1 3 2 7b

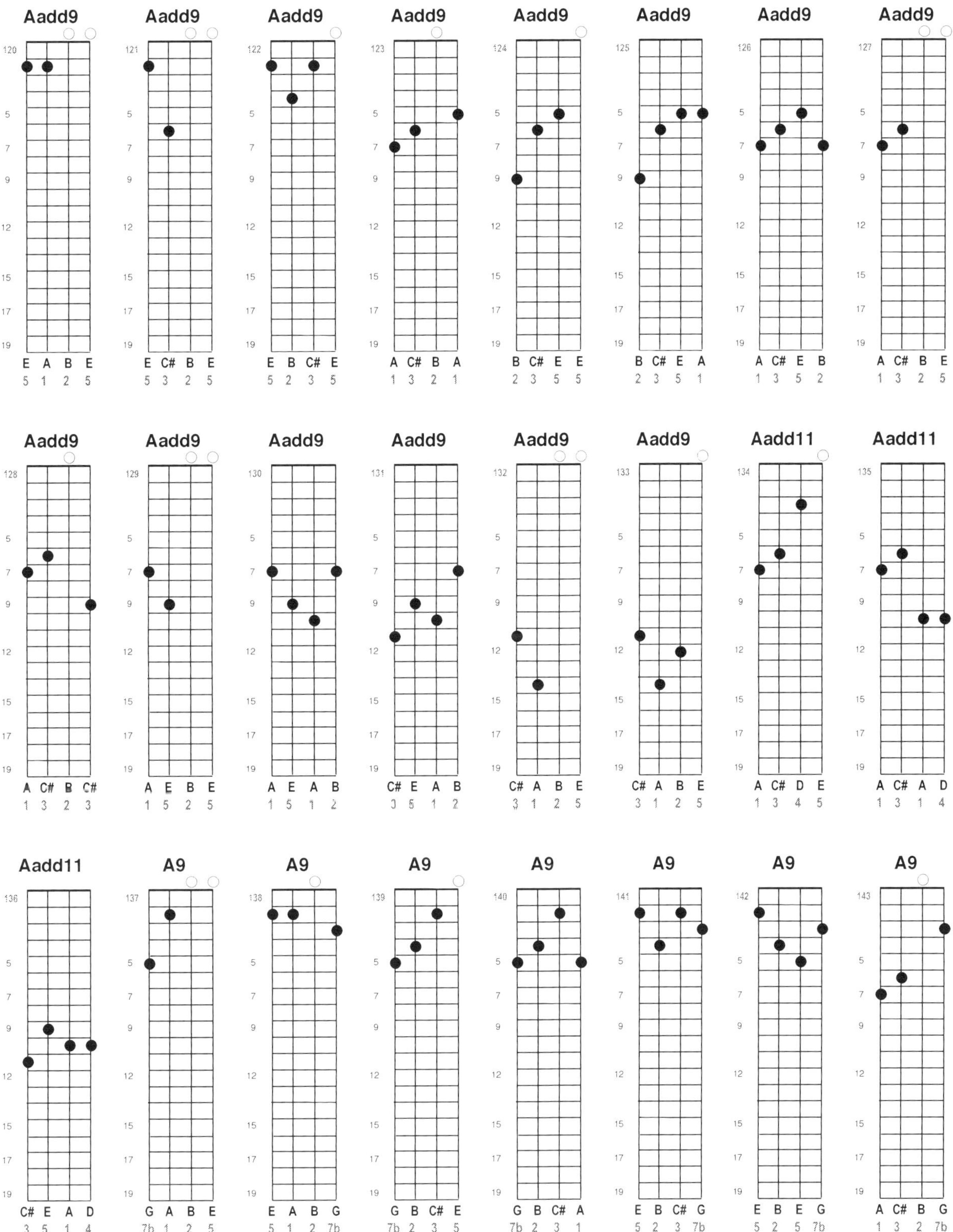

TUNING: D G B E

A9
144
G C# B G
7b 3 2 7b
A9
145
A G B A
1 7b 2 1
A9
146
G C# B E
7b 3 2 5
A9
147
G C# G B
7b 3 7b 2
A9
148
G C# E B
7b 3 5 2
A9
149
B C# G E
2 3 7b 5
A9
150
B C# G B
2 3 7b 2
A9
151
A C# G B
1 3 7b 2
A9
152
B C# G C#
2 3 7b 3
A9
153
A G B E
1 7b 2 5
A9
154
A E G B
1 5 7b 2
A9
155
C# G A B
3 7b 1 2
A9
156
A G G B
1 7b 7b 2
A9
157
B E G B
2 5 7b 2
A9
158
B E G E
2 5 7b 5
A9
159
B E G C#
2 5 7b 3
A9
160
B G A E
2 7b 1 5
A9
161
C# G B E
3 7b 2 5
A9
162
C# G B E
3 7b 2 5
A9
163
C# G B E
3 7b 2 5
A9
164
C# G B E
3 7b 2 5
A9
165
C# G B E
3 7b 2 5
A9
166
E G B E
5 7b 2 5
A9
167
E G B E
5 7b 2 5

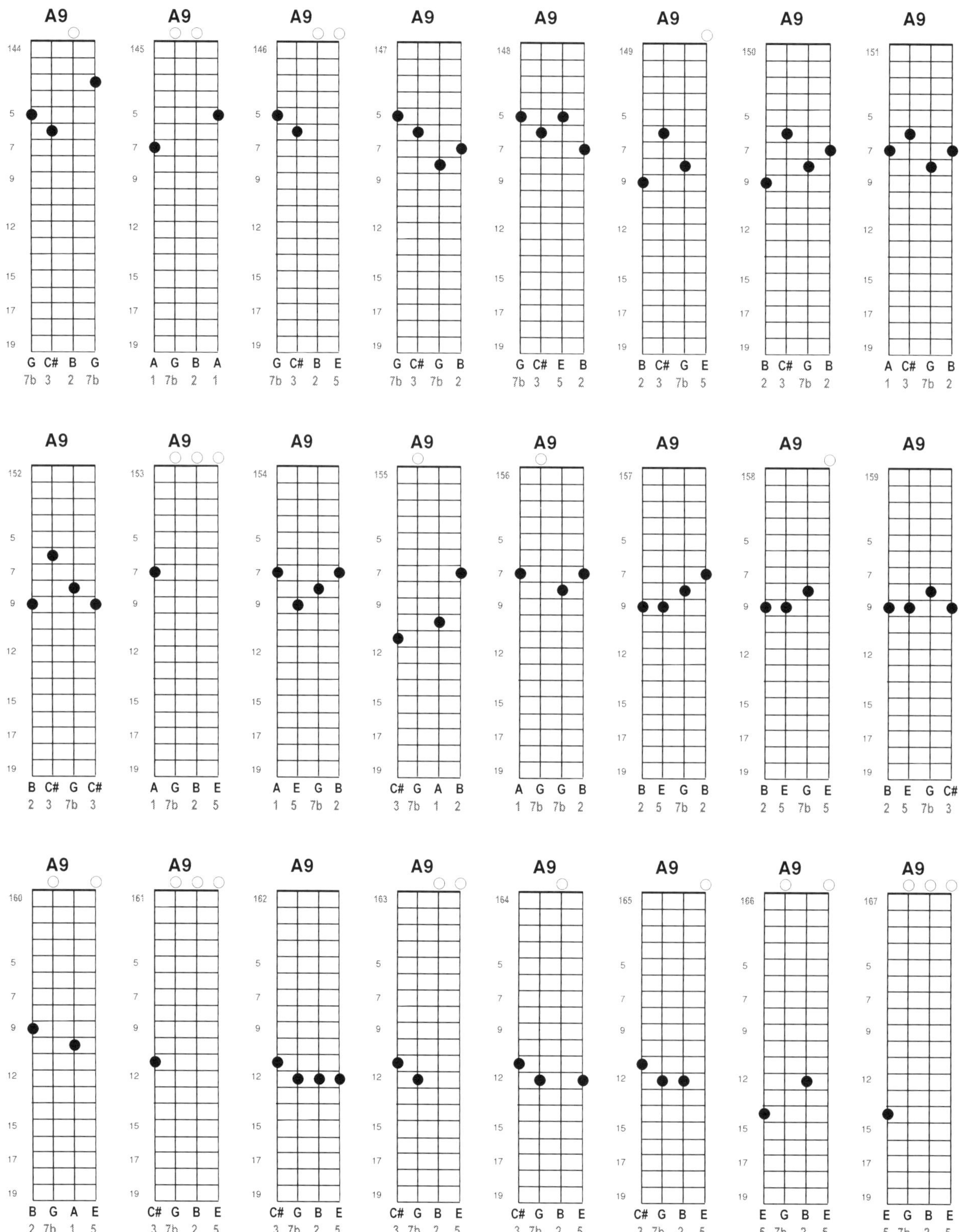

TUNING: D G B E

A11
168
E B D E
5 2 4 5
A11
169
A D G B
1 4 7b 2
A11
170
B E G D
2 5 7b 4
A11
171
D G B E
4 7b 2 5
A11
172
D G B E
4 7b 2 5
A6/7
173
E G C# F#
5 7b 3 6
A6/7
174
E G D F#
5 7b 4 6
A6/7
175
G C# F# A
7b 3 6 1
A6/7
176
G C# F# E
7b 3 6 5
A13
177
G C# F# B
7b 3 6 2
A13
178
C# G B F#
3 7b 2 6
A13
179
C# G B F#
3 7b 2 6
A6/9
180
A C# B F#
1 3 2 6
A6/9
181
E A B F#
5 1 2 6
A6/9
182
F# B E A
6 2 5 1
A6/9
183
B E F# A
2 5 6 1
A6/9
184
B C# F# A
2 3 6 1
A6/9
185
A C# F# B
1 3 6 2
A6/9
186
A F# B E
1 6 2 5
A6/9
187
B E F# C#
2 5 6 3
A6/9
188
B F# A E
2 6 1 5
A6/9
189
C# F# B E
3 6 2 5
A6/9
190
E F# B E
5 6 2 5
Adim
191
D# A C x
5b 1 3b x

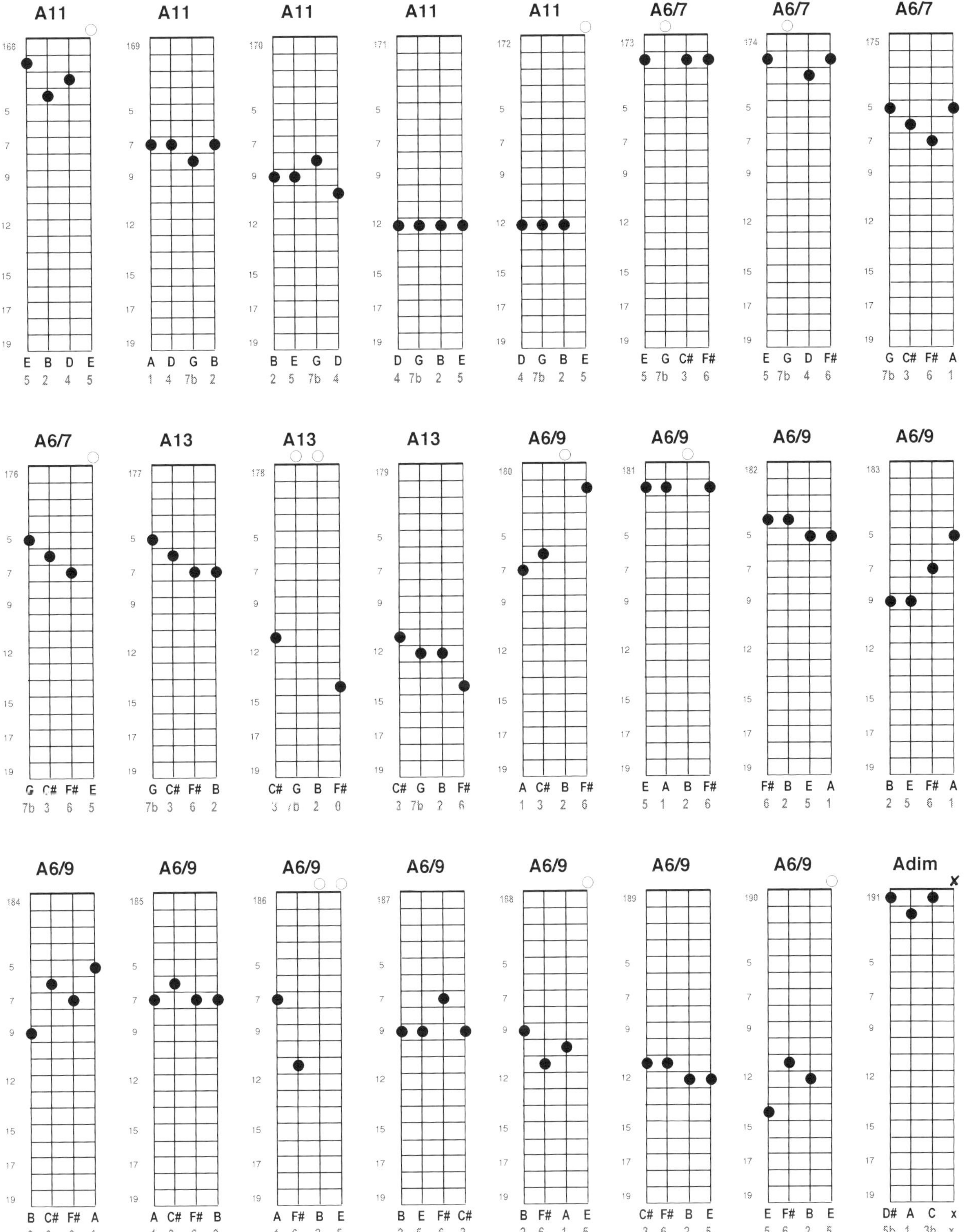

TUNING: D G B E

Adim 192 D# A C F# 5b 1 3b 6
Adim 193 F# A D# x 6 1 5b x
Adim 194 F# C D# x 6 3b 5b x
Adim 195 F# C D# A 6 3b 5b 1
Adim 196 A C F# x 1 3b 6 x
Adim 197 A C F# E 1 3b 6 5
Adim 198 A D# F# x 1 5b 6 x
Adim 199 A D# F# C 1 5b 6 3b
Adim 200 C D# A x 3b 5b 1 x
Adim 201 C F# A x 3b 6 1 x
Adim 202 C F# A D# 3b 6 1 5b
A+ 203 F A C# x 5# 1 3 x
A+ 204 F C# F x 5# 3 5# x
A+ 205 A C# F A 1 3 5# 1
A+ 206 A C# F x 1 3 5# x
A+ 207 C# F A C# 3 5# 1 3
A+ 208 C# F A x 3 5# 1 x
Am6 209 F# A C E 6 1 3b 5
Am6 210 E A C F# 5 1 3b 6
Am6 211 E C E F# 5 3b 5 6
Am6 212 F# C E F# 6 3b 5 6
Am6 213 F# C F# E 6 3b 6 5
Am6 214 F# C E A 6 3b 5 1
Am6 215 F# C F# A 6 3b 6 1
5
7
9
12
15
17
19

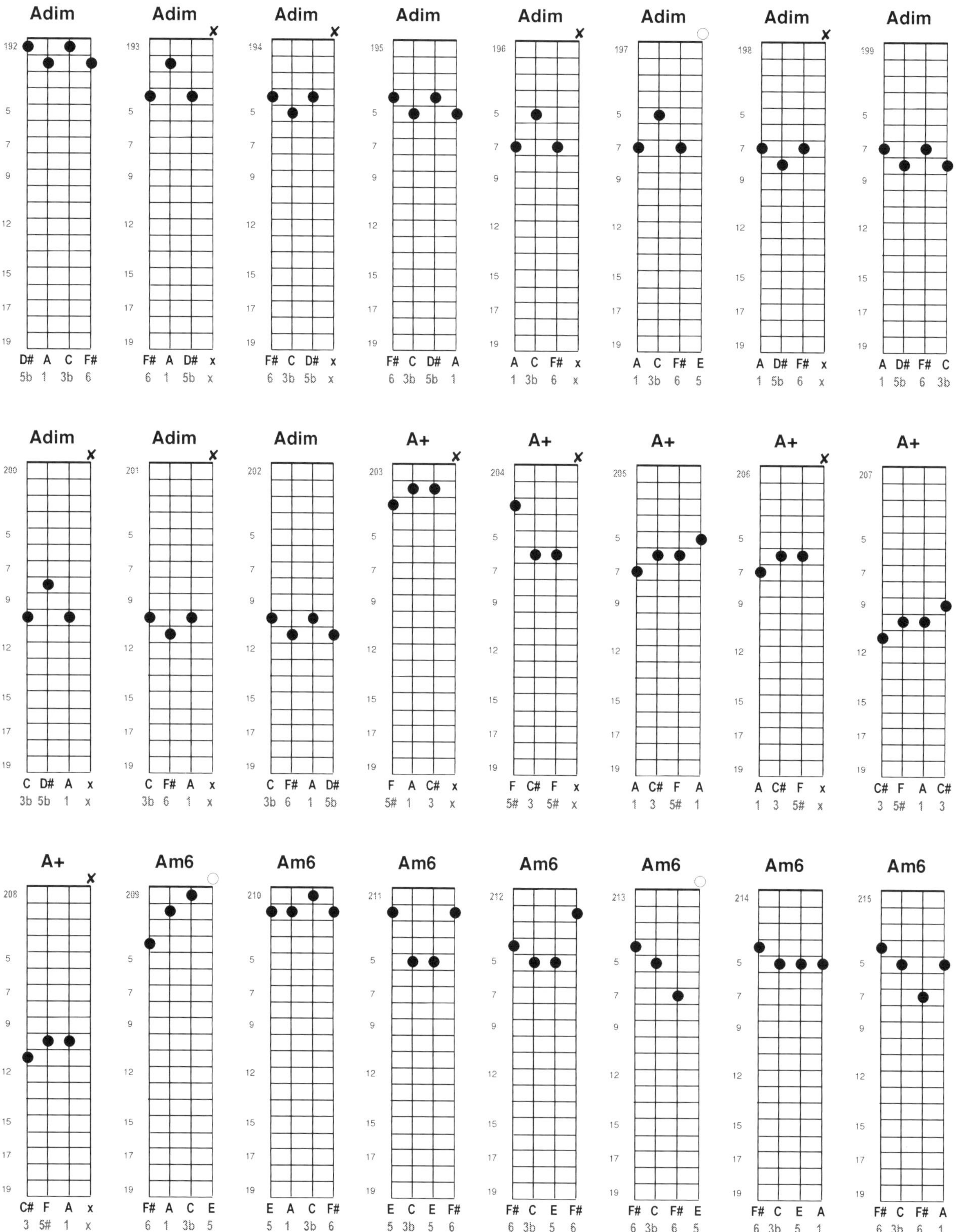

TUNING: D G B E

Am6
216
A C F# A
1 3b 6 1
Am6
217
A C F# C
1 3b 6 3b
Am6
218
C E F# E
3b 5 6 5
Am6
219
A E F# C
1 5 6 3b
Am6
220
C E F# C
3b 5 6 3b
Am6
221
C F# A E
3b 6 1 5
Am6
222
C F# C E
3b 6 3b 5
Am6
223
C F# A E
3b 6 1 5
Am6
224
C F# C E
3b 6 3b 5
Am6
225
E F# C E
5 6 3b 5
Am6
226
E F# C F#
5 6 3b 6
Am6/7
227
E G C F#
5 7b 3b 6
Am6/7
228
G C E F#
7b 3b 5 6
Am6/7
229
C F# G E
3b 6 7b 5
Am6/9
230
F# C E B
6 3b 5 2
Am6/9
231
A C F# B
1 3b 6 2
Am6/9
232
B C F# A
2 3b 6 1
Am6/9
233
C E F# B
3b 5 6 2
Am6/9
234
C F# B E
3b 6 2 5
Am13
235
F# C B G
6 3b 2 7b
Am13
236
C G B E
3b 7b 2 5
Am13
237
C G B F#
3b 7b 2 6
Am9
238
B C G A
2 3b 7b 1
Am9
239
G C G B
7b 3b 7b 2

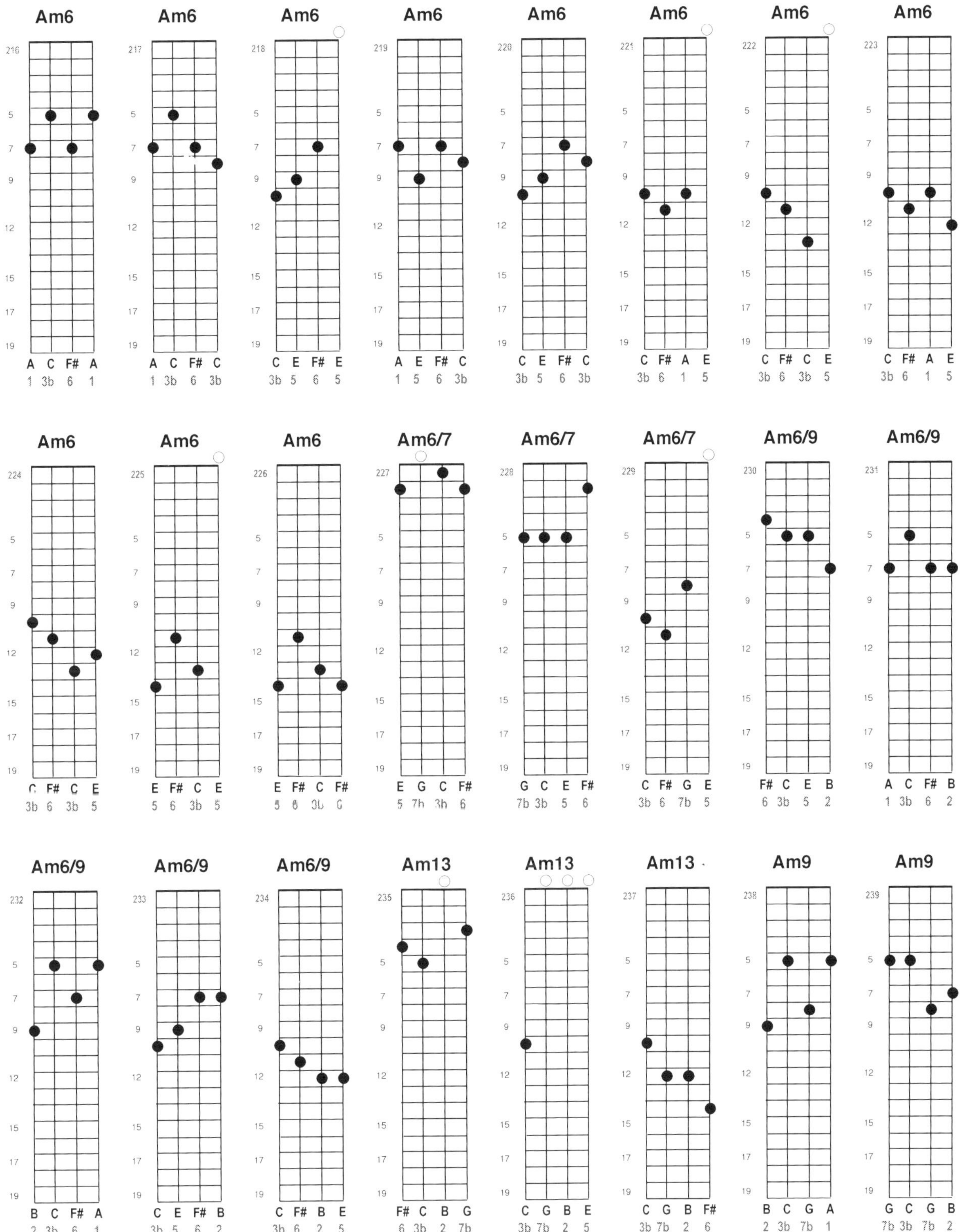

TUNING: D G B E

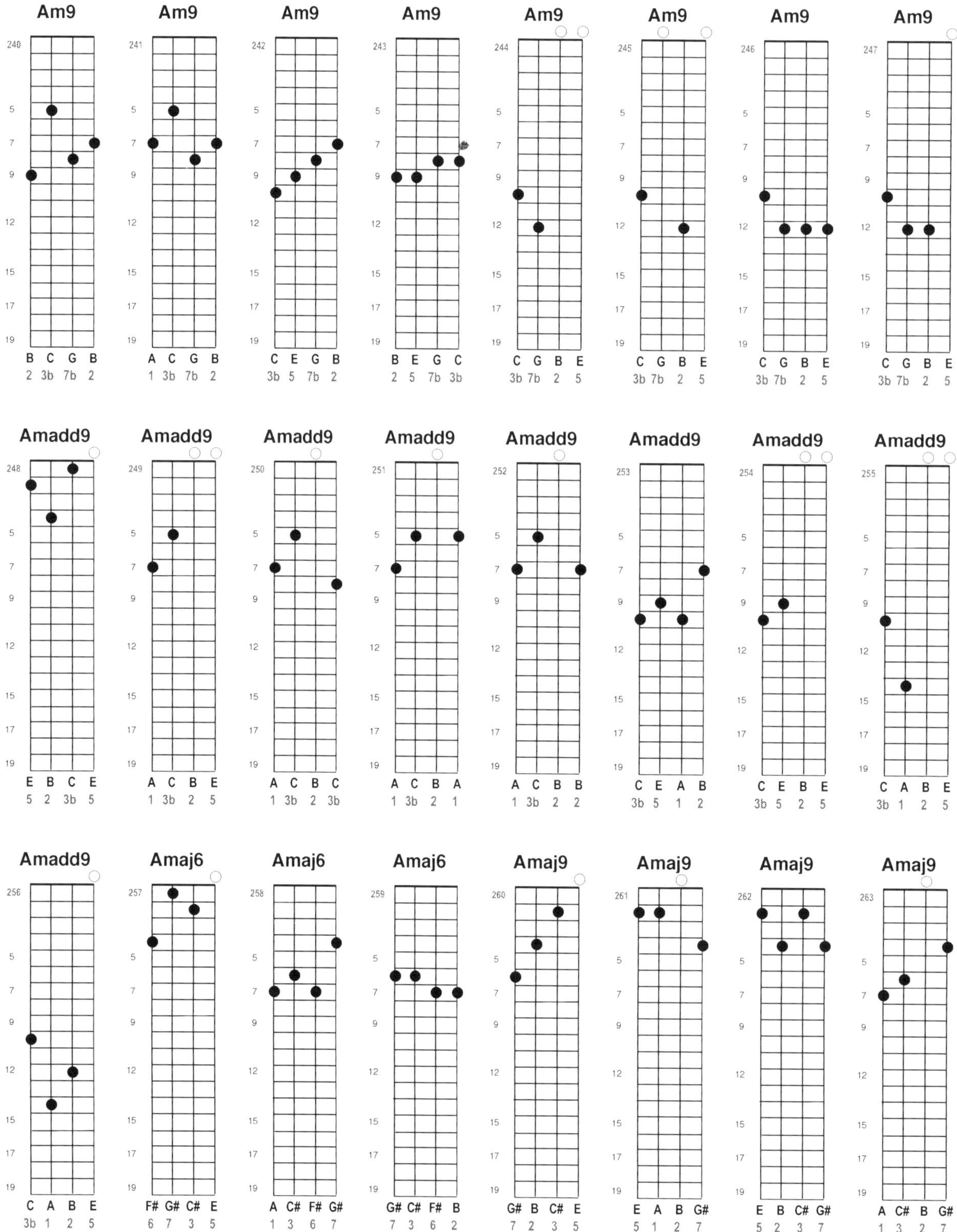

TUNING: D G B E

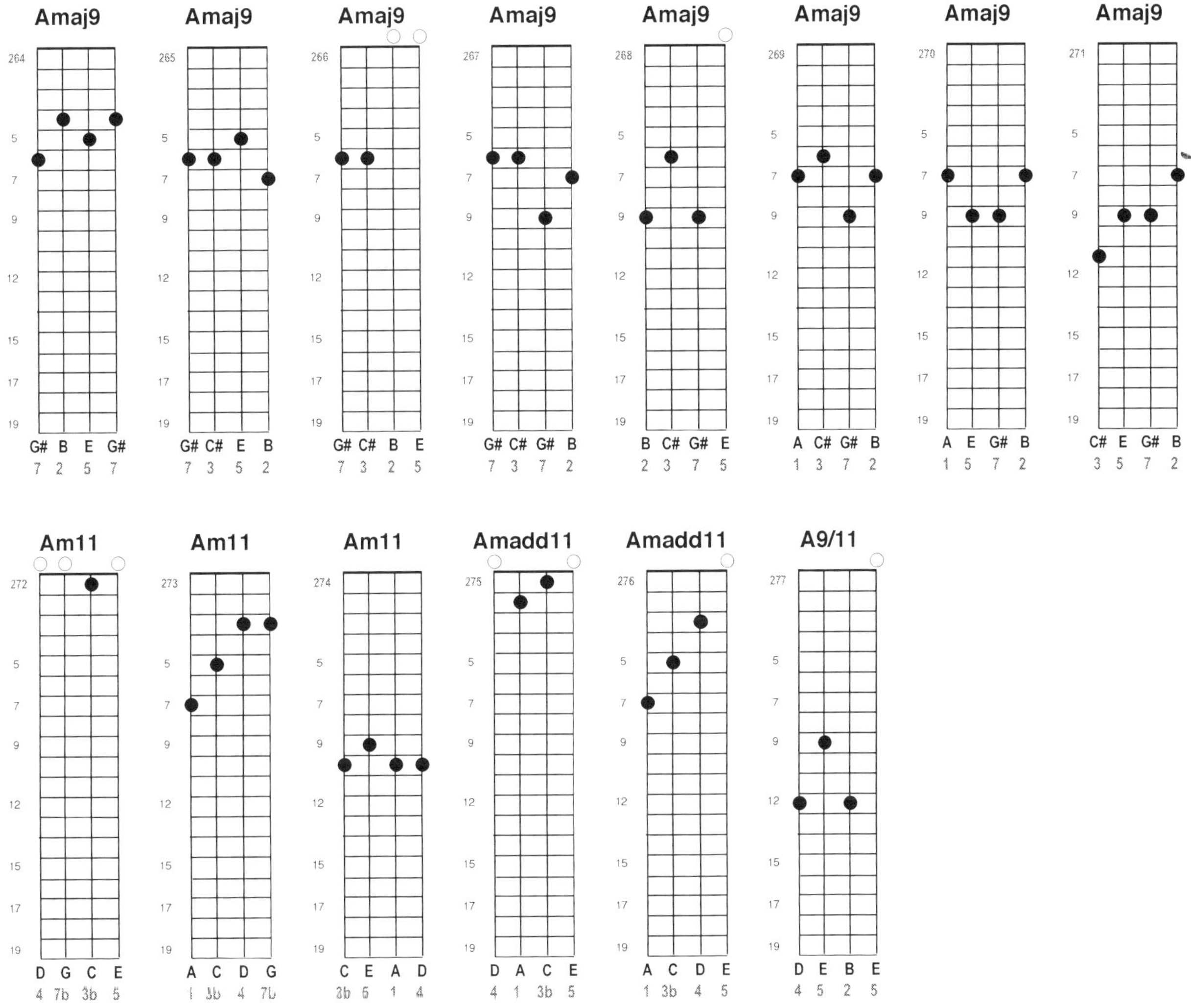

Its difficult to be rigorous about chord structure with a 4-string instrument, since some of the more extended chords have 5 or 6 notes in them, and there are bound to be any number of missing notes.

A 9th chord might have no 5th, or no 3rd. An 11th chord, which "technically" has a 1-3-5-7-9-11 spelling, might have a ninth and it might not. In general, I have left out chords with missing roots, though not always. 9th chords without roots still sound like 9th chords to my ears, though other types of chords don't.

Baritone Ukulele Chords

TUNING: D G B E

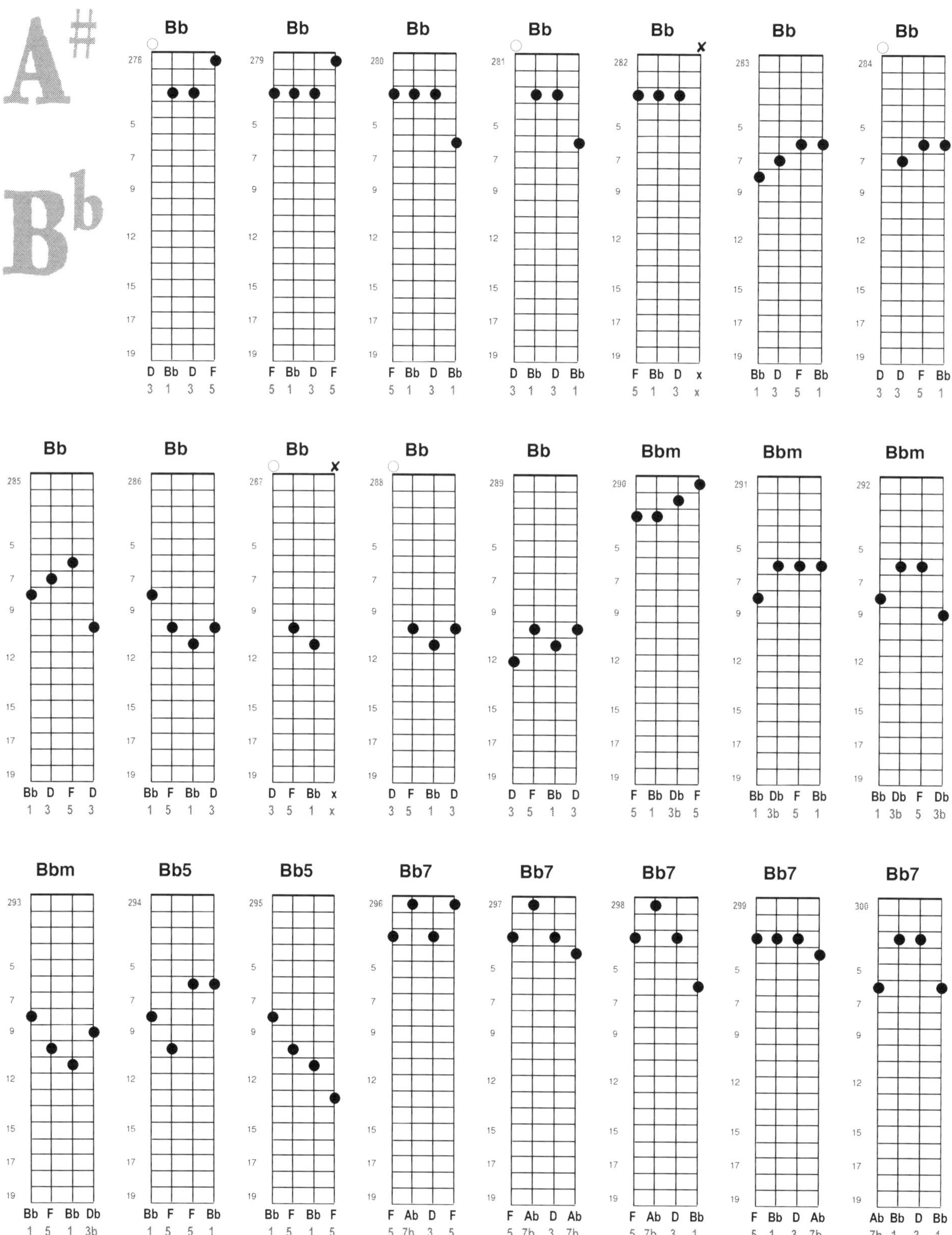

TUNING: D G B E

Bb7
301
D Bb D Ab
3 1 3 7b
Bb7
302
D Bb F Ab
3 1 5 7b
Bb7
303
Bb D F Ab
1 3 5 7b
Bb7
304
Ab D F Bb
7b 3 5 1
Bb7
305
D F Ab Bb
3 5 7b 1
Bb7
306
Bb D Ab Bb
1 3 7b 1
Bb7
307
Bb F Ab Bb
1 5 7b 1
Bb7
308
Bb D Ab D
1 3 7b 3
Bb7
309
Bb F Ab D
1 5 7b 3
Bb7
310
D F Ab x
3 5 7b x
Bb7
311
D F Ab D
3 5 7b 3
Bbm7
312
F Ab Db F
5 7b 3b 5
Bbm7
313
Ab Db F Bb
7b 3b 5 1
Bbm7
314
Ab Db Ab Bb
7b 3b 7b 1
Bbm7
315
Bb Db Ab Bb
1 3b 7b 1
Bbm7
316
Bb Db Ab Db
1 3b 7b 3b
Bbm7
317
Bb F Ab Db
1 5 7b 3b
Bbmaj7
318
F A D F
5 7 3 5
Bbmaj7
319
D Bb D A
3 1 3 7
Bbmaj7
320
F Bb D A
5 1 3 7
Bbmaj7
321
D Bb F A
3 1 5 7
Bbmaj7
322
Bb D F A
1 3 5 7
Bbmaj7
323
A D F Bb
7 3 5 1
Bbmaj7
324
Bb D A Bb
1 3 7 1

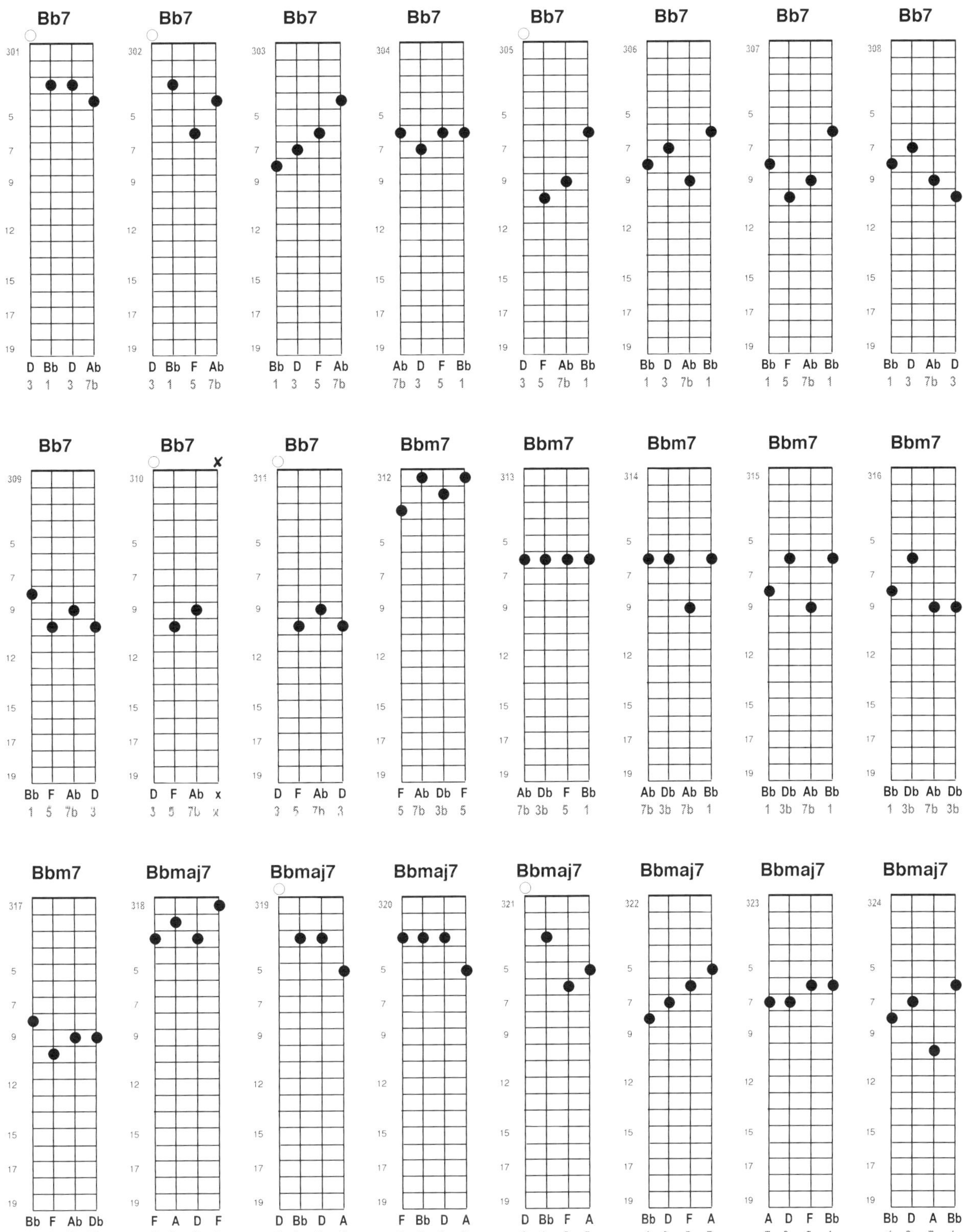

Baritone Ukulele Chords

TUNING: D G B E

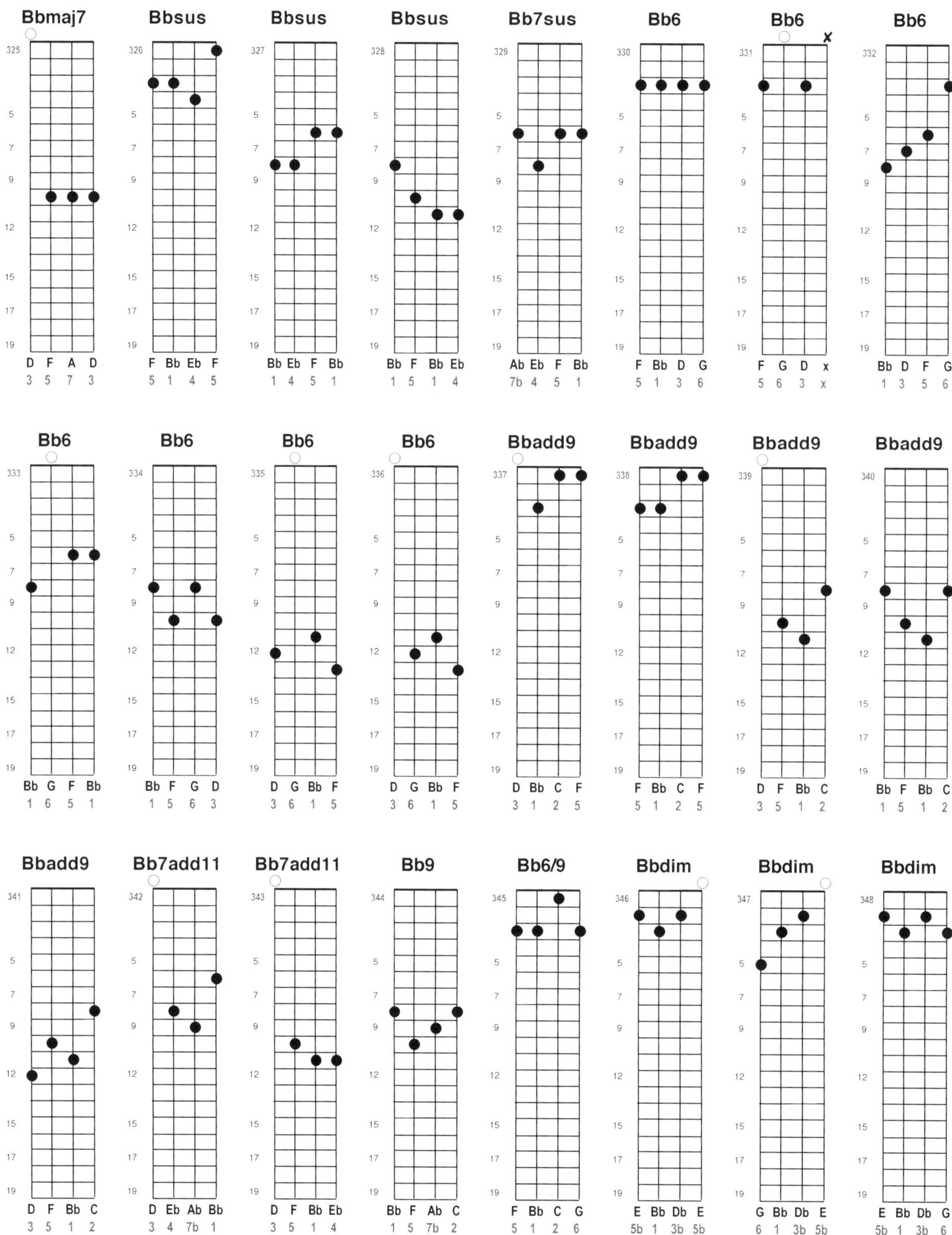

TUNING: D G B E

Bbdim
349
Bb Db E E
1 3b 5b 5b
Bbdim
350
G Db E Bb
6 3b 5b 1
Bbdim
351
Bb Db G E
1 3b 6 5b
Bbdim
352
Bb E G Db
1 5b 6 3b
Bbdim
353
Db E Bb E
3b 5b 1 5b
Bbdim
354
Db G Bb E
3b 6 1 5b
Bbdim
355
Db G Bb E
3b 6 1 5b
Bbdim
356
Db G Bb E
3b 6 1 5b
Bb+
357
D Bb D F#
3 1 3 5#
Bb+
358
D D F# Bb
3 3 5# 1
Bb+
359
D F# Bb D
3 5# 1 3
Bbm6
360
Bb Db G Bb
1 3b 6 1
Bbm6
361
Bb F G Db
1 5 6 3b
Bbmadd9
362
Db F Bb C
3b 5 1 2
Bbmaj9
363
Bb F A C
1 5 7 2
Bbmaj9
364
D F A C
3 5 7 2
Bbm11
365
Bb Db Eb Ab
1 3b 4 7b
Bb?
366
F Bb D E
5 1 3 5b
Bb?
367
Bb D F E
1 3 5 5b
Bb?
368
D F Bb E
3 5 1 5b

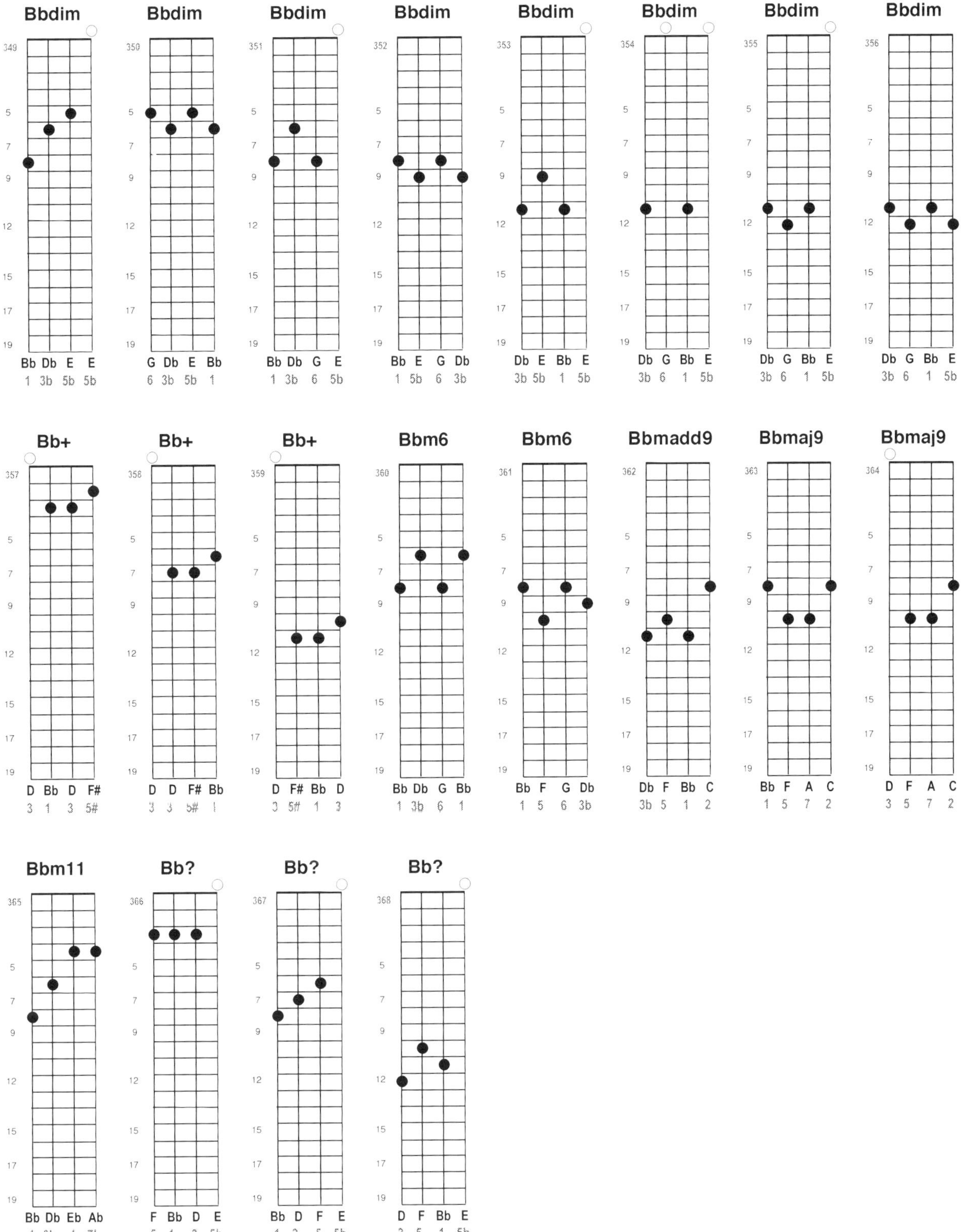

TUNING: D G B E

B

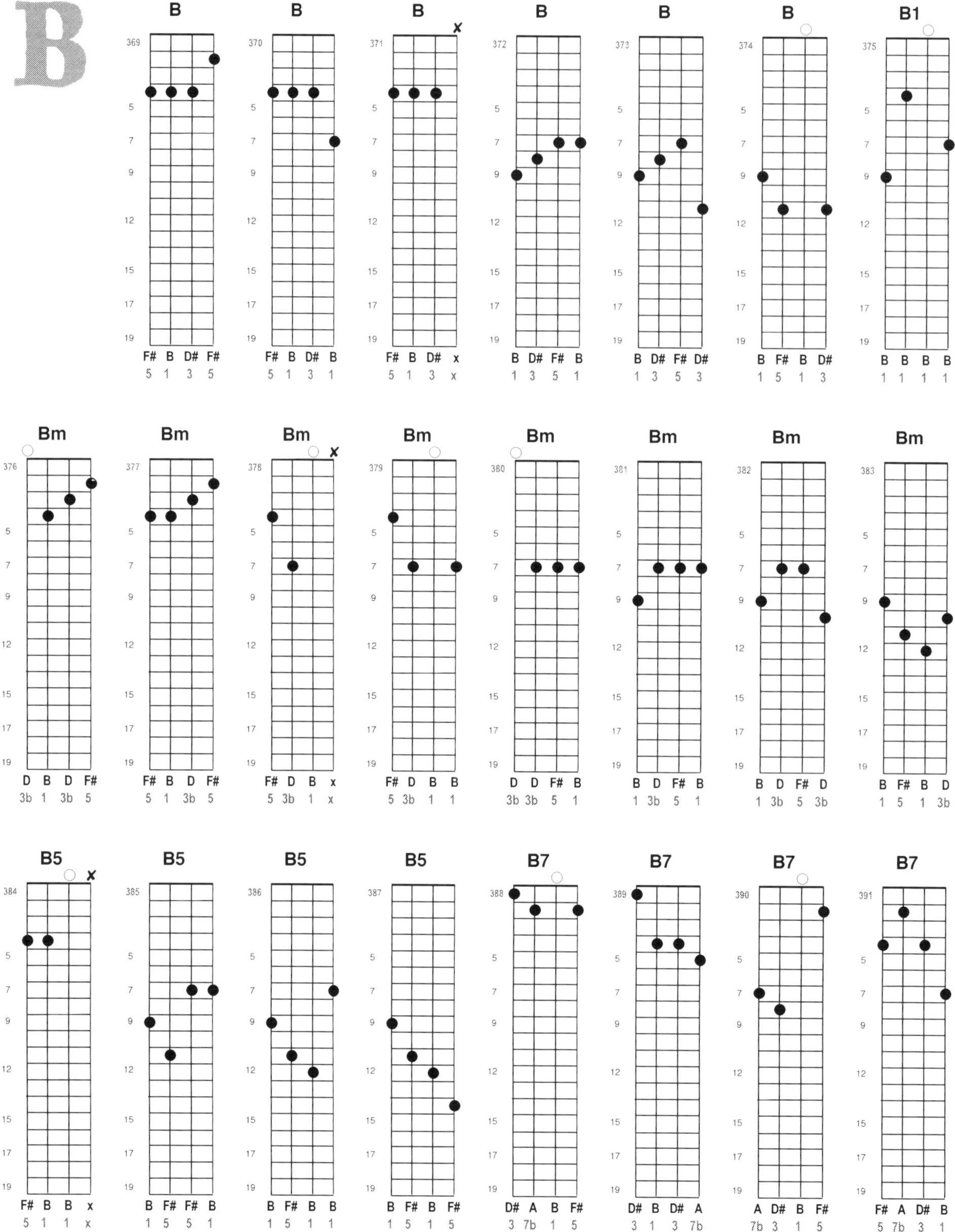

TUNING: D G B E

B7
392
F# B D# A
5 1 3 7b
B7
393
A B D# B
7b 1 3 1
B7
394
A D# B A
7b 3 1 7b
B7
395
B D# B A
1 3 1 7b
B7
396
B D# F# A
1 3 5 7b
B7
397
A D# F# B
7b 3 5 1
B7
398
A D# B B
7b 3 1 1
B7
399
A D# A B
7b 3 7b 1
B7
400
B F# A B
1 5 7b 1
B7
401
B D# A B
1 3 7b 1
B7
402
B D# A D#
1 3 7b 3
B7
403
D# A B x
3 7b 1 x
B7
404
D# A B F#
3 7b 1 5
Bm7
405
D A B F#
3b 7b 1 5
Bm7
406
F# A D F#
5 7b 3b 5
Bm7
407
F# B D A
5 1 3b 7b
Bm7
408
A D F# B
7b 3b 5 1
Bm7
409
A D A B
7b 3b 7b 1
Bm7
410
D F# A B
3b 5 7b 1
Bm7
411
B D A B
1 3b 7b 1
Bm7
412
B D A D
1 3b 7b 3b
Bm7
413
B F# A D
1 5 7b 3b
Bmaj7
414
F# A# D# F#
5 7 3 5
Bmaj7
415
F# B D# A#
5 1 3 7

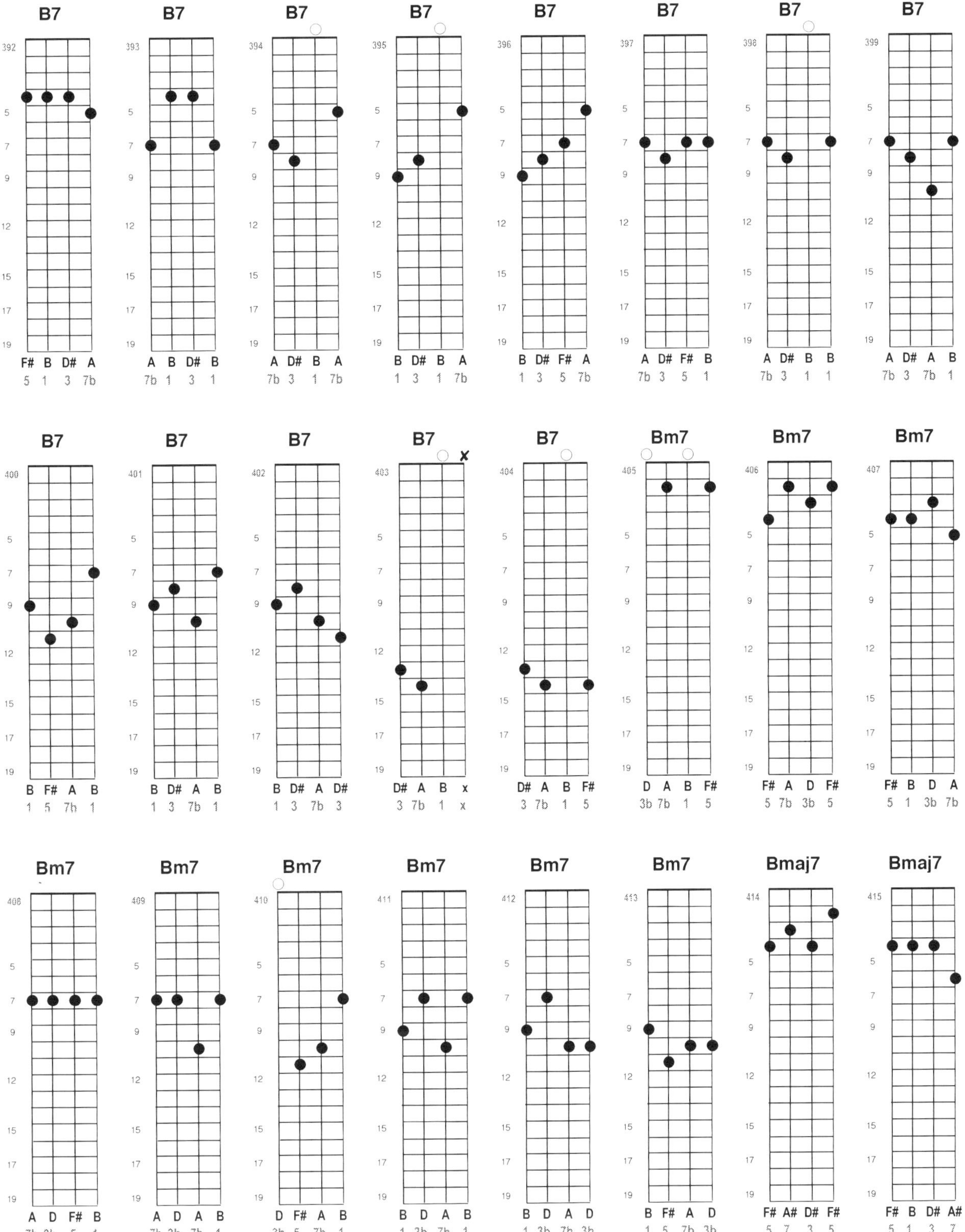

TUNING: D G B E

Bmaj7
416
5 7 9 12 15 17 19
B D# F# A#
1 3 5 7
Bmaj7
417
A# D# F# B
7 3 5 1
Bmaj7
418
B D# A# B
1 3 7 1
Bsus
419
F# B E F#
5 1 4 5
Bsus
420
F# B B E
5 1 1 4
Bsus
421
B E F# B
1 4 5 1
Bsus
422
B E B E
1 4 1 4
Bsus
423
B F# B E
1 5 1 4
Bsus
424
E F# B E
4 5 1 4
B7sus
425
F# A B E
5 7b 1 4
B7sus
426
F# A E F#
5 7b 4 5
B7sus
427
A E F# B
7b 4 5 1
B7sus
428
E A B E
4 7b 1 4
B6
429
D# G# B F#
3 6 1 5
B6
430
F# B D# G#
5 1 3 6
B6
431
B D# F# G#
1 3 5 6
B6
432
B F# G# D#
1 5 6 3
Badd9
433
F# B C# F#
5 1 2 5
Badd9
434
B C# F# B
1 2 5 1
Badd9
435
B D# F# C#
1 3 5 2
Badd9
436
D# F# B C#
3 5 1 2
Badd9
437
B F# B C#
1 5 1 2
Badd11
438
F# D# B E
5 3 1 4
Badd11
439
F# B D# E
5 1 3 4

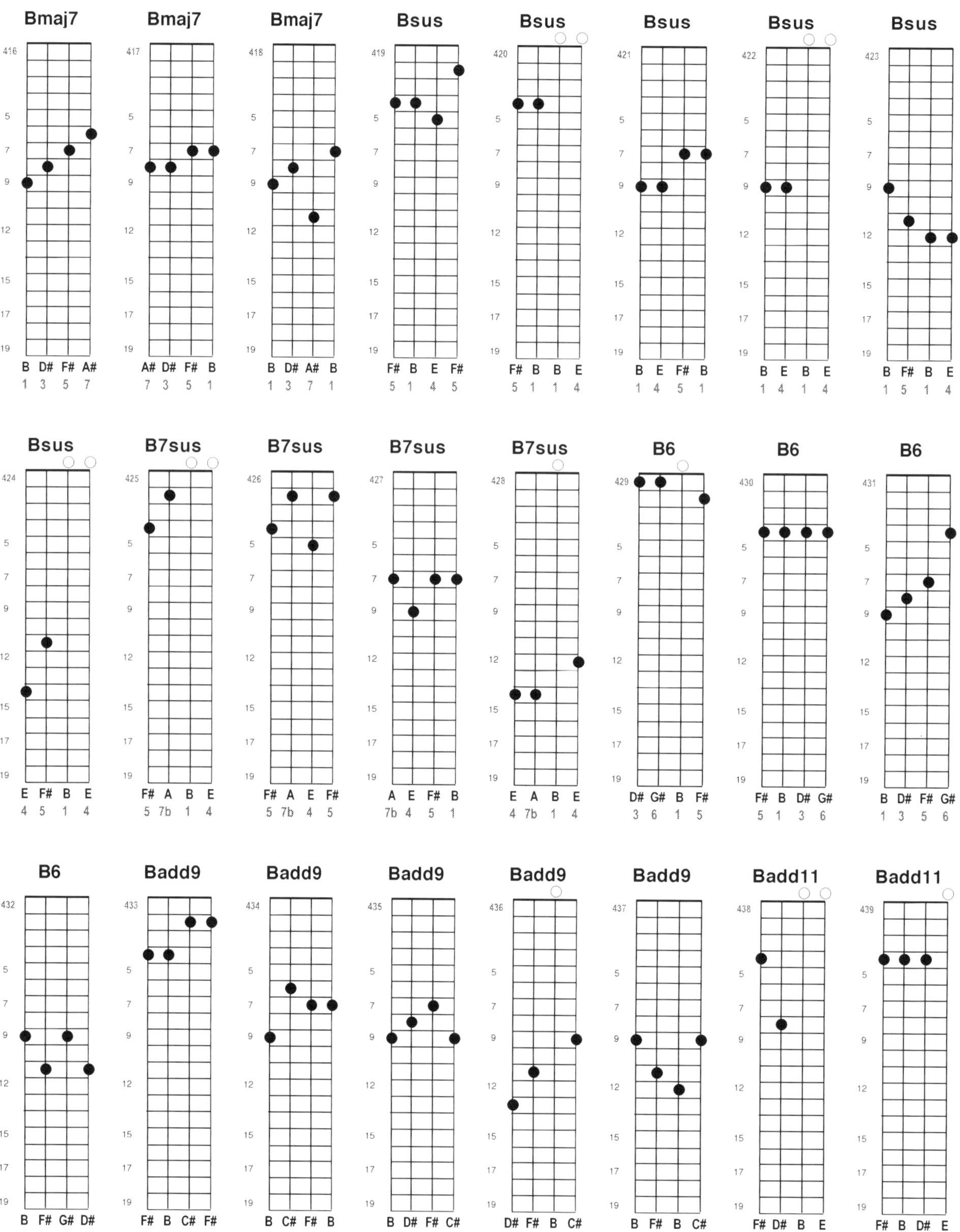

TUNING: D G B E

Badd11
B D# B E
1 3 1 4
Badd11
D# F# B E
3 5 1 4
B7add11
A D# B E
7b 3 1 4
B9
D# A C# F#
3 7b 2 5
B9
F# A C# F#
5 7b 2 5
B9
F# C# B A
5 2 1 7b
B9
A D# F# C#
7b 3 5 2
B9
B F# A C#
1 5 7b 2
B11
F# C# B E
5 2 1 4
B11
A C# F# E
7b 2 5 4
B6/7
F# A D# G#
5 7b 3 6
B6/7
A D# B G#
7b 3 1 6
B6/9
F# B C# G#
5 1 2 6
B6/9
F# C# B G#
5 2 1 6
B6/9
G# D# B C#
6 3 1 2
B6/9
G# C# F# B
6 2 5 1
Bdim
D G# B F
3b 6 1 5b
Bdim
D B D F
3b 1 3b 5b
Bdim
F B D F
5b 1 3b 5b
Bdim
F B D G#
5b 1 3b 6
Bdim
D D F G#
3b 3b 5b 6
Bdim
D B F G#
3b 1 5b 6
Bdim
G# D F B
6 3b 5b 1
Bdim
D F G# B
3b 5b 6 1

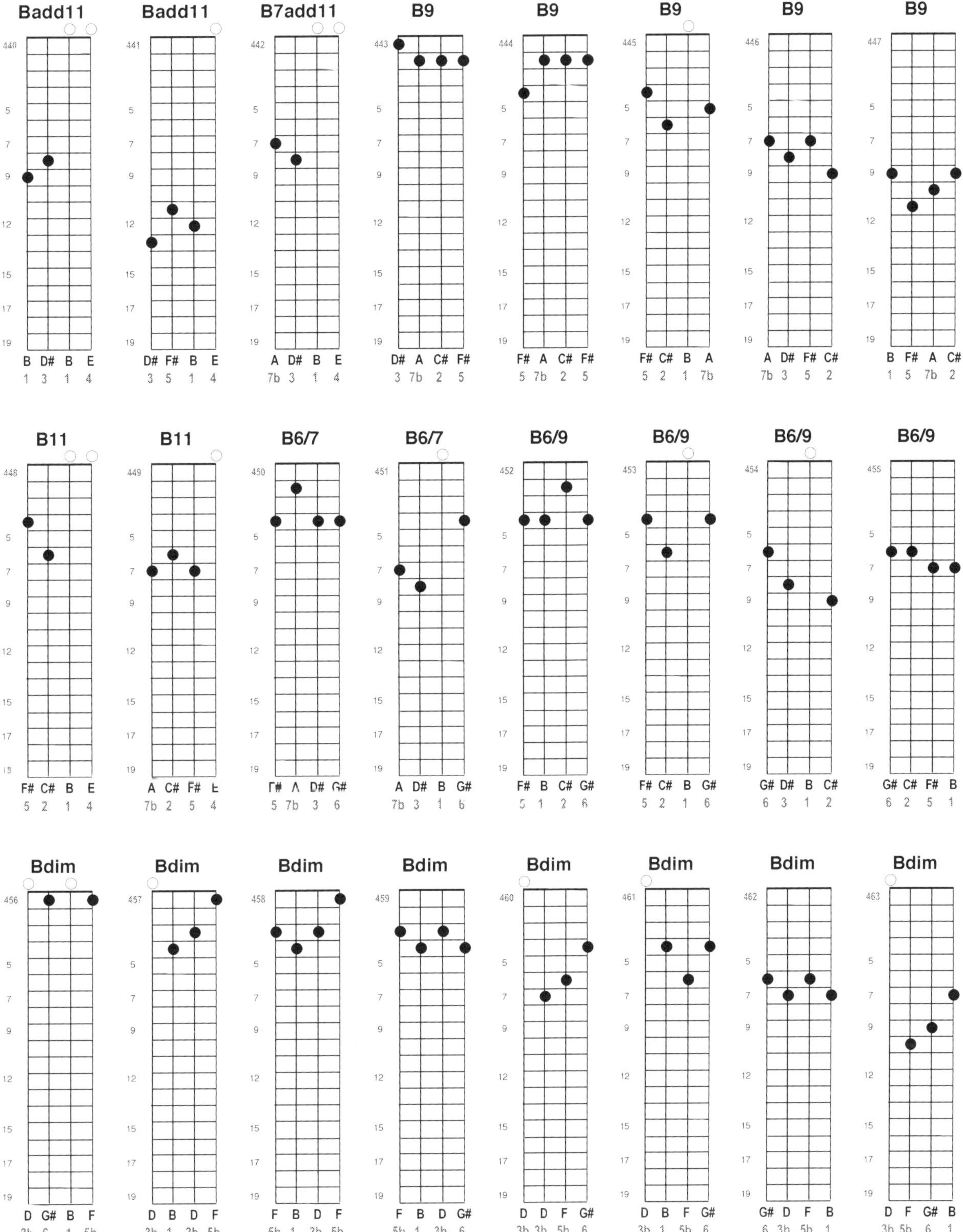

TUNING: D G B E

Bdim
464
B F G# D
1 5b 6 3b
Bdim
465
D F B D
3b 5b 1 3b
Bdim
466
D F B D
3b 5b 1 3b
Bdim
467
D G# B D
3b 6 1 3b
B+
468
D# G B G
3 5# 1 5#
B+
469
G B D# G
5# 1 3 5#
B+
470
B D# G B
1 3 5# 1
B+
471
D# G B D#
3 5# 1 3
B+
472
D# G B D#
3 5# 1 3
B+
473
D# G B D#
3 5# 1 3
B+
474
D# G B D#
3 5# 1 3
Bm6
475
D G# B F#
3b 6 1 5
Bm6
476
B D G# B
1 3b 6 1
Bm6
477
B F# G# D
1 5 6 3b
Bm9
478
D A C# F#
3b 7b 2 5
Bm9
479
D B C# F#
3b 1 2 5
Bm9
480
B D A C#
1 3b 7b 2
Bm9
481
D F# B C#
3b 5 1 2
Bm9
482
D F# B C#
3b 5 1 2
Bm9
483
D F# A C#
3b 5 7b 2
Bmadd9
484
D C# B F#
3b 2 1 5
Bmadd9
485
B D F# C#
1 3b 5 2
Bmadd9
486
D F# B C#
3b 5 1 2
Bmaj9
487
B F# A# C#
1 5 7 2

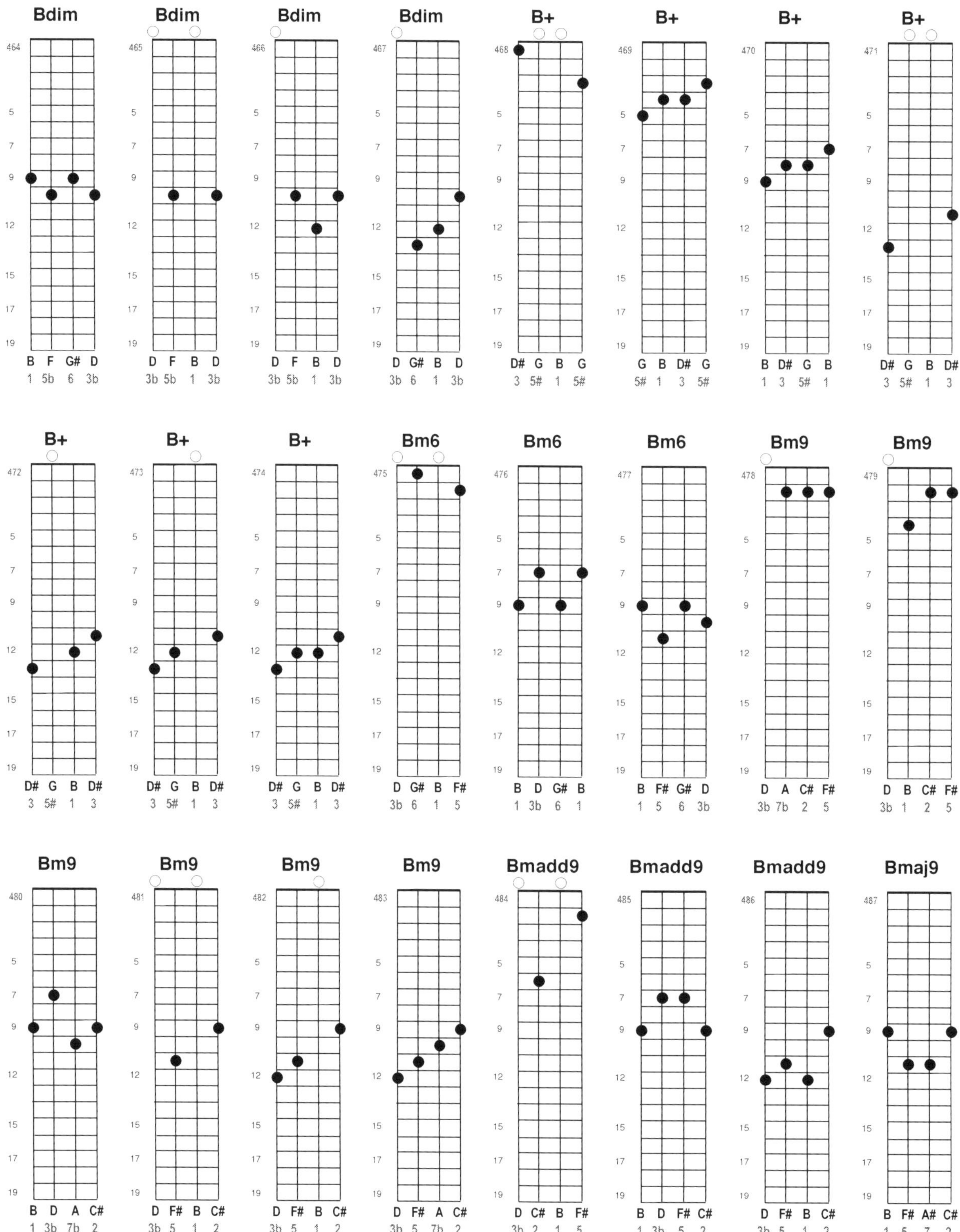

TUNING: D G B E

Bm11
Bmadd11
Bmadd11
Bmadd11
Bmadd11
488
489
490
491
492
5
7
9
12
15
17
19
B D E A
1 3b 4 7b
F# B D E
5 1 3b 4
F# D B E
5 3b 1 4
B D B E
1 3b 1 4
B D F# E
1 3b 5 4

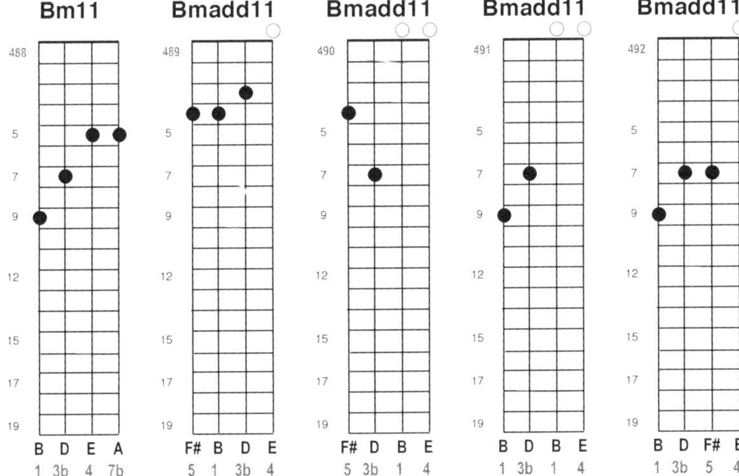

TUNING: D G B E

C

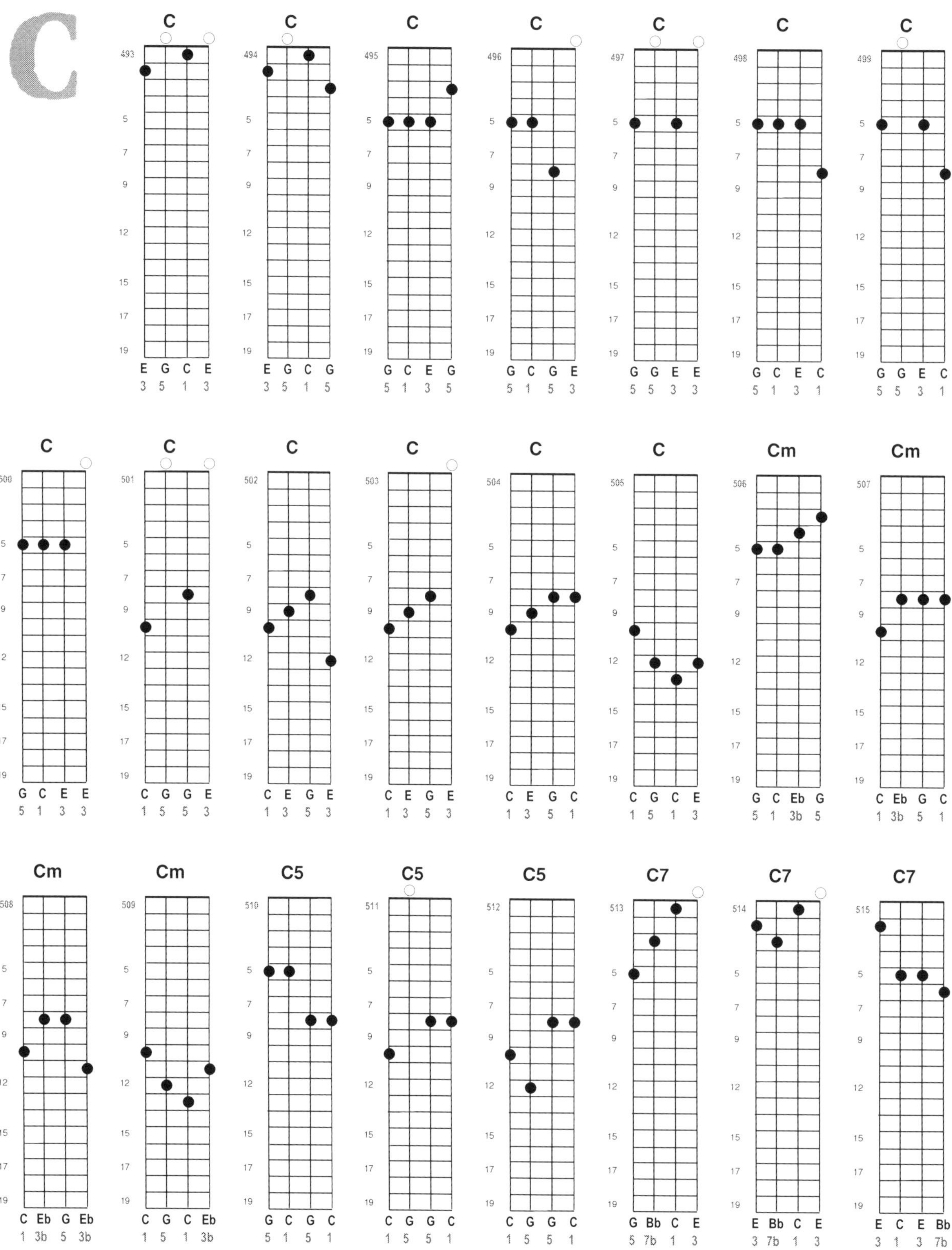

TUNING: D G B E

C7
516
G Bb E E
5 7b 3 3
C7
517
G Bb E G
5 7b 3 5
C7
518
G Bb E Bb
5 7b 3 7b
C7
519
G Bb E C
5 7b 3 1
C7
520
Bb C E C
7b 1 3 1
C7
521
G G E Bb
5 5 3 7b
C7
522
Bb C G E
7b 1 5 3
C7
523
C E G Bb
1 3 5 7b
C7
524
Bb E G C
7b 3 5 1
C7
525
Bb E Bb C
7b 3 7b 1
C7
526
C G Bb C
1 5 7b 1
C7
527
C E Bb C
1 3 7b 1
C7
528
C E Bb E
1 3 7b 3
C7
529
C E Bb E
1 3 7b 3
C7
530
C G Bb E
1 5 7b 3
C7
531
C G Bb E
1 5 7b 3
Cm7
532
G C Eb Bb
5 1 3b 7b
Cm7
533
Bb Eb G C
7b 3b 5 1
Cm7
534
C Eb Bb C
1 3b 7b 1
Cm7
535
C Eb Bb Eb
1 3b 7b 3b
Cm7
536
C G Bb Eb
1 5 7b 3b
Cmaj7
537
E B C E
3 7 1 3
Cmaj7
538
E G B E
3 5 7 3
Cmaj7
539
E G B G
3 5 7 5

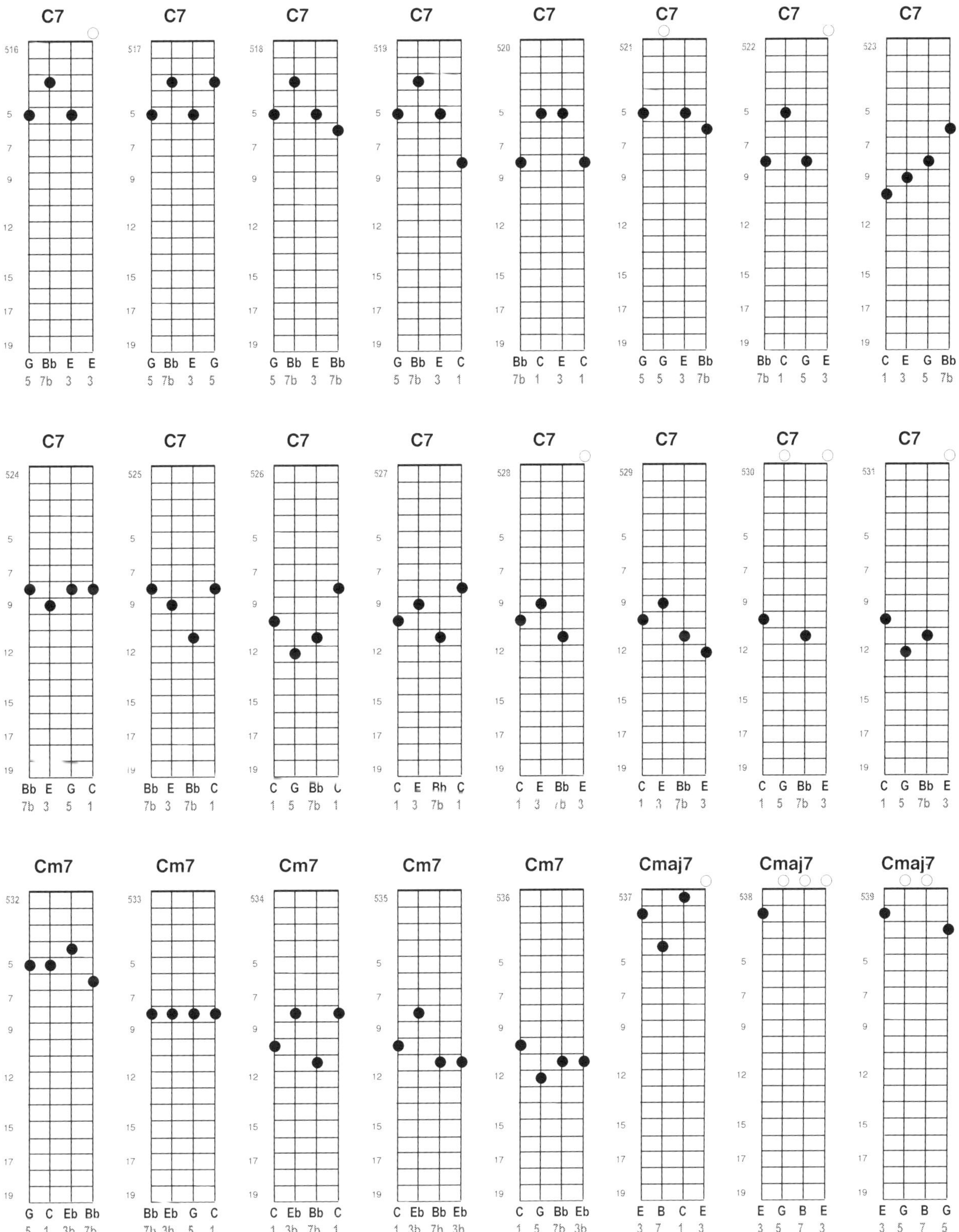

TUNING: D G B E

Cmaj7 540 G C B G 5 1 7 5
Cmaj7 541 G B E G 5 7 3 5
Cmaj7 542 G B E E 5 7 3 3
Cmaj7 543 G C B E 5 1 7 3
Cmaj7 544 G C E B 5 1 3 7
Cmaj7 545 C E G B 1 3 5 7
Cmaj7 546 B G G E 7 5 5 3
Cmaj7 547 B E G C 7 3 5 1
Cmaj7 548 C E B C 1 3 7 1
Cmaj7 549 C E B E 1 3 7 3
Cmaj7 550 C E B E 1 3 7 3
Cmaj7 551 C G B E 1 5 7 3
Cmaj7 552 C G B E 1 5 7 3
Cmaj7 553 C G B E 1 5 7 3
Csus 554 F G C F 4 5 1 4
Csus 555 G C F G 5 1 4 5
Csus 556 C F G C 1 4 5 1
Csus 557 C G C F 1 5 1 4
C7sus 558 G Bb F G 5 7b 4 5
C7sus 559 Bb F G C 7b 4 5 1
C6 560 G C E A 5 1 3 6
C6 561 A C G E 6 1 5 3
C6 562 C E G A 1 3 5 6
C6 563 A G G E 6 5 5 3

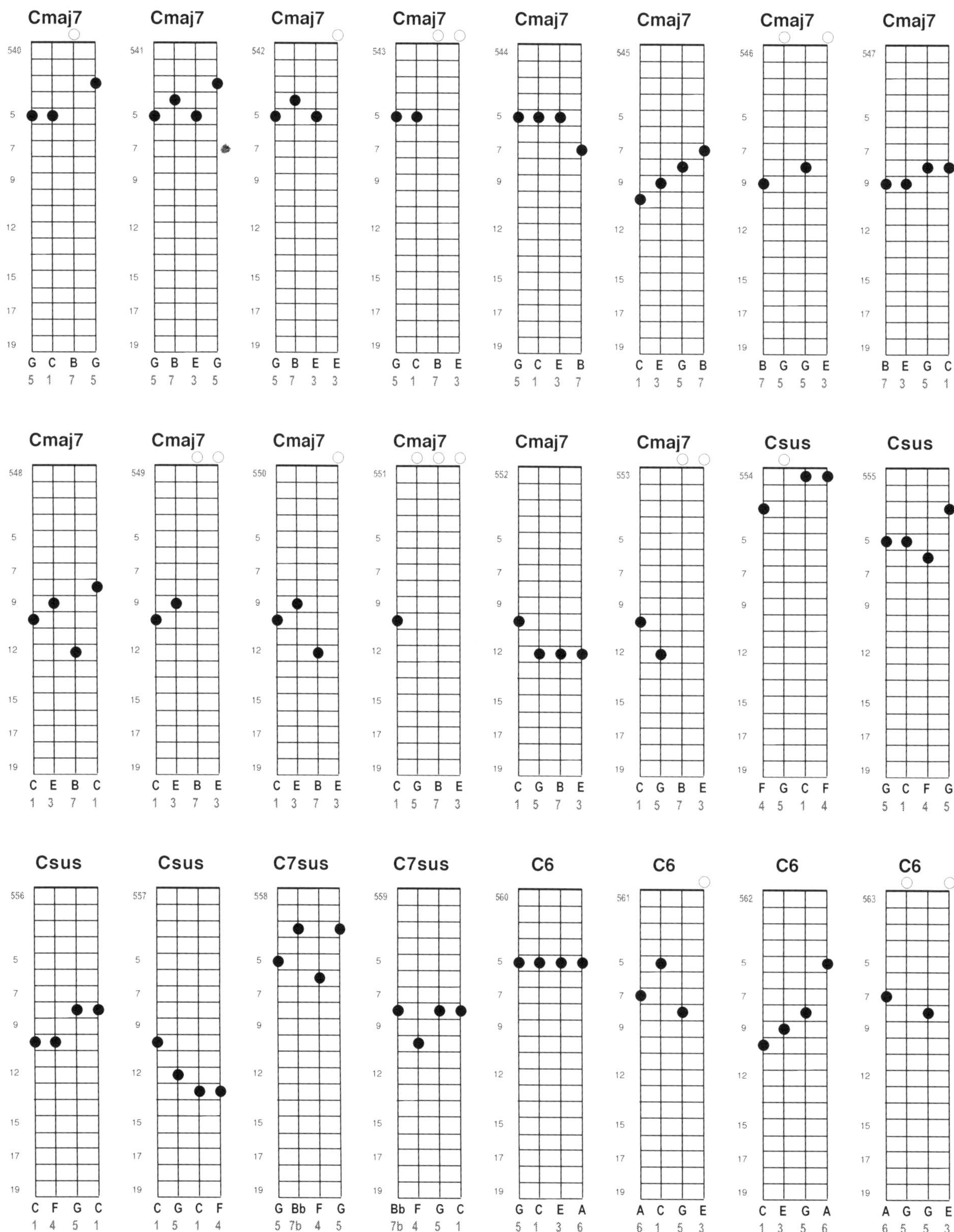

TUNING: D G B E

C6
564
C G A E
1 5 6 3
Cadd9
565
E G D E
3 5 2 3
Cadd9
566
G C D G
5 1 2 5
Cadd9
567
G C D E
5 1 2 3
Cadd9
568
G D E C
5 2 3 1
Cadd9
569
C D G E
1 2 5 3
Cadd9
570
C G C D
1 5 1 2
Cadd11
571
C F C E
1 4 1 3
C7add11
572
E Bb C F
3 7b 1 4
C9
573
E Bb D C
3 7b 2 5
C9
574
Bb D G E
7b 2 5 3
C9
575
Bb D G C
7b 2 5 1
C9
576
Bb E G D
7b 3 5 2
C9
577
C G Bb D
1 5 7b 2
C6/7
578
G Bb E A
5 7b 3 6
C6/7
579
Bb E A C
7b 3 6 1
C6/9
580
G C D A
5 1 2 6
C6/9
581
C D A E
1 2 6 3
C6/9
582
C G A D
1 5 6 2
Cdim
583
Eb A C F#
3b 6 1 5b
Cdim
584
F# C Eb F#
5b 1 3b 5b
Cdim
585
F# C Eb A
5b 1 3b 6
Cdim
586
A Eb F# C
6 3b 5b 1
Cdim
587
C F# A Eb
1 5b 6 3b

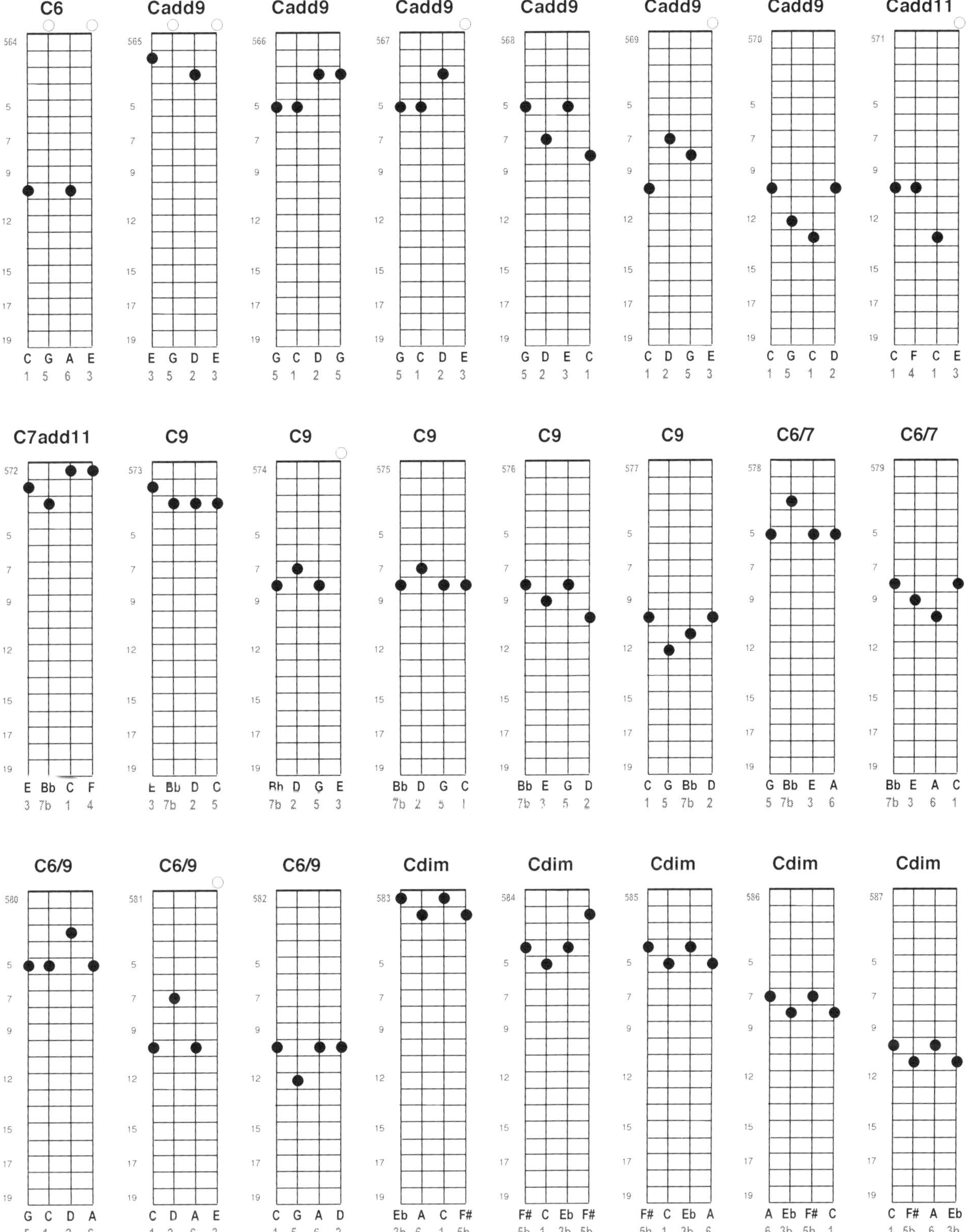

TUNING: D G B E

588 C+ E G# C E 3 5# 1 3
589 C+ G# C E G# 5# 1 3 5#
590 C+ G# C E E 5# 1 3 3
591 C+ C E G# C 1 3 5# 1
592 C+ C E G# E 1 3 5# 3
593 C+ E G# C E 3 5# 1 3
594 Cm6 Eb A C G 3b 6 1 5
595 Cm6 G C Eb A 5 1 3b 6
596 Cm6 C Eb A C 1 3b 6 1
597 Cm6 C G A Eb 1 5 6 3b
598 Cm6 C G A Eb 1 5 6 3b
599 Cmaj9 C D B E 1 2 7 3
600 Cmaj9 C G B D 1 5 7 2
601 Cm11 C Eb F Bb 1 3b 4 7b

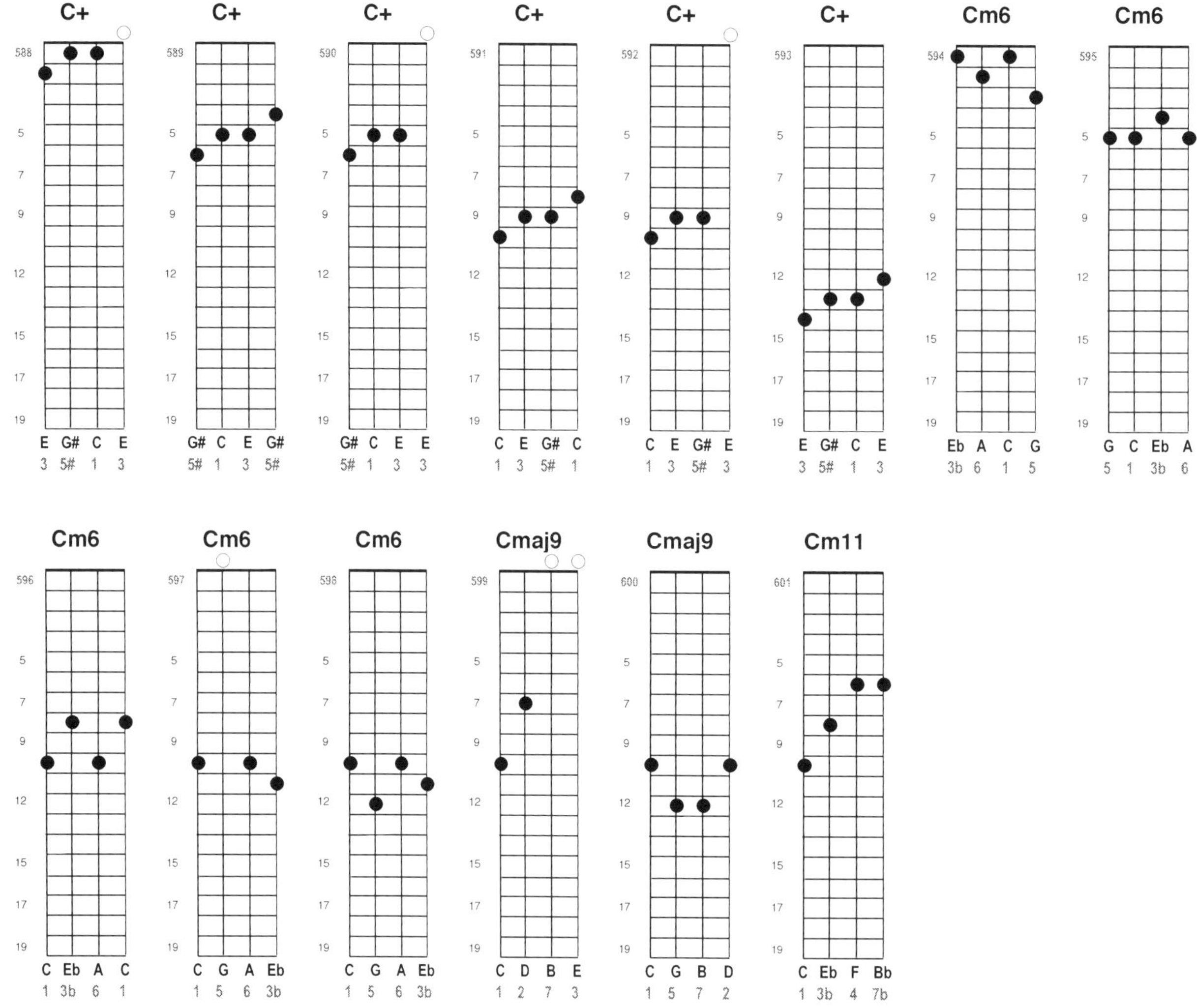

TUNING: D G B E

C#
Db
C#
602
E# G# C# E#
3 5 1 3
C#
603
G# C# E# G#
5 1 3 5
C#
604
G# C# E# C#
5 1 3 1
C#
605
C# E# G# C#
1 3 5 1
C#
606
C# E# G# E#
1 3 5 3
C#m
607
E G# C# E
3b 5 1 3b
C#m
608
G# C# E G#
5 1 3b 5
C#m
609
G# C# E E
5 1 3b 3b
C#m
610
C# E G# C#
1 3b 5 1
C#m
611
C# E C# E
1 3b 5 3b
C#m
612
C# G# C# E
1 5 1 3b
C#m
613
C# G# C# E
1 5 1 3b
C#5
614
C# G# G# C#
1 5 5 1
C#7
615
E# G# B E#
3 5 7b 3
C#7
616
E# B C# G#
3 7b 1 5
C#7
617
E# C# B G#
3 1 7b 5
C#7
618
E# C# E# B
3 1 3 7b
C#7
619
G# C# B G#
5 1 7b 5
C#7
620
G# B E# G#
5 7b 3 5
C#7
621
G# B E# B
5 7b 3 7b
C#7
622
G# B E# C#
5 7b 3 1
C#7
623
G# C# E# B
5 1 3 7b
C#7
624
B C# E# C#
7b 1 3 1

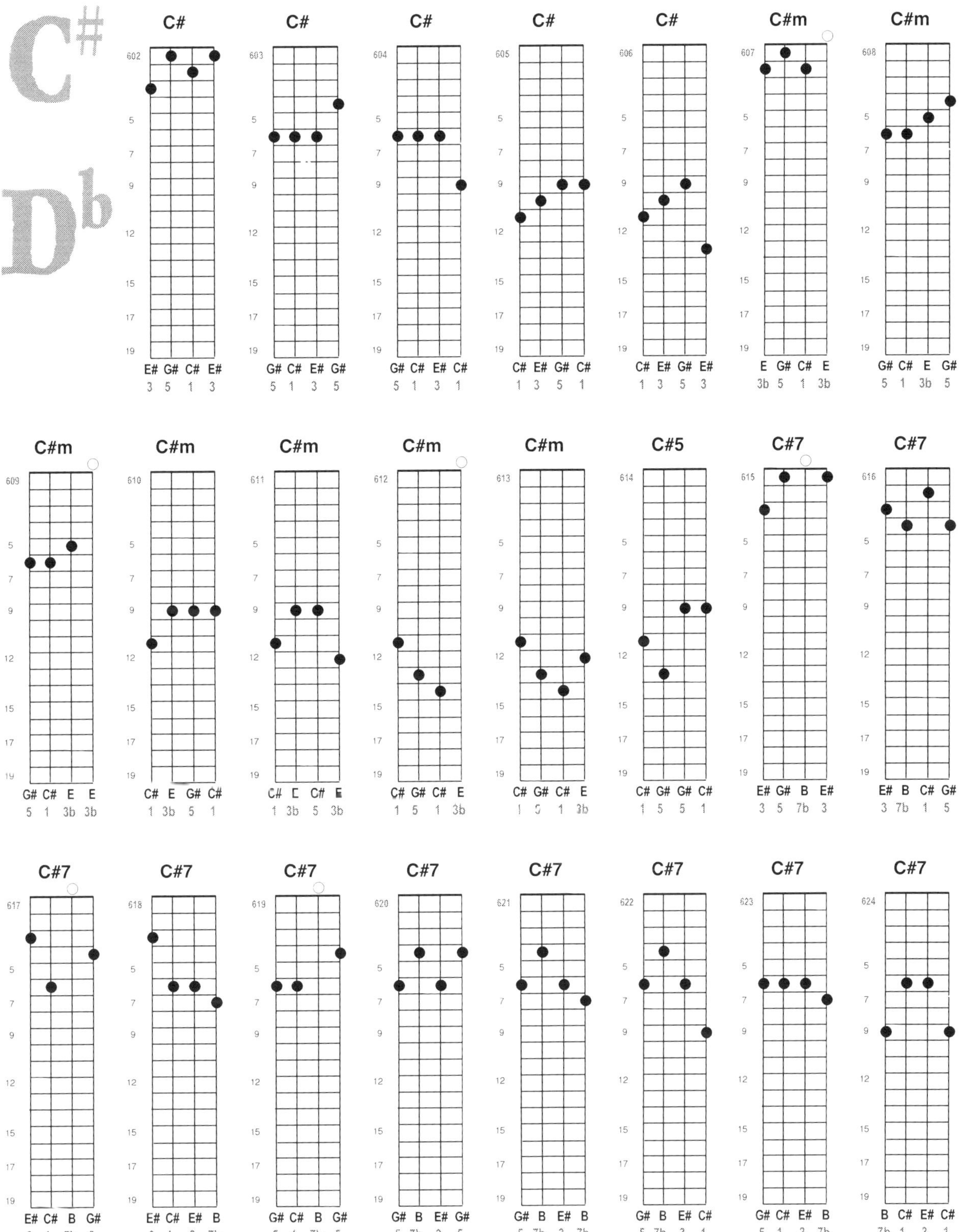

TUNING: D G B E

C#7
625
C# E# G# B
1 3 5 7b
C#7
626
B E# G# C#
7b 3 5 1
C#7
627
C# E# B C#
1 3 7b 1
C#7
628
C# G# B C#
1 5 7b 1
C#7
629
C# E# B C#
1 3 7b 1
C#7
630
C# E# B E#
1 3 7b 3
C#m7
631
E B C# E
3b 7b 1 3b
C#m7
632
G# C# B E
5 1 7b 3b
C#m7
633
B C# G# E
7b 1 5 3b
C#m7
634
B E G# C#
7b 3b 5 1
C#m7
635
B E B C#
7b 3b 7b 1
C#m7
636
C# E B E
1 3b 7b 3b
C#m7
637
C# E B C#
1 3b 7b 1
C#m7
638
C# E B E
1 3b 7b 3b
C#m7
639
C# G# B E
1 5 7b 3b
C#m7
640
C# G# B E
1 5 7b 3b
C#maj7
641
E# G# B# E#
3 5 7 3
C#maj7
642
G# B# E# G#
5 7 3 5
C#maj7
643
G# C# E# B#
5 1 3 7
C#maj7
644
C# E# G# B#
1 3 5 7
C#maj7
645
B# E# G# C#
7 3 5 1
C#sus
646
G# C# F# G#
5 1 4 5
C#sus
647
C# F# G# C#
1 4 5 1
C#sus
648
C# G# C# F#
1 5 1 4

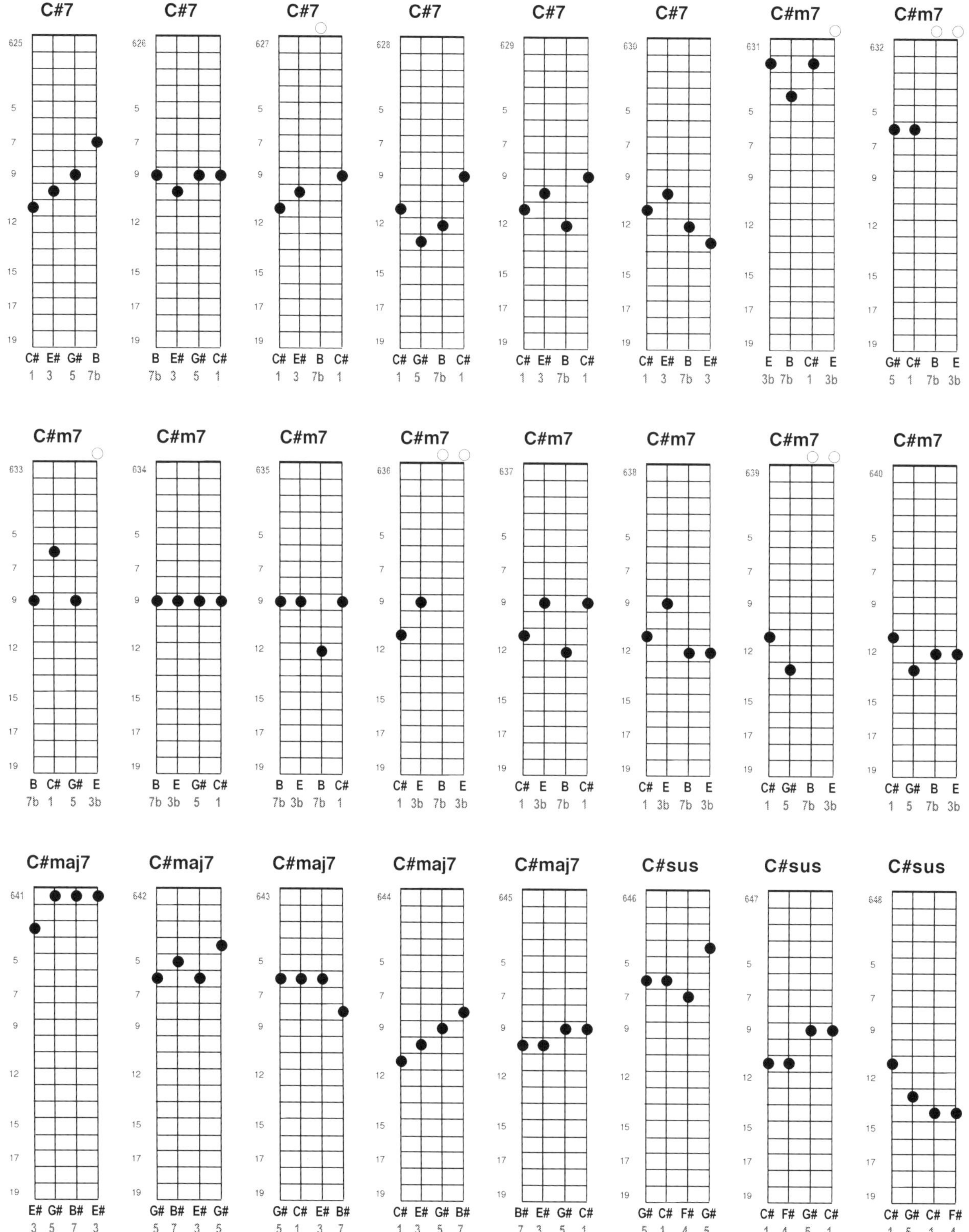

TUNING: D G B E

649 C#7sus
G# B F# G#
5 7b 4 5
650 C#7sus
F# C# B G#
4 1 7b 5
651 C#6
G# C# E# A#
5 1 3 6
652 C#6
C# E# G# A#
1 3 5 6
653 C#add9
G# C# D# G#
5 1 2 5
654 C#7add11
E# G# B F#
3 5 7b 4
655 C#9
E# B D# G#
3 7b 2 5
656 C#9
G# B D# G#
5 7b 2 5
657 C#9
B D# G# C#
7b 2 5 1
658 C#9
B E# C# D#
7b 3 5 2
659 C#6/7
G# B E# A#
5 7b 3 6
660 C#6/7
B E# A# C#
7b 3 6 1
661 C#6/9
G# C# D# A#
5 1 2 6
662 C#dim
G A# C# E
5b 6 1 3b
663 C#dim
E A# C# G
3b 6 1 5b
664 C#dim
G C# E E
5b 1 3b 3b
665 C#dim
A# C# E E
6 1 3b 3b
666 C#dim
G C# E A#
5b 1 3b 6
667 C#dim
A# C# G E
6 1 5b 3b
668 C#dim
C# E G E
1 3b 5b 3b
669 C#dim
A# E G C#
6 3b 5b 1
670 C#dim
C# G A# E
1 5b 6 3b
671 C#+
E# A C# E#
3 5# 1 3
672 C#+
A C# E# A
5# 1 3 5#

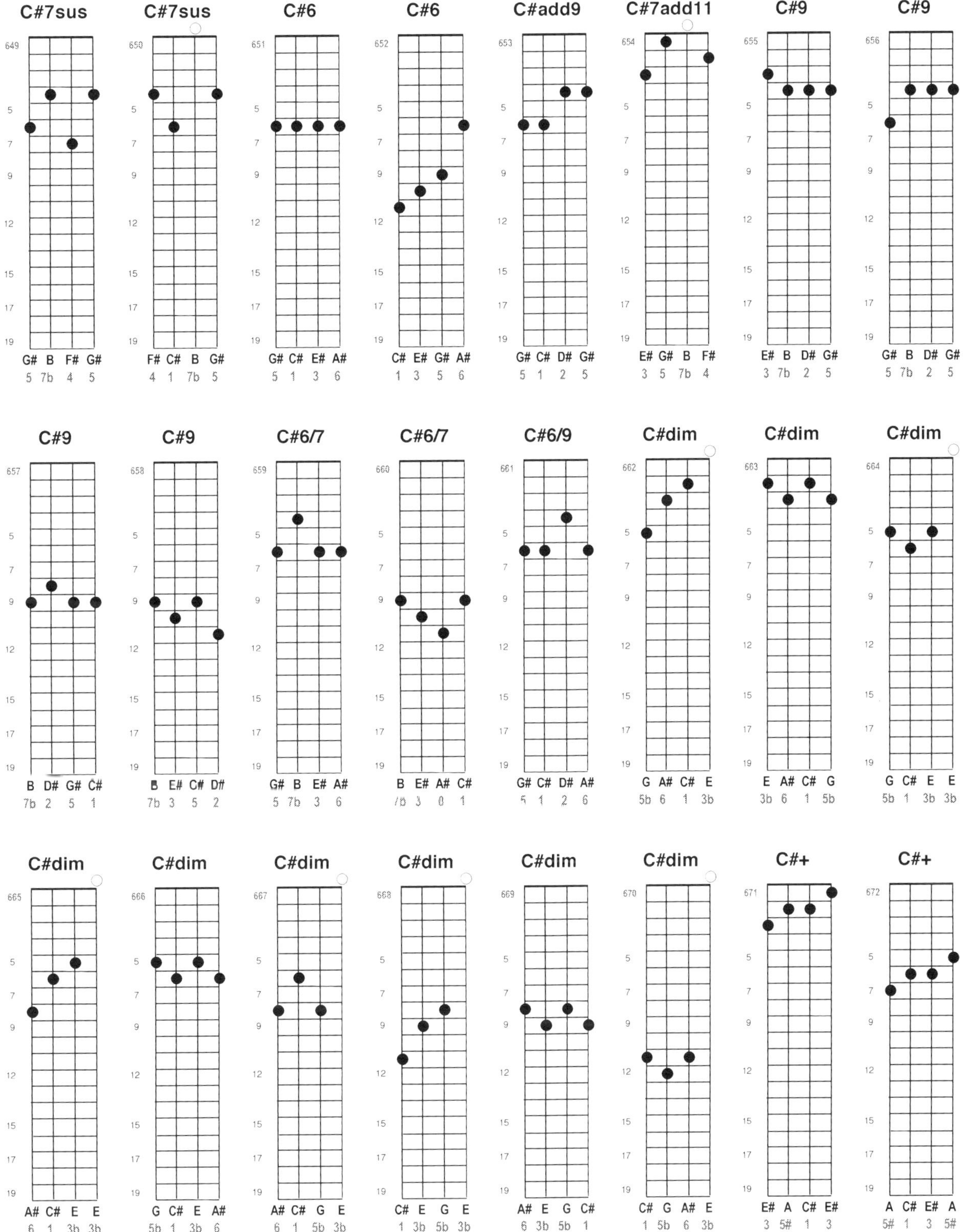

TUNING: D G B E

No.	Chord	Notes	Degrees
673	C#+	C# E# A C#	1 3 5# 1
674	C#m6	E A# C# E	3b 6 1 3b
675	C#m6	E A# C# G#	3b 6 1 5
676	C#m6	A# C# G# E	6 1 5 3b
677	C#m6	C# E A# E	1 3b 6 3b
678	C#m6	C# E A# C#	1 3b 6 1
679	C#m6	C# G# A# E	1 5 6 3b
680	C#m6	C# G# A# E	1 5 6 3b
681	C#m9	E B D# G#	3b 7b 2 5
682	C#m9	G# D# B E	5 2 7b 3b
683	C#m9	C# D# B E	1 2 7b 3b
684	C#m9	B E G# D#	7b 3b 5 2
685	C#m9	B E B D#	7b 3b 7b 2
686	C#maj9	C# G# B# D#	1 5 7 2
687	C#m11	F# C# D# E	4 1 2 3b
688	C#m11	C# E F# B	1 3b 4 7b

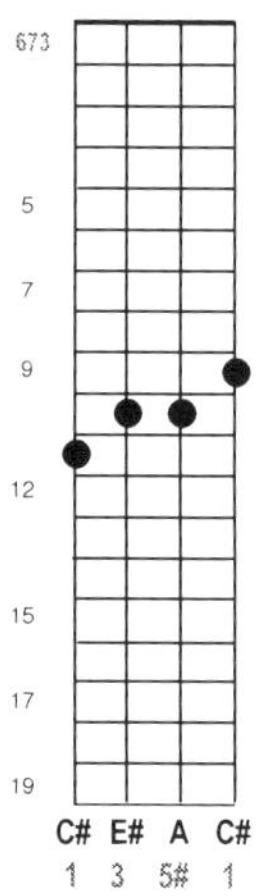

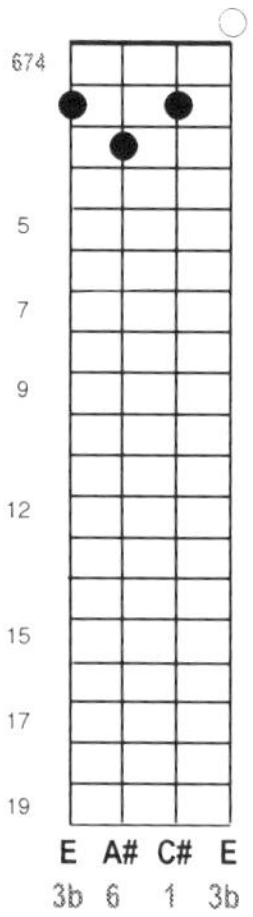

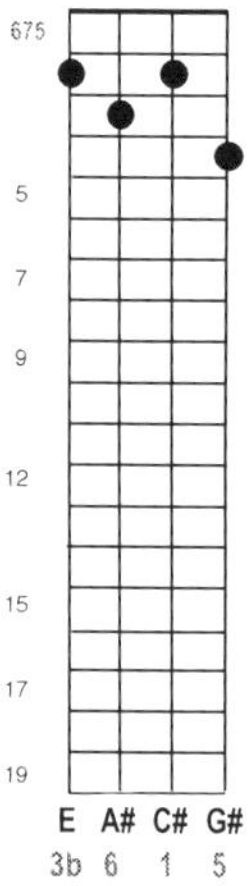

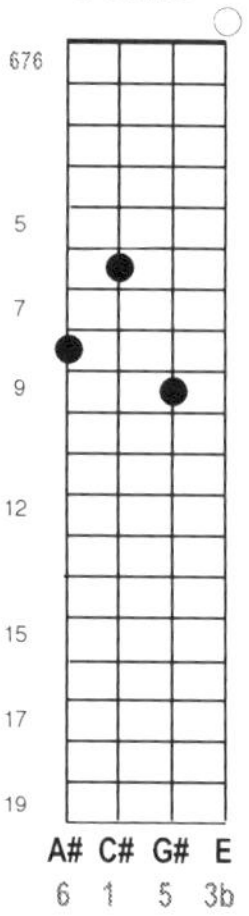

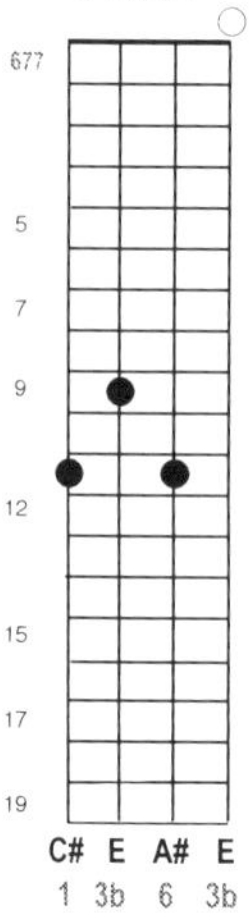

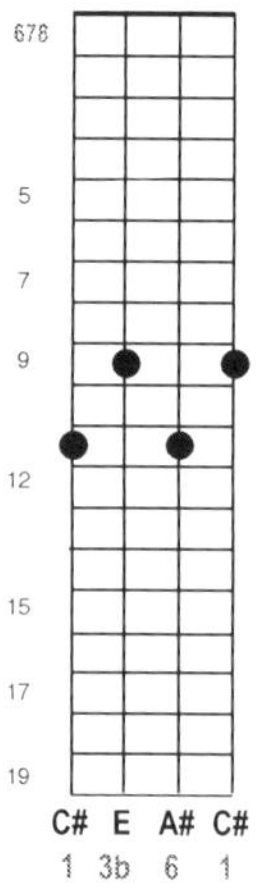

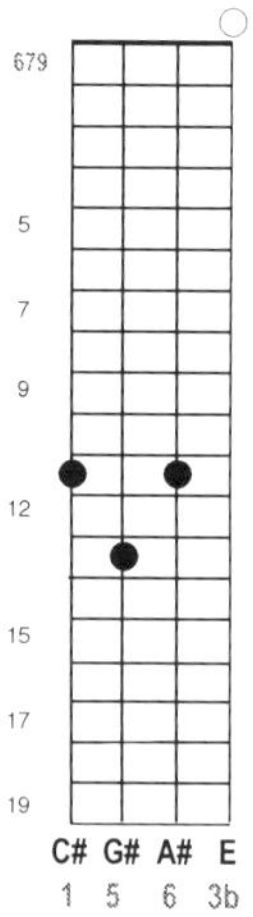

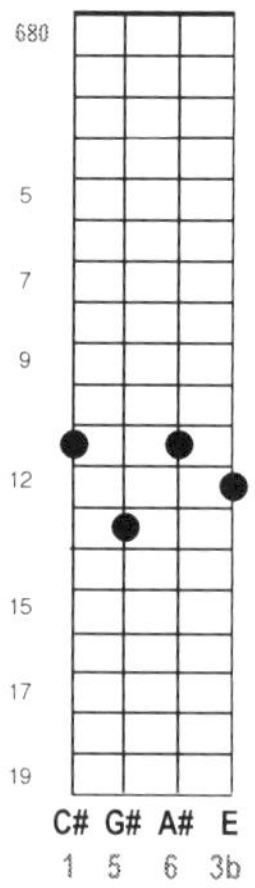

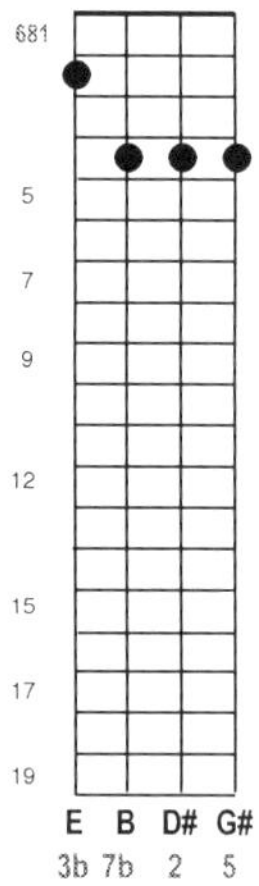

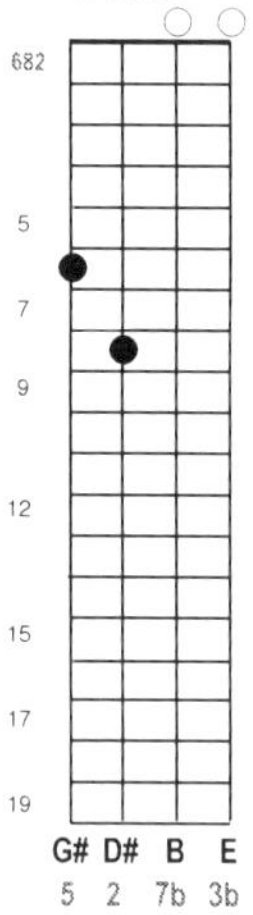

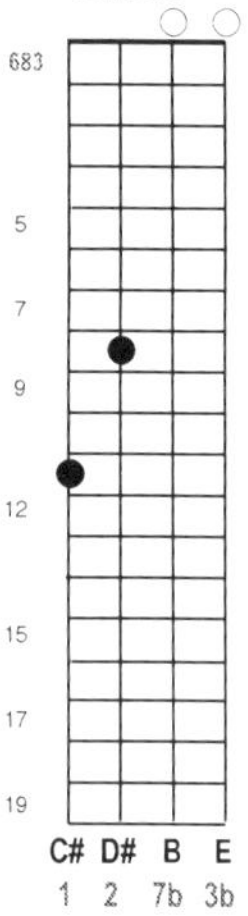

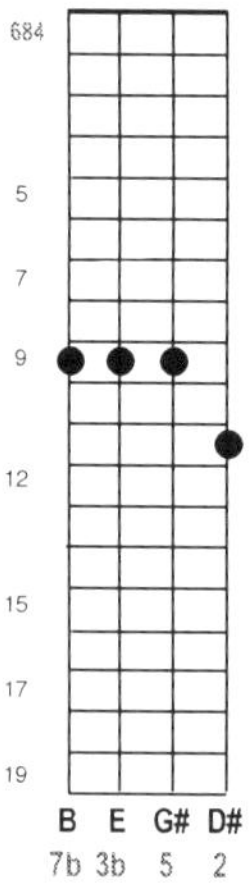

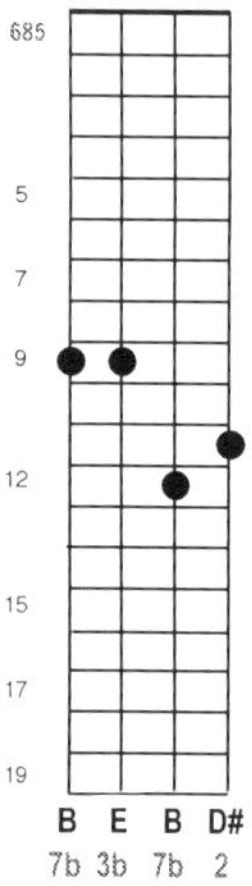

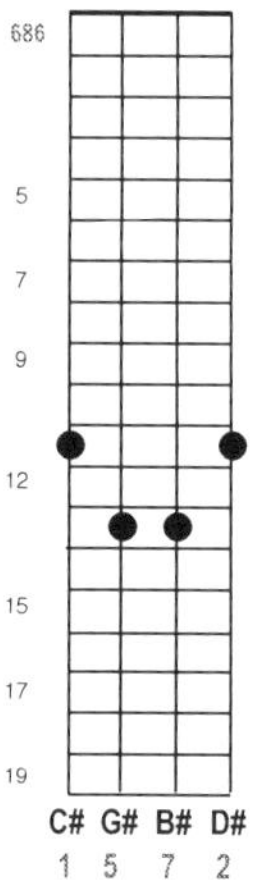

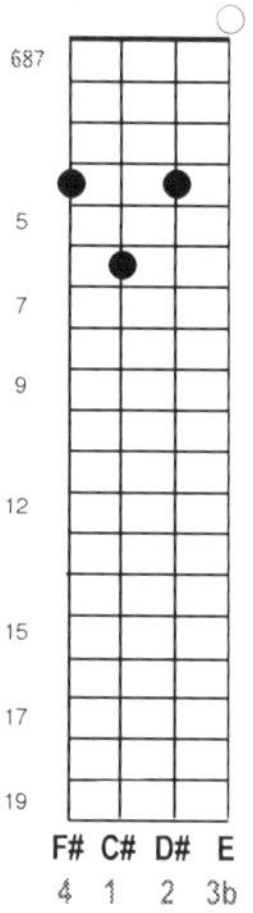

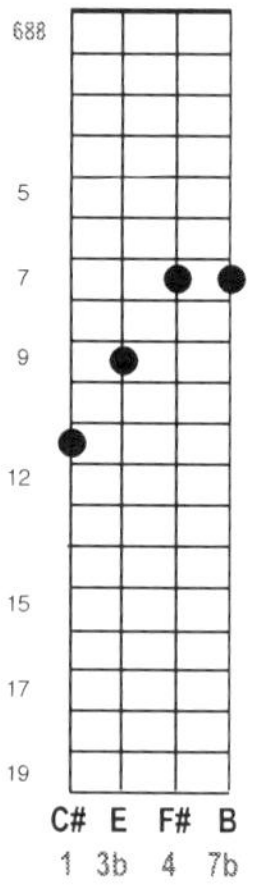

C#m11

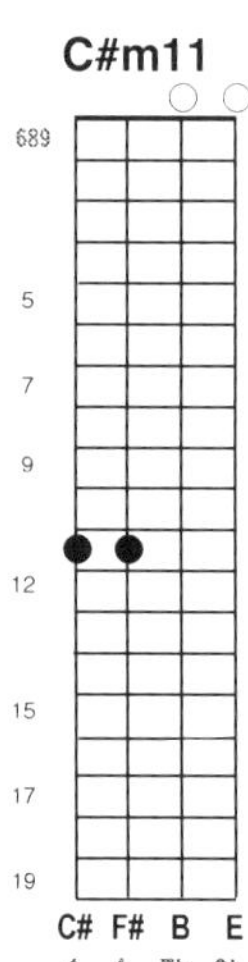

TUNING: D G B E

D

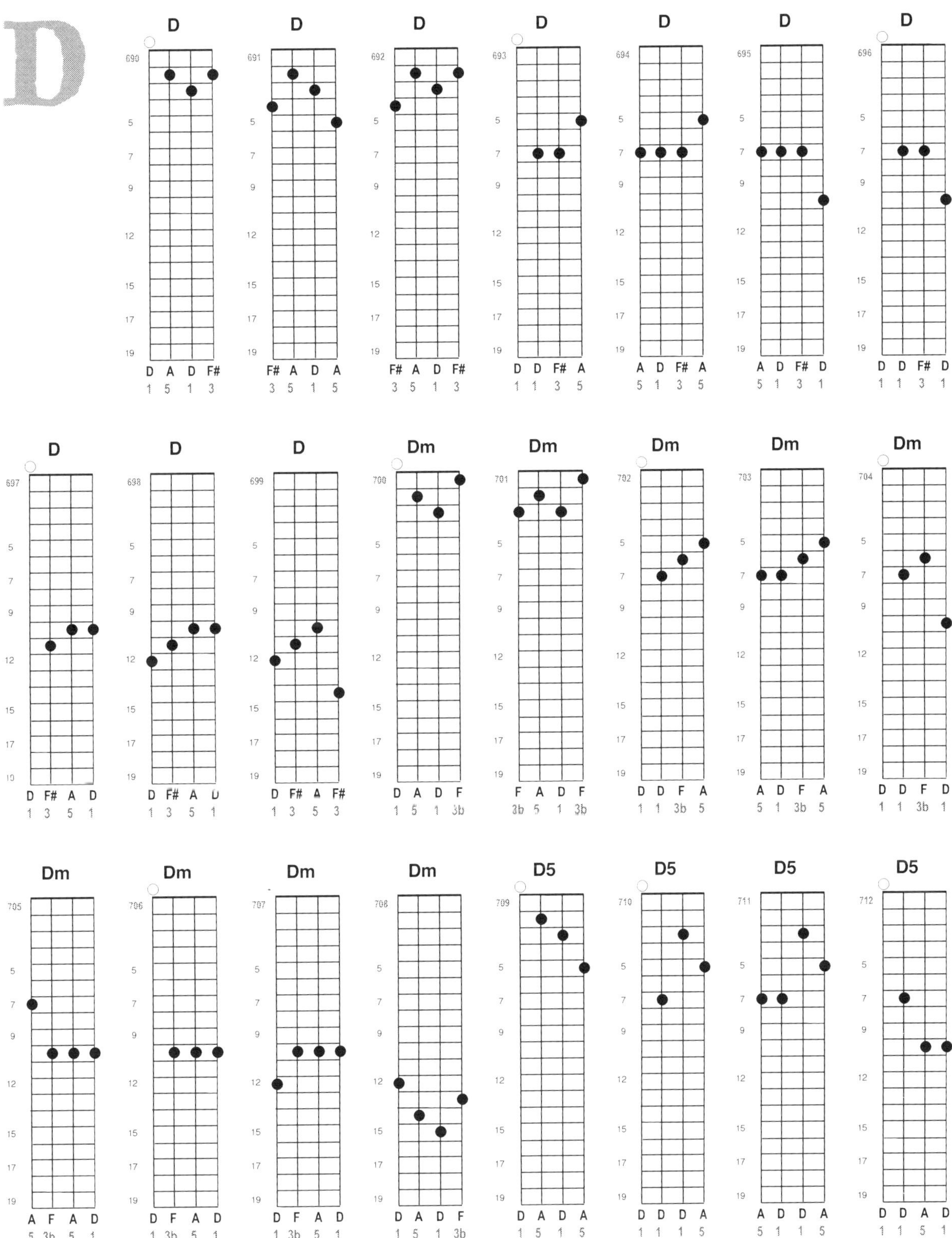

TUNING: D G B E

D7
713
D A C F#
1 5 7b 3
D7
714
D A C A
1 5 7b 5
D7
715
F# C D F#
3 7b 1 3
D7
716
D C D A
1 7b 1 5
D7
717
F# C D A
3 7b 1 5
D7
718
F# D F# C
3 1 3 7b
D7
719
D C F# A
1 7b 3 5
D7
720
D C F# C
1 7b 3 7b
D7
721
A C F# A
5 7b 3 5
D7
722
D C F# D
1 7b 3 1
D7
723
A C F# C
5 7b 3 7b
D7
724
A C F# D
5 7b 3 1
D7
725
A D F# C
5 1 3 7b
D7
726
D D F# C
1 1 3 7b
D7
727
A D A C
5 1 5 7b
D7
728
C D F# D
7b 1 3 1
D7
729
D F# A C
1 3 5 7b
D7
730
C F# A C
7b 3 5 7b
D7
731
D F# A C
1 3 5 7b
D7
732
C F# A D
7b 3 5 1
D7
733
D A C D
1 5 7b 1
D7
734
D F# C D
1 3 7b 1
Dm7
735
D A C F
1 5 7b 3b
Dm7
736
D C D F
1 7b 1 3b

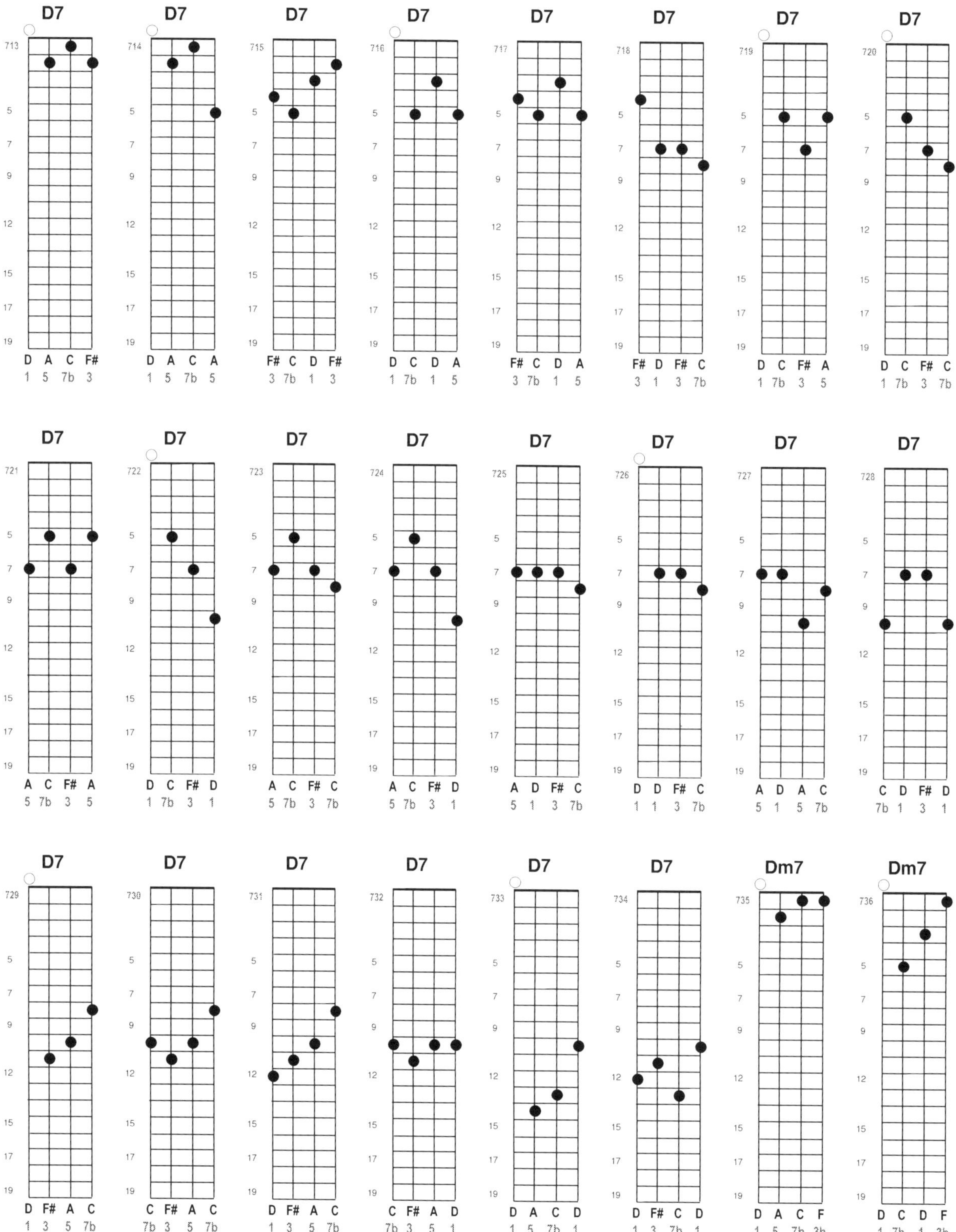

TUNING: D G B E

Dm7 737 D C F A 1 7b 3b 5
Dm7 738 A C F A 5 7b 3b 5
Dm7 739 D D F C 1 1 3b 7b
Dm7 740 D F A C 1 3b 5 7b
Dm7 741 C F A D 7b 3b 5 1
Dm7 742 D F C D 1 3b 7b 1
Dm7 743 D F C D 1 3b 7b 1
Dm7 744 D F C F 1 3b 7b 3b
Dmaj7 745 D A C# F# 1 5 7 3
Dmaj7 746 F# A C# F# 3 5 7 3
Dmaj7 747 D C# F# A 1 7 3 5
Dmaj7 748 A C# F# A 5 7 3 5
Dmaj7 749 D C# F# D 1 7 3 1
Dmaj7 750 A D F# C# 5 1 3 7
Dmaj7 751 D D F# C# 1 1 3 7
Dmaj7 752 D D A C# 1 1 5 7
Dmaj7 753 D F# A C# 1 3 5 7
Dmaj7 754 D F# A C# 1 3 5 7
Dmaj7 755 C# F# A D 7 3 5 1
Dsus 756 D A D G 1 5 1 4
Dsus 757 D D G A 1 1 4 5
Dsus 758 A D G A 5 1 4 5
Dsus 759 D D G D 1 1 4 1
Dsus 760 A D G D 5 1 4 1

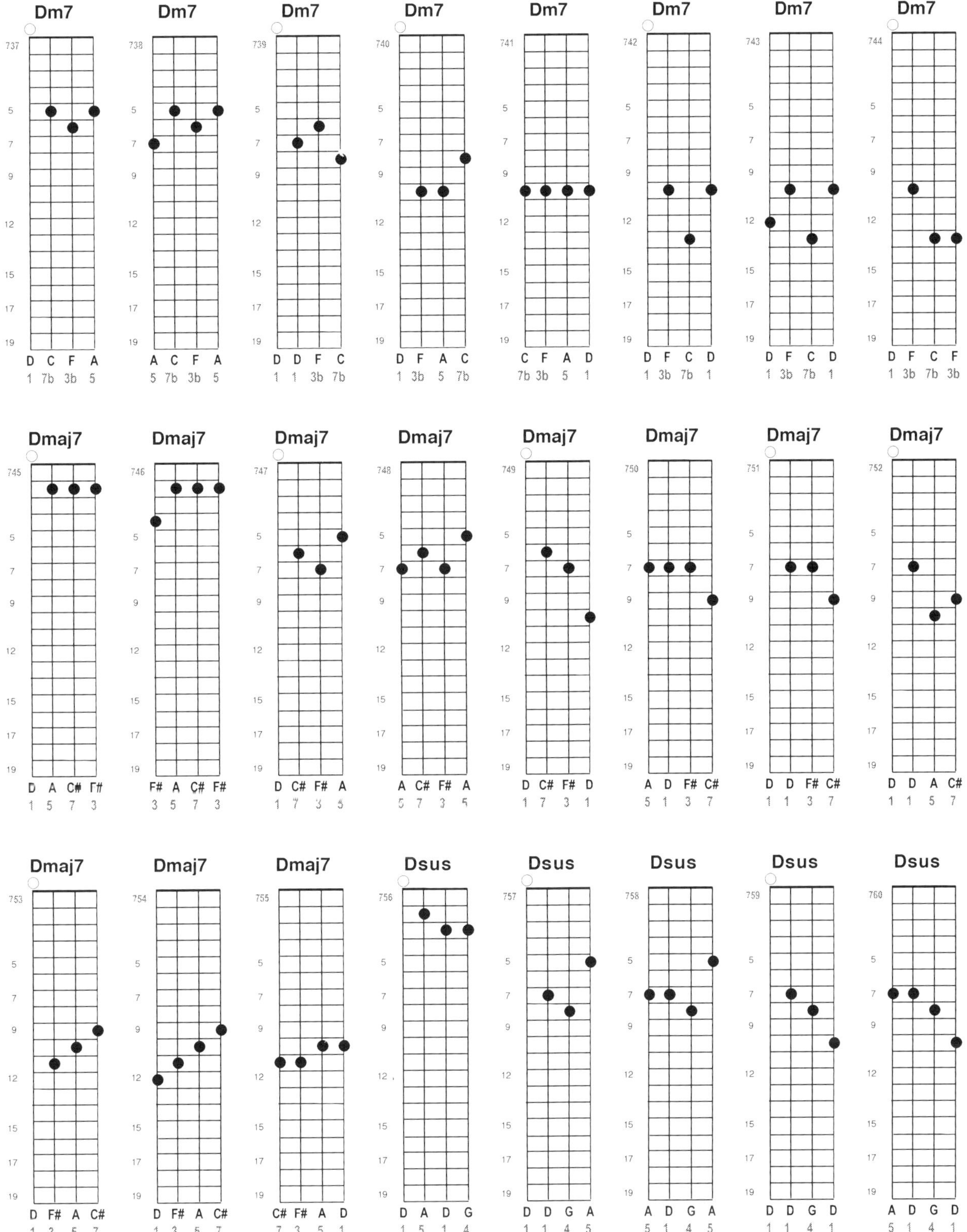

TUNING: D G B E

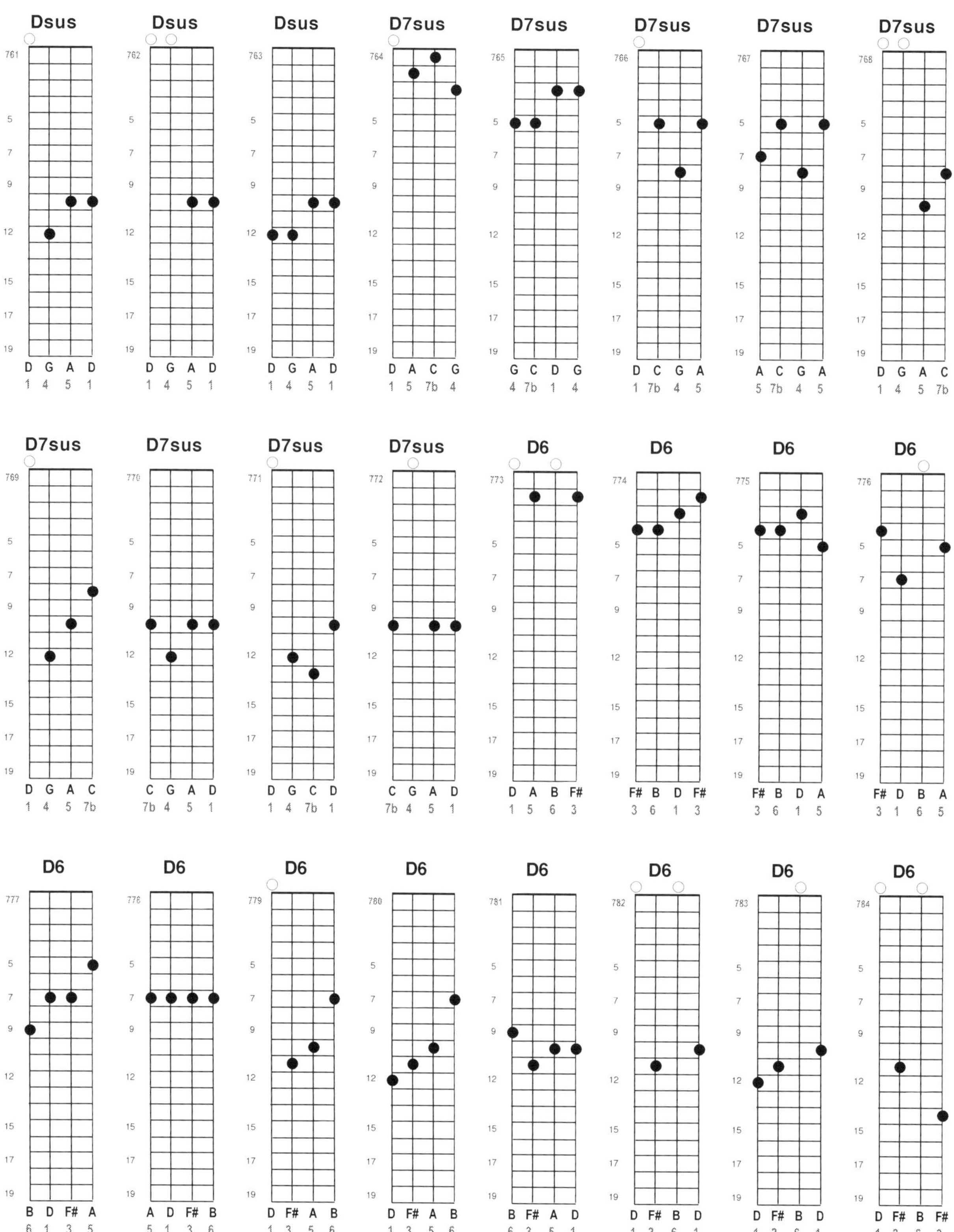

TUNING: D G B E

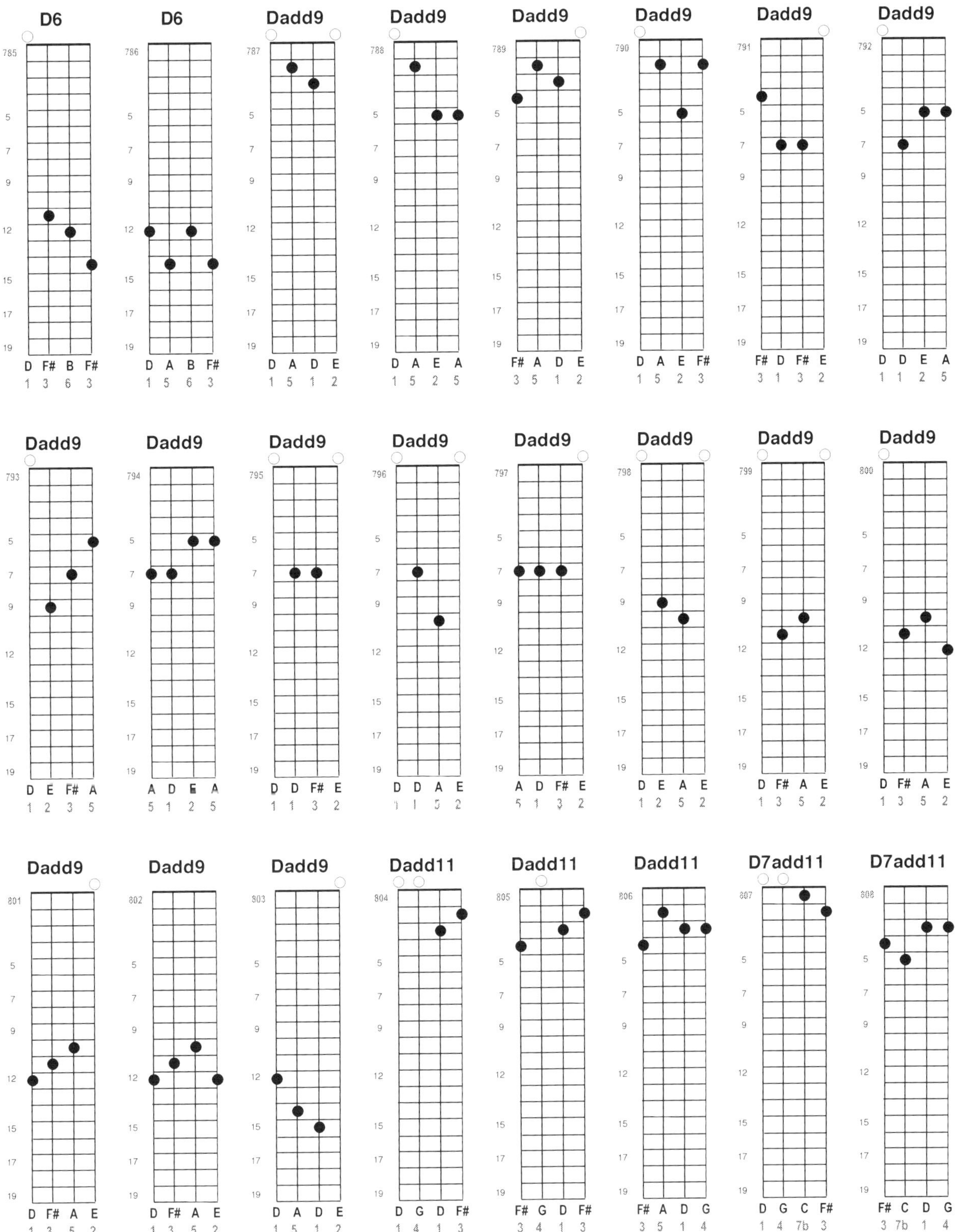

TUNING: D G B E

D7add11
D9
D9
D9
D9
D9
D9
D9
809
810
811
812
813
814
815
816
A G F# C
5 4 3 7b
D A C E
1 5 7b 2
F# A C E
3 5 7b 2
F# C D E
3 7b 1 2
F# C E A
3 7b 2 5
F# C F# E
3 7b 3 2
F# C E E
3 7b 2 2
D C F# E
1 7b 3 2
D9
D9
D9
D9
D9
D9
D9
D9
817
818
819
820
821
822
823
824
D C E C
1 7b 2 7b
A C E A
5 7b 2 5
D C E A
1 7b 2 5
D D E C
1 1 2 7b
C D A E
7b 1 5 2
D E F# C
1 2 3 7b
D E A C
1 2 5 7b
C E A D
7b 2 5 1
D9
D9
D9
D9
D11
D11
D11
D11
825
826
827
828
829
830
831
832
C F# A E
7b 3 5 2
C F# A E
7b 3 5 2
D F# C E
1 3 7b 2
D F# C E
1 3 7b 2
D G C E
1 4 7b 2
G C D E
4 7b 1 2
G C D E
4 7b 1 2
D C E G
1 7b 2 4

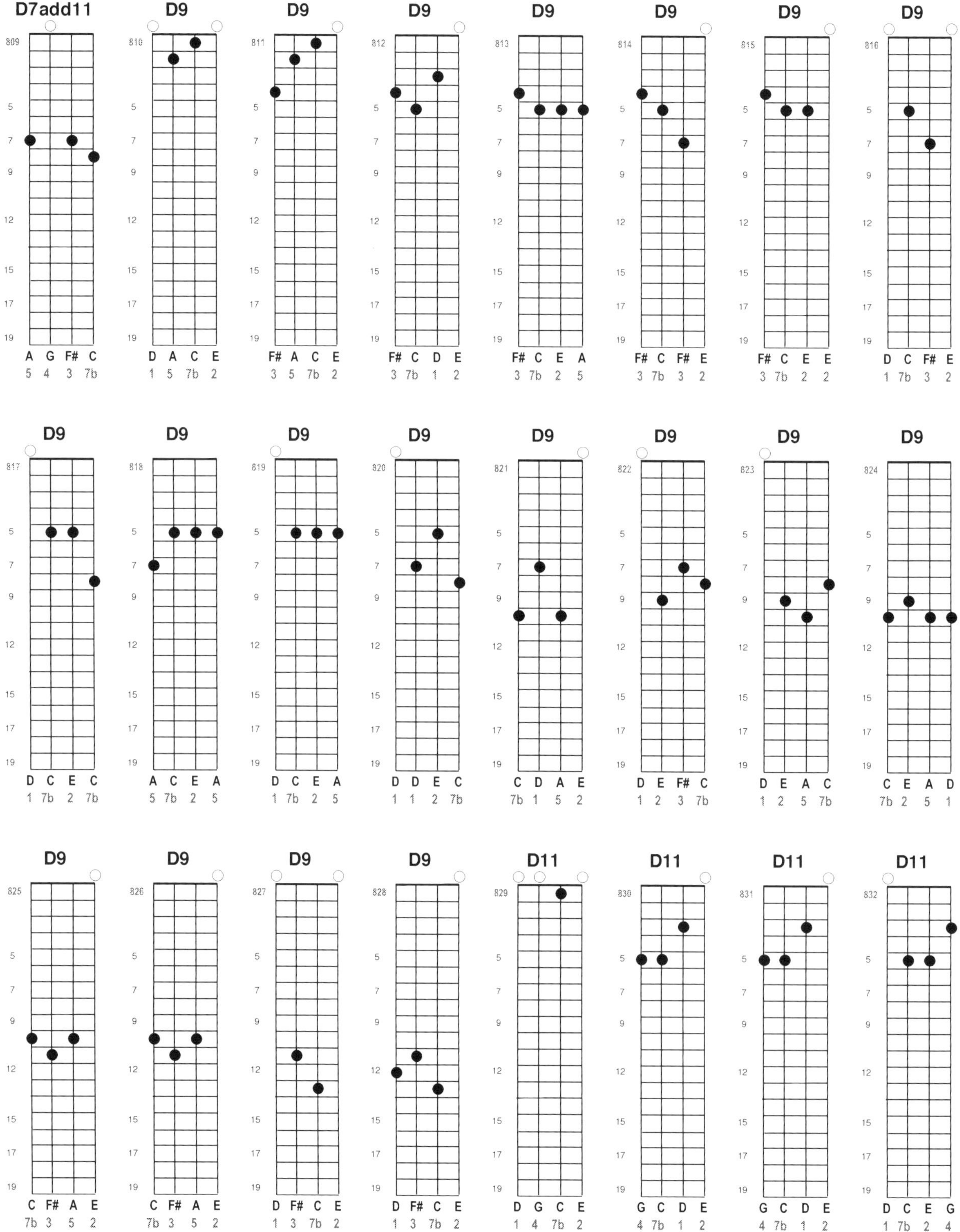

TUNING: D G B E

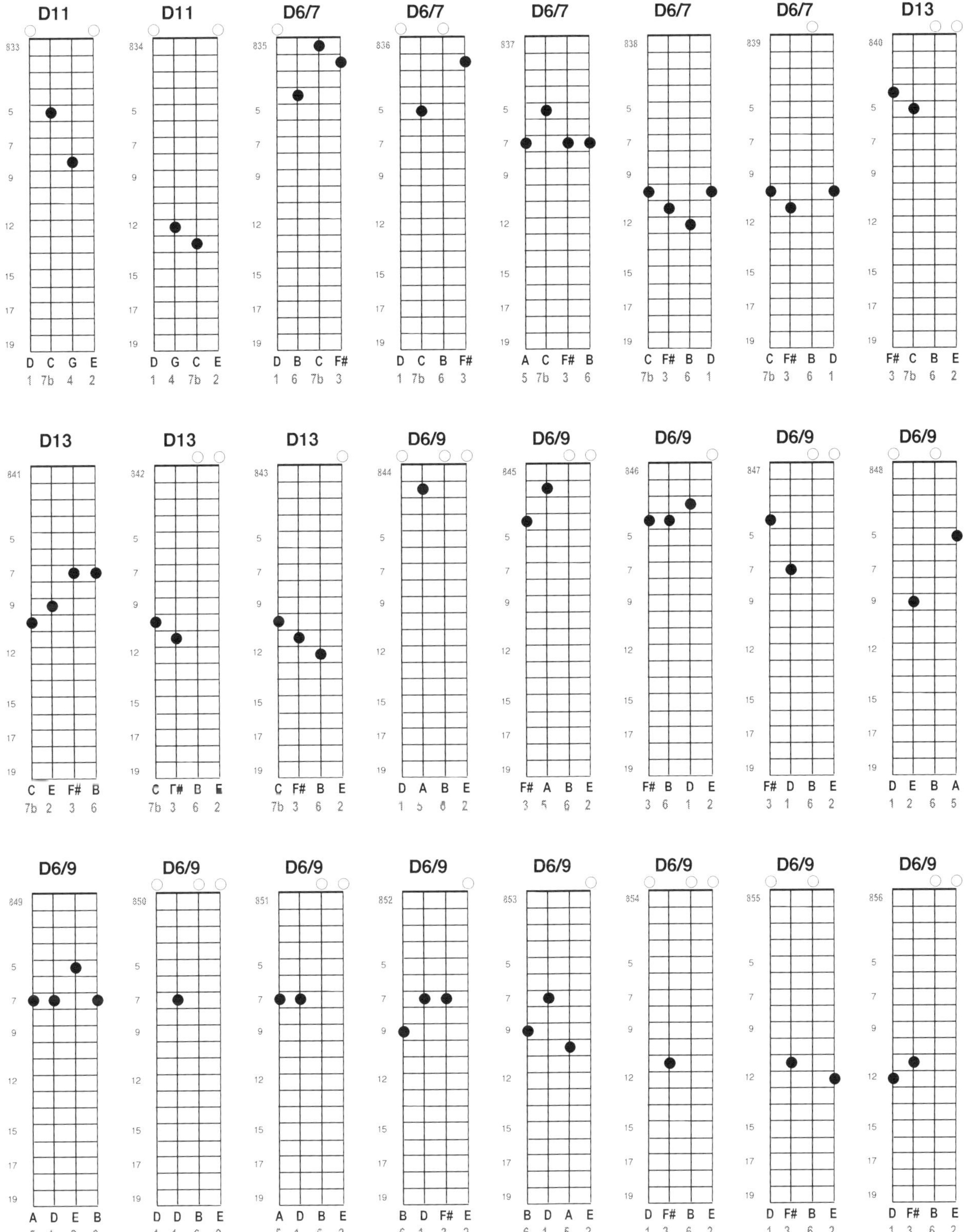

Baritone Ukulele Chords

TUNING: D G B E

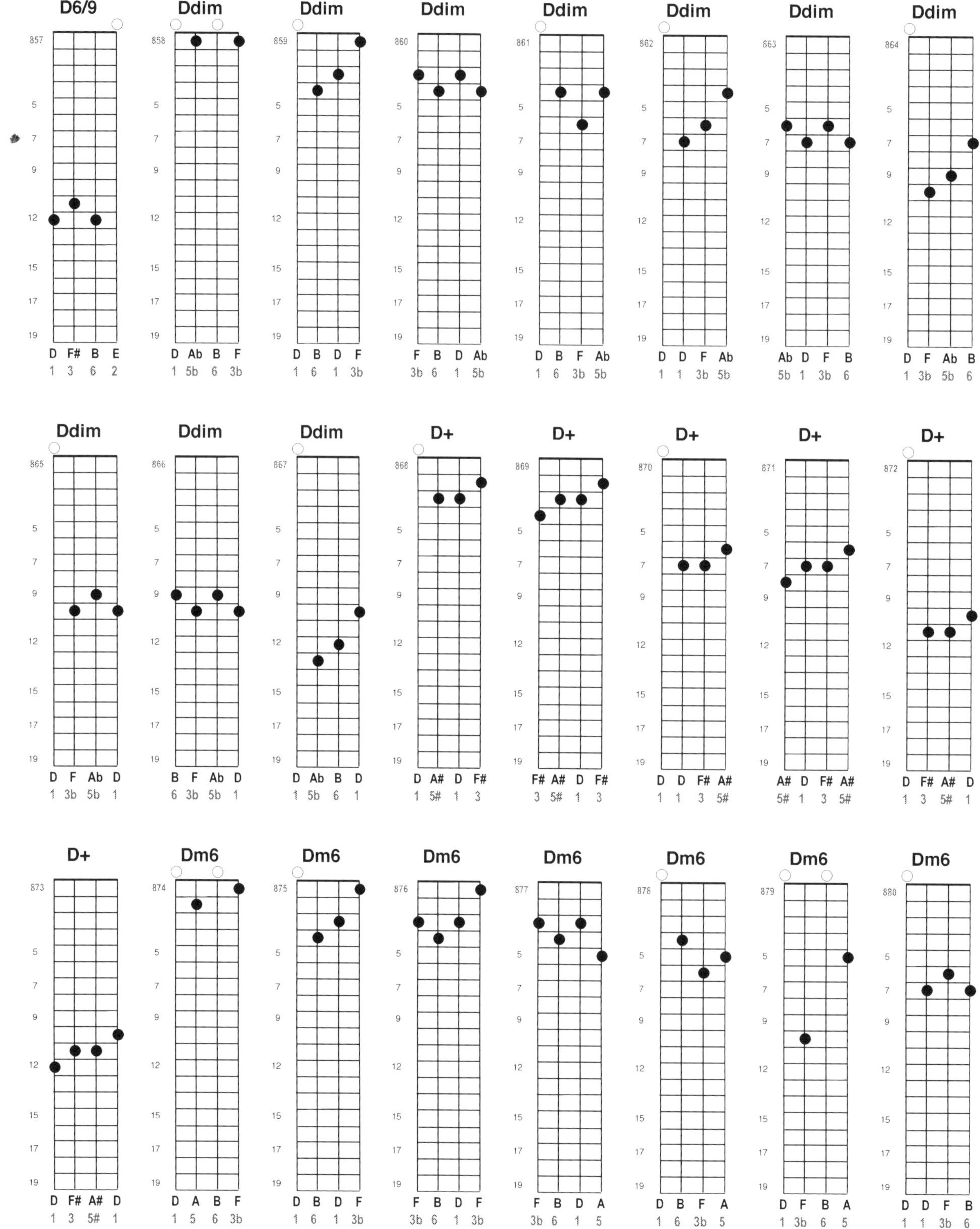

TUNING: D G B E

Dm6
881
D F A B
1 3b 5 6
Dm6
882
D F B D
1 3b 6 1
Dm6
883
D F B D
1 3b 6 1
Dm6
884
D A B F
1 5 6 3b
Dm6
885
D A B F
1 5 6 3b
Dm6/7
886
D B C F
1 6 7b 3b
Dm6/9
887
F A B E
3b 5 6 2
Dm6/9
888
F B B E
3b 6 6 2
Dm6/9
889
F B D E
3b 6 1 2
Dm6/9
890
A B F E
5 6 3b 2
Dm6/9
891
D F B E
1 3b 6 2
Dm13
892
F C B E
3b 7b 6 2
Dm13
893
F C E B
3b 7b 2 6
Dm13
894
C D B E
7b 1 6 2
Dm13
895
C F B E
7b 3b 6 2
Dm13
896
C F B E
7b 3b 6 2
Dm9
897
F A C E
3b 5 7b 2
Dm9
898
F C D E
3b 7b 1 2
Dm9
899
D C F E
1 7b 3b 2
Dm9
900
A C F E
5 7b 3b 2
Dm9
901
D E F C
1 2 3b 7b
Dm9
902
D F C E
1 3b 7b 2
Dm9
903
C F A E
7b 3b 5 2
Dm9
904
C F A E
7b 3b 5 2

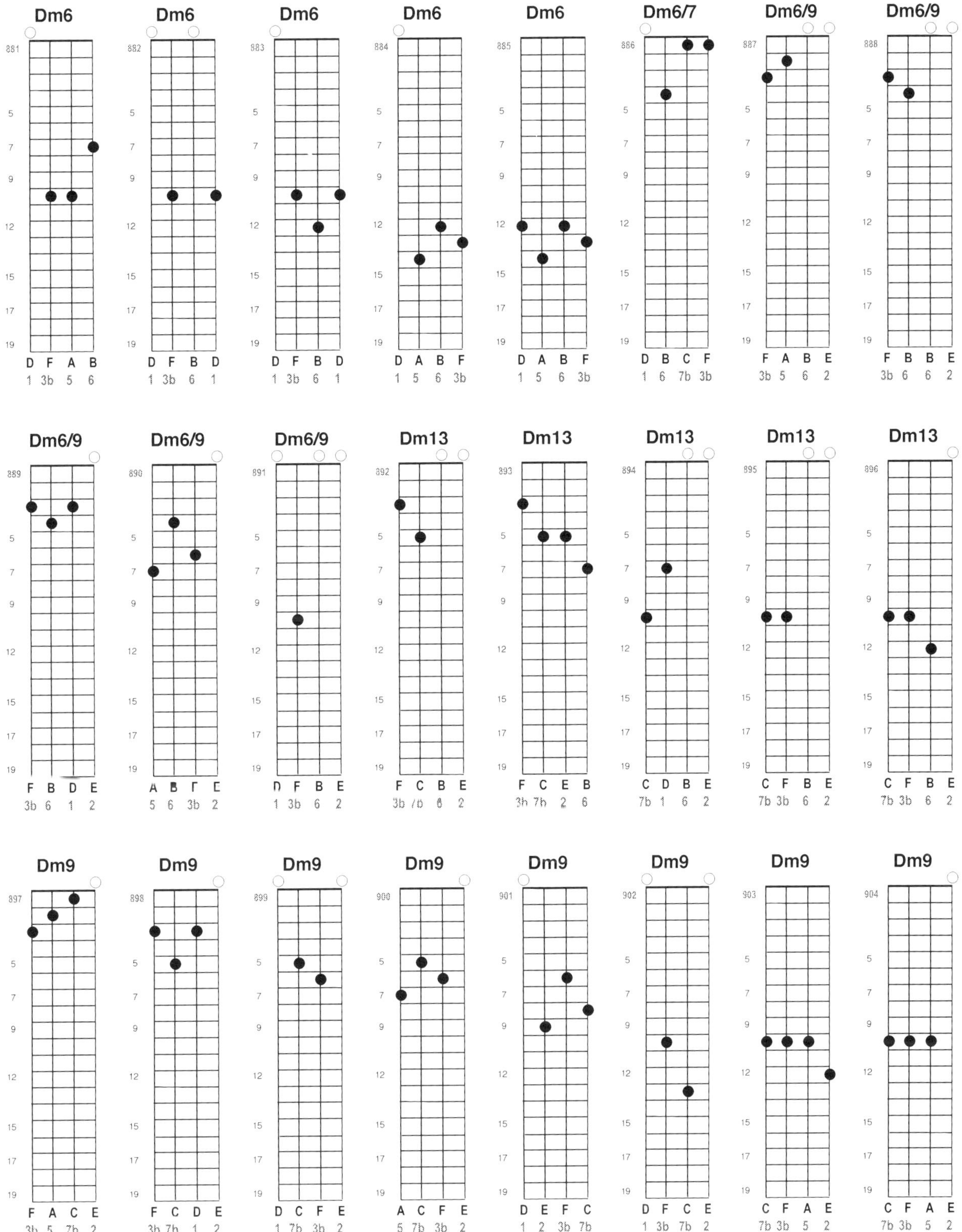

TUNING: D G B E

Dm9
905
D F C E
1 3b 7b 2
Dm9
906
D F C E
1 3b 7b 2
Dm9
907
D F C E
1 3b 7b 2
Dmadd9
908
F A D E
3b 5 1 2
Dmadd9
909
D F E A
1 3b 2 5
Dmadd9
910
D D F E
1 1 3b 2
Dmadd9
911
A D F E
5 1 3b 2
Dmadd9
912
D F A E
1 3b 5 2
Dmadd9
913
D F A E
1 3b 5 2
Dmaj6
914
D B C# F#
1 6 7 3
Dmaj6
915
D F# B C#
1 3 6 7
Dmaj9
916
D A C# E
1 5 7 2
Dmaj9
917
F# C# D E
3 7 1 2
Dmaj9
918
A C# E E
5 7 2 2
Dmaj9
919
D C# F# E
1 7 3 2
Dmaj9
920
A C# F# E
5 7 3 2
Dmaj9
921
D E F# C#
1 2 3 7
Dmaj9
922
C# F# A E
7 3 5 2
Dmaj9
923
D F# C# E
1 3 7 2
Dmaj9
924
D F# C# E
1 3 7 2
Dmaj9
925
D A C# E
1 5 7 2
Dm11
926
D G C F
1 4 7b 3b
Dm11
927
C F G E
7b 3b 4 2
Dm11
928
D F G C
1 3b 4 7b

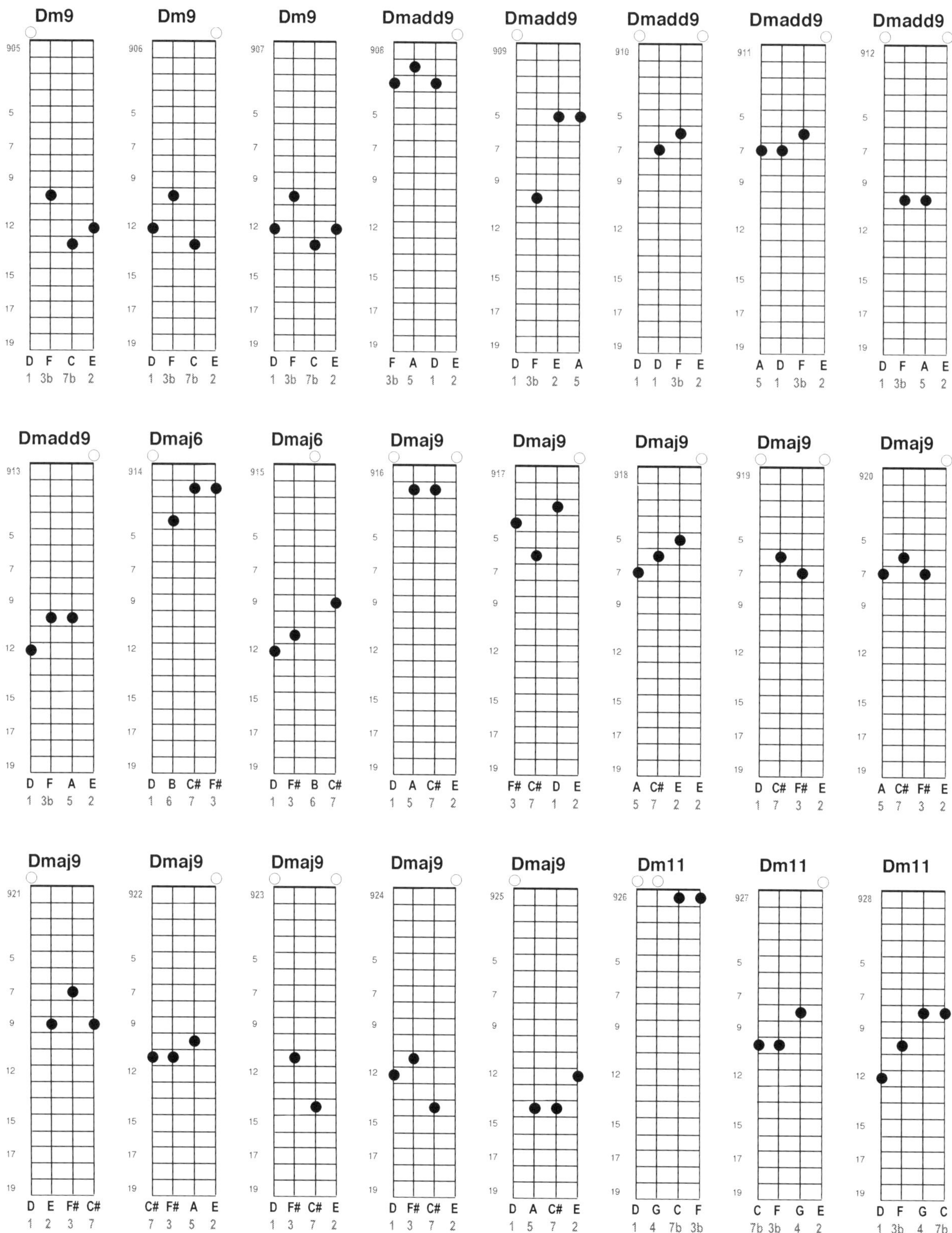

TUNING: D G B E

D9/11
929
D A E G
1 5 2 4
D9/11
930
D G D E
1 4 1 2
D9/11
931
F# G D E
3 4 1 2
D9/11
932
D G F# E
1 4 3 2
D9/11
933
D D G E
1 1 4 2
D9/11
934
D F# G E
1 3 4 2
D9/11
935
D G A E
1 4 5 2
5
7
9
12
15
17
19

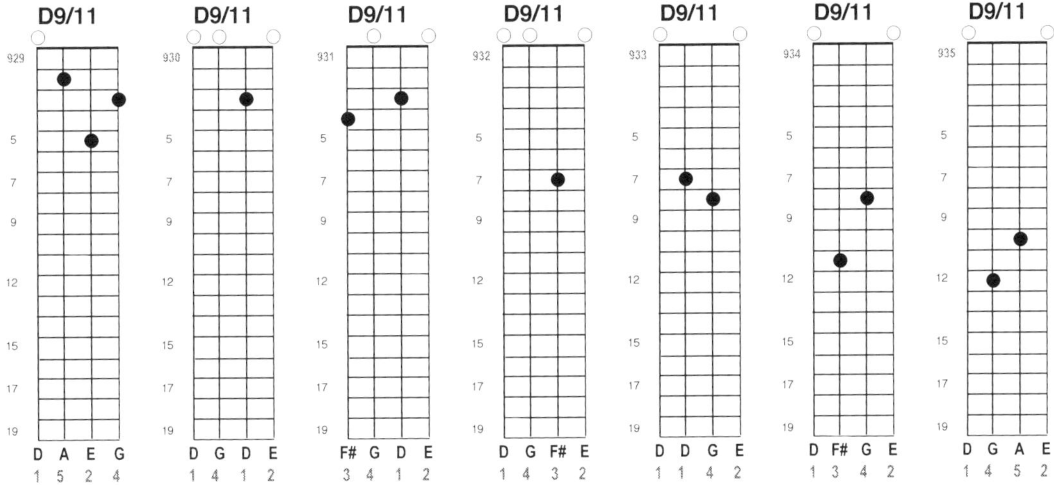

TUNING: D G B E

D# Eb

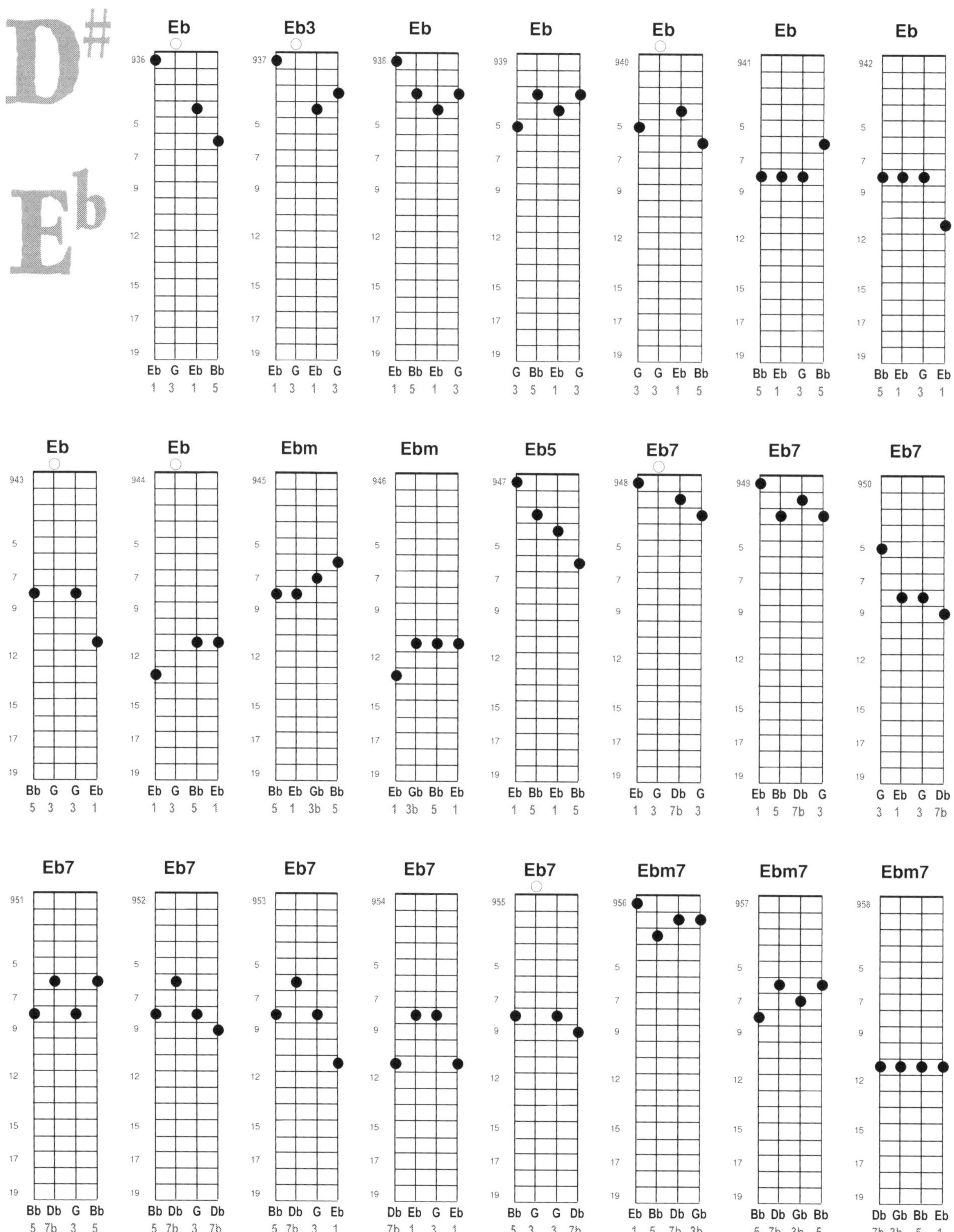

TUNING: D G B E

Ebmaj7
959
G Bb D G
3 5 7 3
Ebmaj7
960
G G D Bb
3 3 7 5
Ebmaj7
961
Bb D G Bb
5 7 3 5
Ebmaj7
962
Bb Eb G D
5 1 3 7
Ebmaj7
963
Eb G Bb D
1 3 5 7
Ebsus
964
Eb Bb Eb Ab
1 5 1 4
Ebsus
965
Bb Eb Ab Bb
5 1 4 5
Eb7sus
966
Bb Db Ab Bb
5 7b 4 5
Eb6
967
Eb Bb C G
1 5 6 3
Eb6
968
Bb Eb G C
5 1 3 6
Eb6
969
Bb Eb Bb C
5 1 5 6
Eb6
970
C G Bb Eb
6 3 5 1
Ebadd9
971
Eb Bb Eb F
1 5 1 2
Ebadd9
972
G Bb Eb F
3 5 1 2
Ebadd9
973
Bb Eb F Bb
5 1 2 5
Ebadd9
974
Eb G Bb F
1 3 5 2
Eb7add11
975
Eb G Db Ab
1 3 7b 4
Eb9
976
Eb Bb Db F
1 5 7b 2
Eb9
977
G Db F Bb
3 7b 2 5
Eb9
978
Bb Db F Bb
5 7b 2 5
Eb9
979
Db F Bb Eb
7b 2 5 1
Eb9
980
Db G Bb F
7b 3 5 2
Eb6/7
981
Bb Db G C
5 7b 3 6
Eb6/9
982
Eb G C F
1 3 6 2

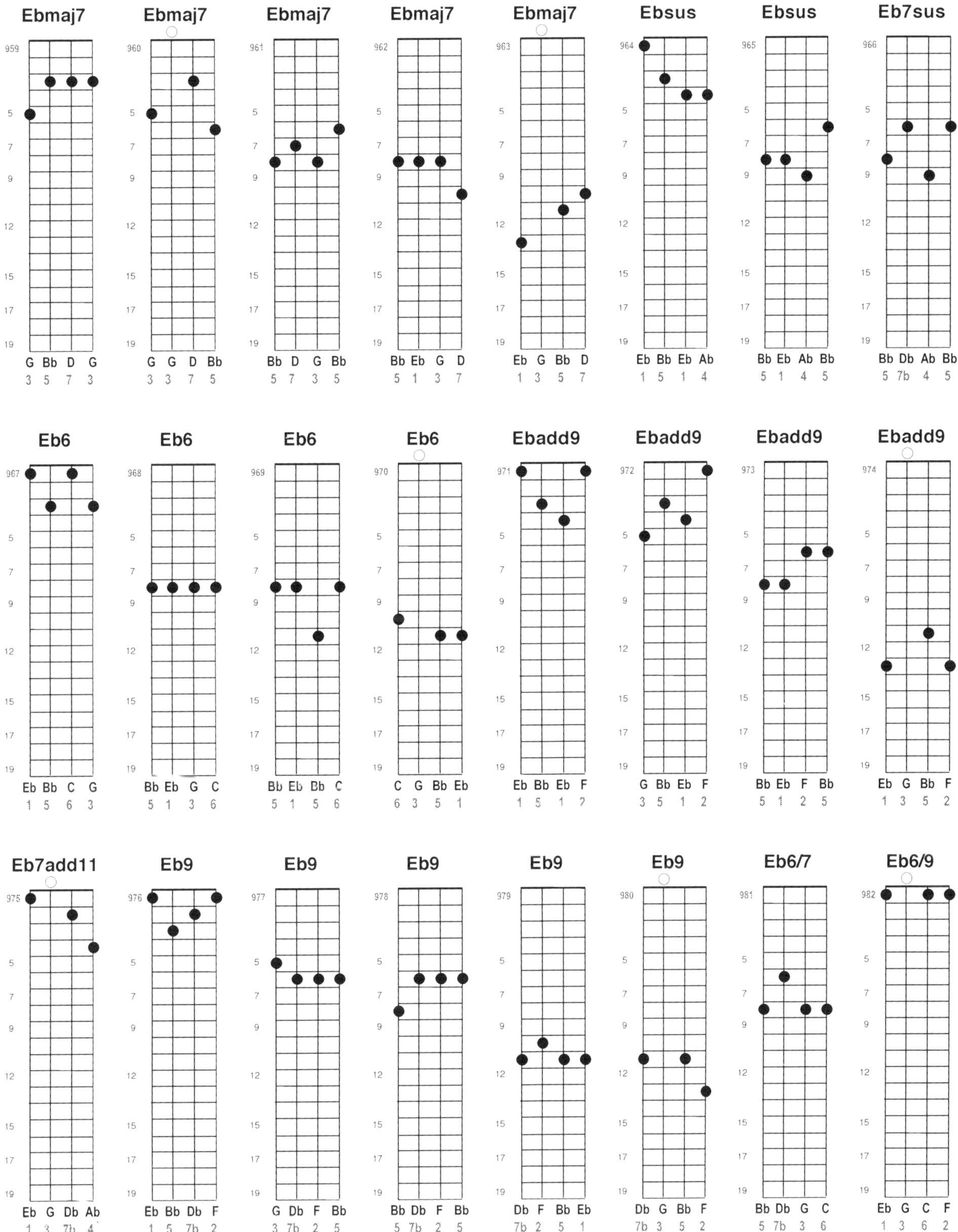

TUNING: D G B E

Eb6/9
Eb6/9
Ebdim
Ebdim
Ebdim
Ebdim
Ebdim
Ebdim
Bb Eb F C
5 1 2 6
Eb G C F
1 3 6 2
Eb A C Gb
1 5b 6 3b
Gb A Eb x
3b 5b 1 x
Gb C Eb Gb
3b 6 1 3b
Gb C Eb A
3b 6 1 5b
A Eb Gb A
5b 1 3b 5b
A Eb Gb x
5b 1 3b x
Ebdim
Eb+
Eb+
Eb+
Eb+
Eb+
Eb+
Ebm6
A Eb Gb C
5b 1 3b 6
Eb G B x
1 3 5# x
G B Eb G
3 5# 1 3
G B Eb x
3 5# 1 x
B Eb G B
5# 1 3 5#
B Eb G x
5# 1 3 x
Eb G B Eb
1 3 5# 1
Eb Bb C Gb
1 5 6 3b
Ebm6
Ebm9
Ebmadd9
Ebmaj9
Ebmaj9
Gb C Eb Bb
3b 6 1 5
Gb Bb Db F
3b 5 7b 2
Gb Bb Eb F
3b 5 1 2
Eb Bb D F
1 5 7 2
F G Eb Bb
2 3 1 5

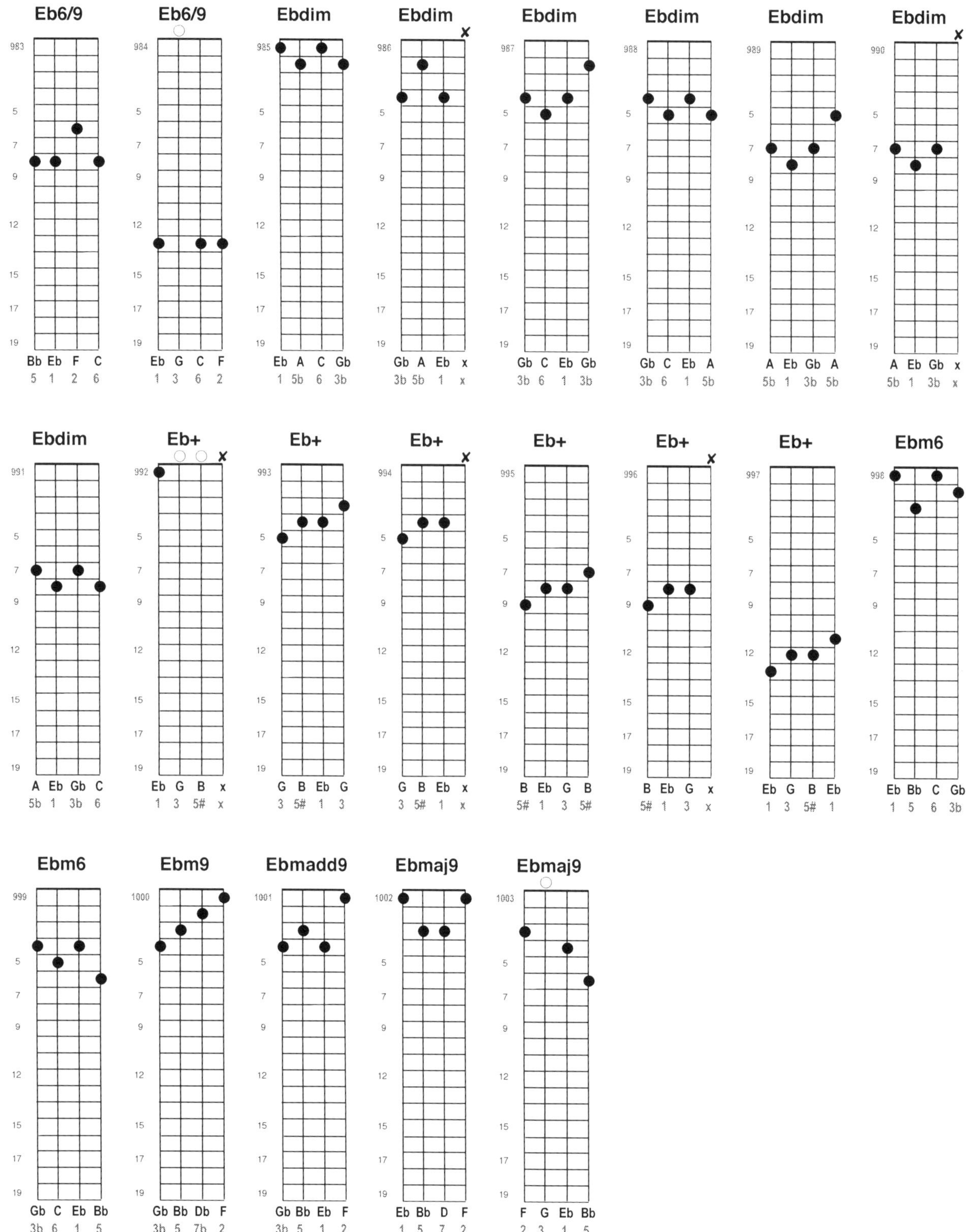

TUNING: D G B E

E

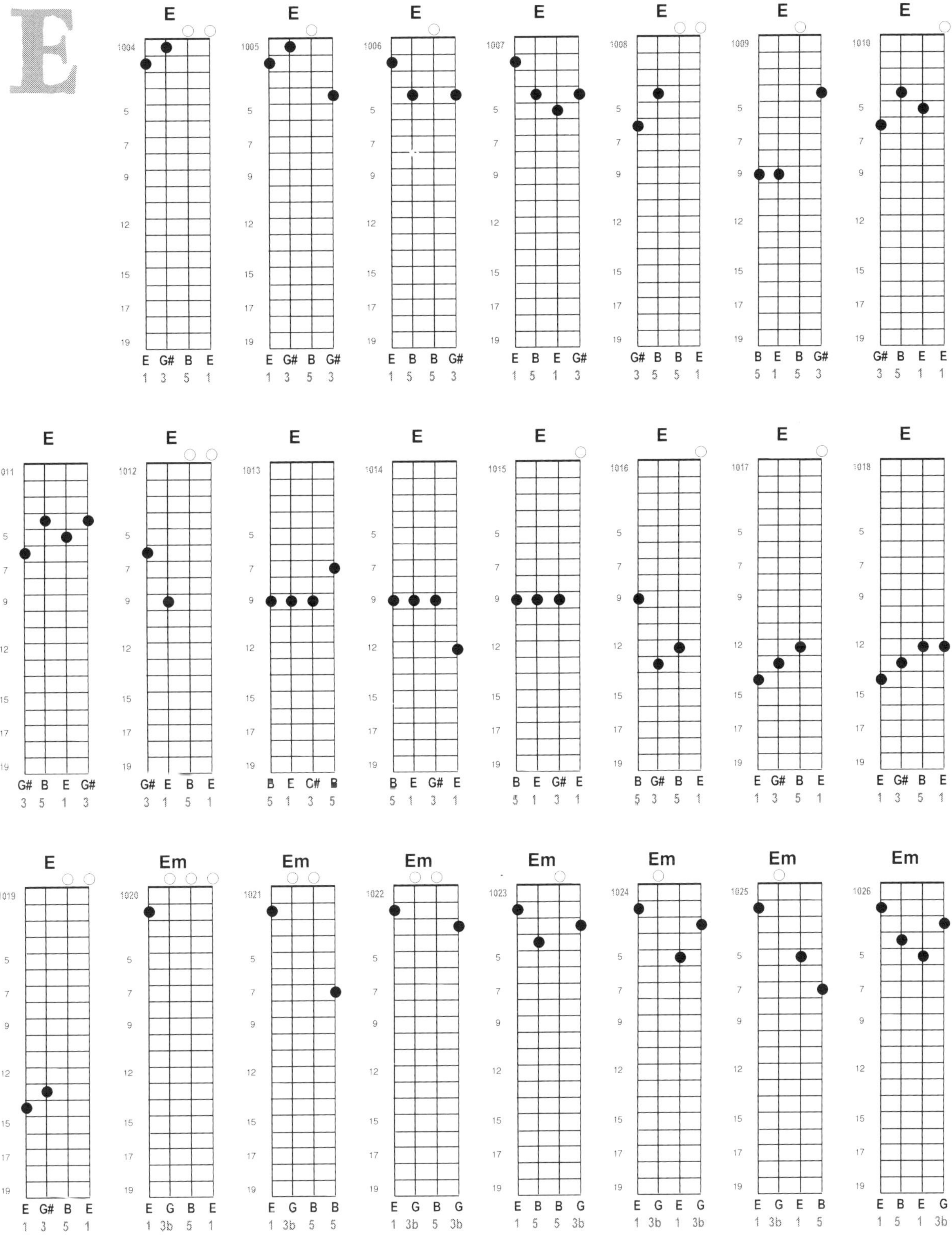

TUNING: D G B E

Em 1027 G B E G 3b 5 1 3b
Em 1028 G B B E 3b 5 5 1
Em 1029 G B E E 3b 5 1 1
Em 1030 G G B E 3b 3b 5 1
Em 1031 G E B E 3b 1 5 1
Em 1032 B E G B 5 1 3b 5
Em 1033 B G G E 5 3b 3b 1
Em 1034 B E G E 5 1 3b 1
Em 1035 B G B E 5 3b 5 1
Em 1036 E G B E 1 3b 5 1
Em 1037 E G B E 1 3b 5 1
E5 1038 E B B E 1 5 5 1
E5 1039 E B B B 1 5 5 5
E5 1040 E B E E 1 5 1 1
E5 1041 E B E B 1 5 1 5
E5 1042 B E E E 5 1 1 1
E5 1043 B E B B 5 1 5 5
E5 1044 B E B E 5 1 5 1
E5 1045 B E B E 5 1 5 1
E7 1046 D G# B E 7b 3 5 1
E7 1047 E G# D E 1 3 7b 1
E7 1048 E G# D G# 1 3 7b 3
E7 1049 E B D E 1 5 7b 1
E7 1050 E B D G# 1 5 7b 3

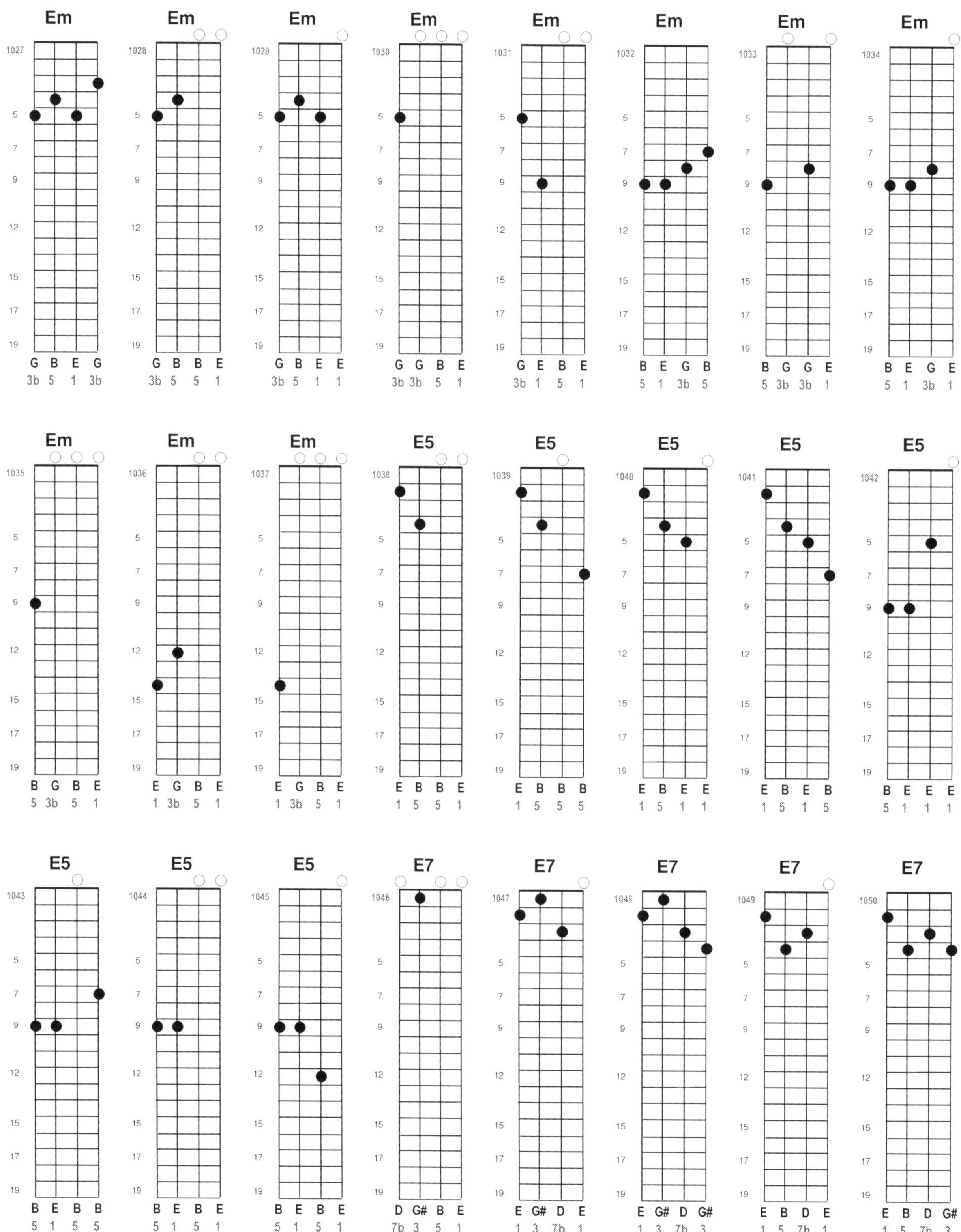

TUNING: D G B E

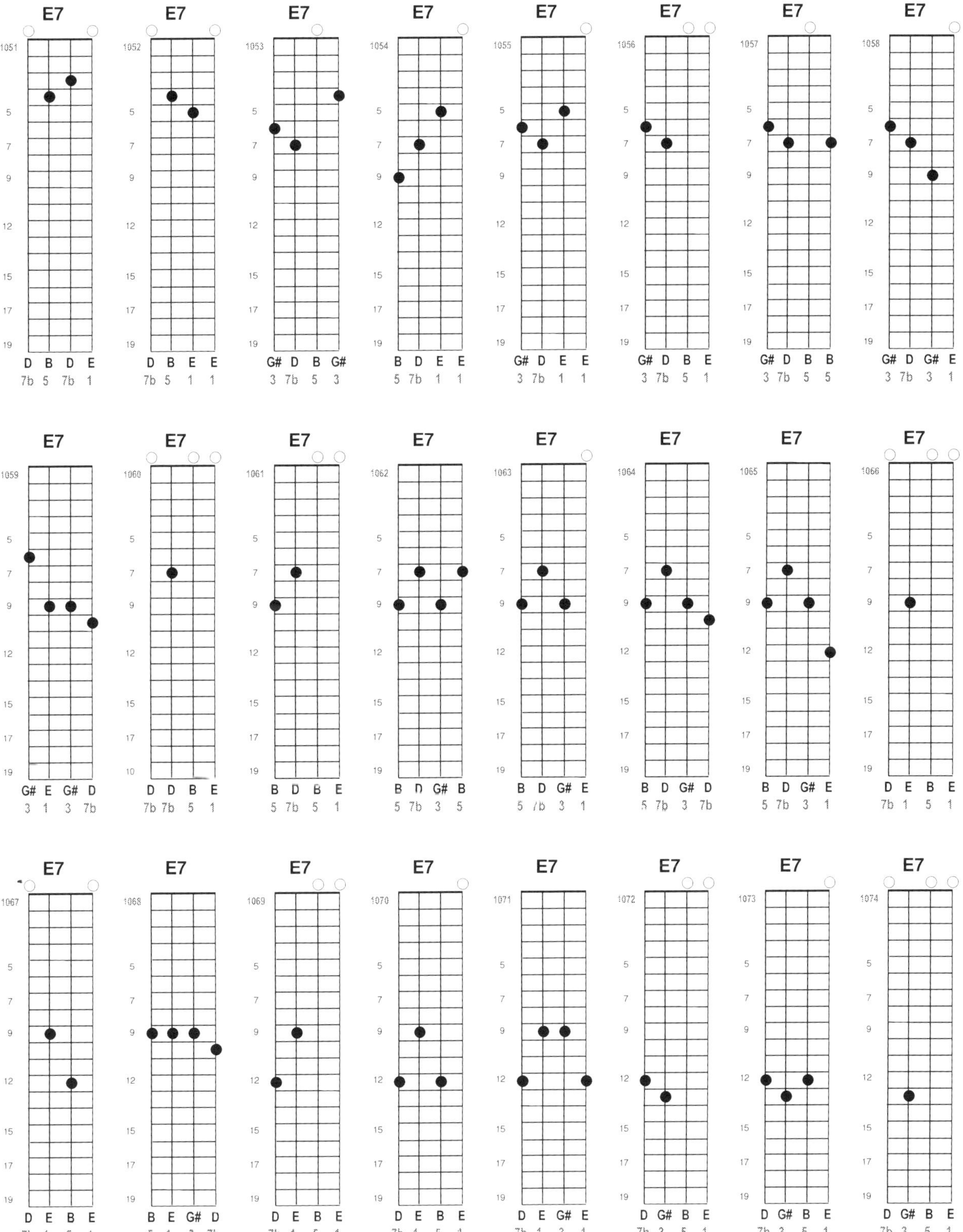

TUNING: D G B E

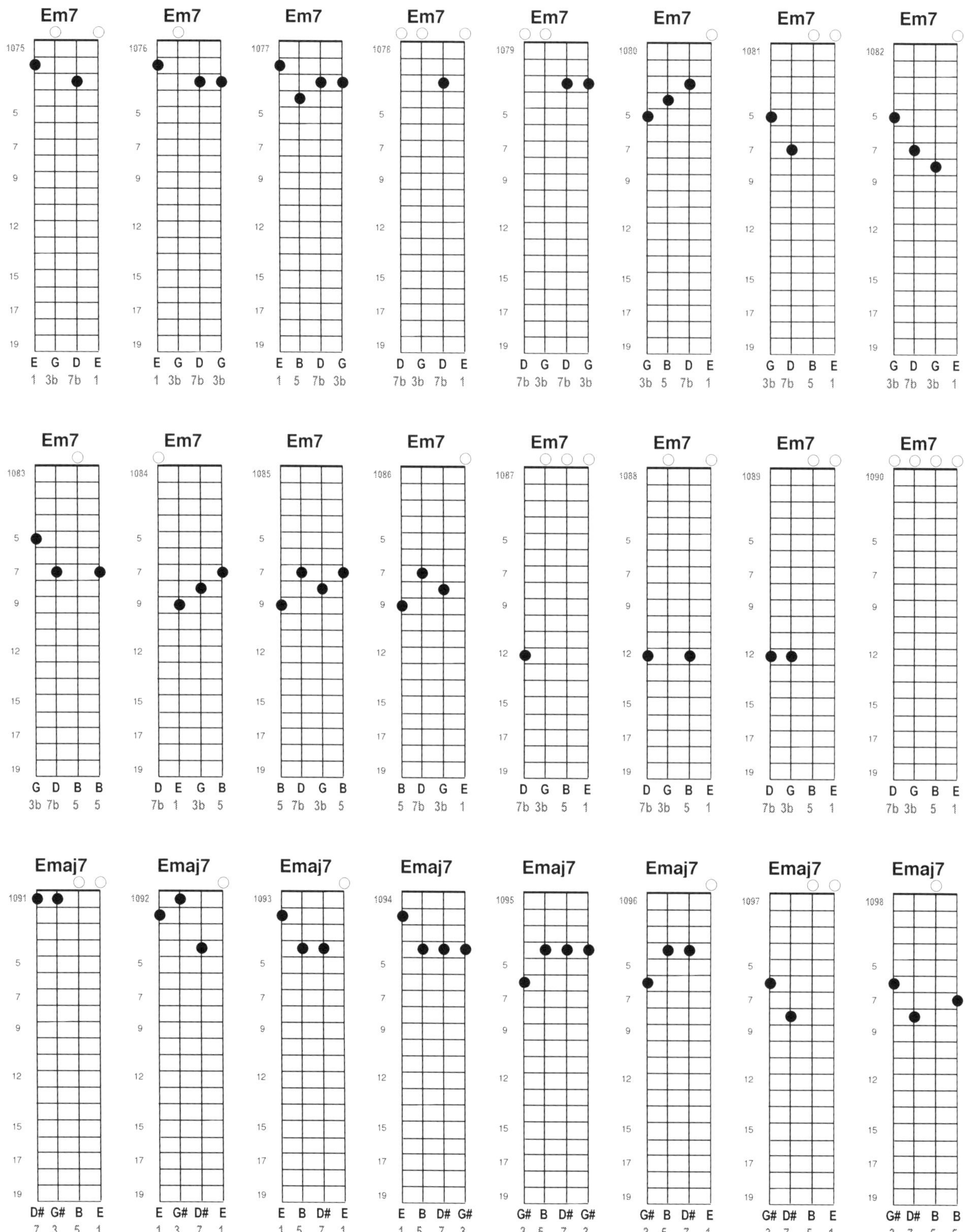

TUNING: D G B E

Emaj7
1099
B D# B B
5 7 5 5
Emaj7
1100
B D# G# B
5 7 3 5
Emaj7
1101
B D# B E
5 7 5 1
Emaj7
1102
B D# G# E
5 7 3 1
Emaj7
1103
B E G# D#
5 1 3 7
Emaj7
1104
D# G# B E
7 3 5 1
Emaj7
1105
D# G# B E
7 3 5 1
Esus
1106
E A B E
1 4 5 1
Esus
1107
E B E A
1 5 1 4
Esus
1108
A B B E
4 5 5 1
Esus
1109
B E B A
5 1 5 4
Esus
1110
A E B E
4 1 5 1
Esus
1111
A E A E
4 1 4 1
Esus
1112
B E A B
5 1 4 5
Esus
1113
B E A E
5 1 4 1
Esus
1114
E A B E
1 4 5 1
E7sus
1115
D A B E
7b 4 5 1
E7sus
1116
E A D E
1 4 7b 1
E7sus
1117
A D B E
4 7b 5 1
E7sus
1118
B D A E
5 7b 4 1
E7sus
1119
B D A B
5 7b 4 5
E7sus
1120
D A B E
7b 4 5 1
E7sus
1121
D A B E
7b 4 5 1
E7sus
1122
D A D E
7b 4 7b 1

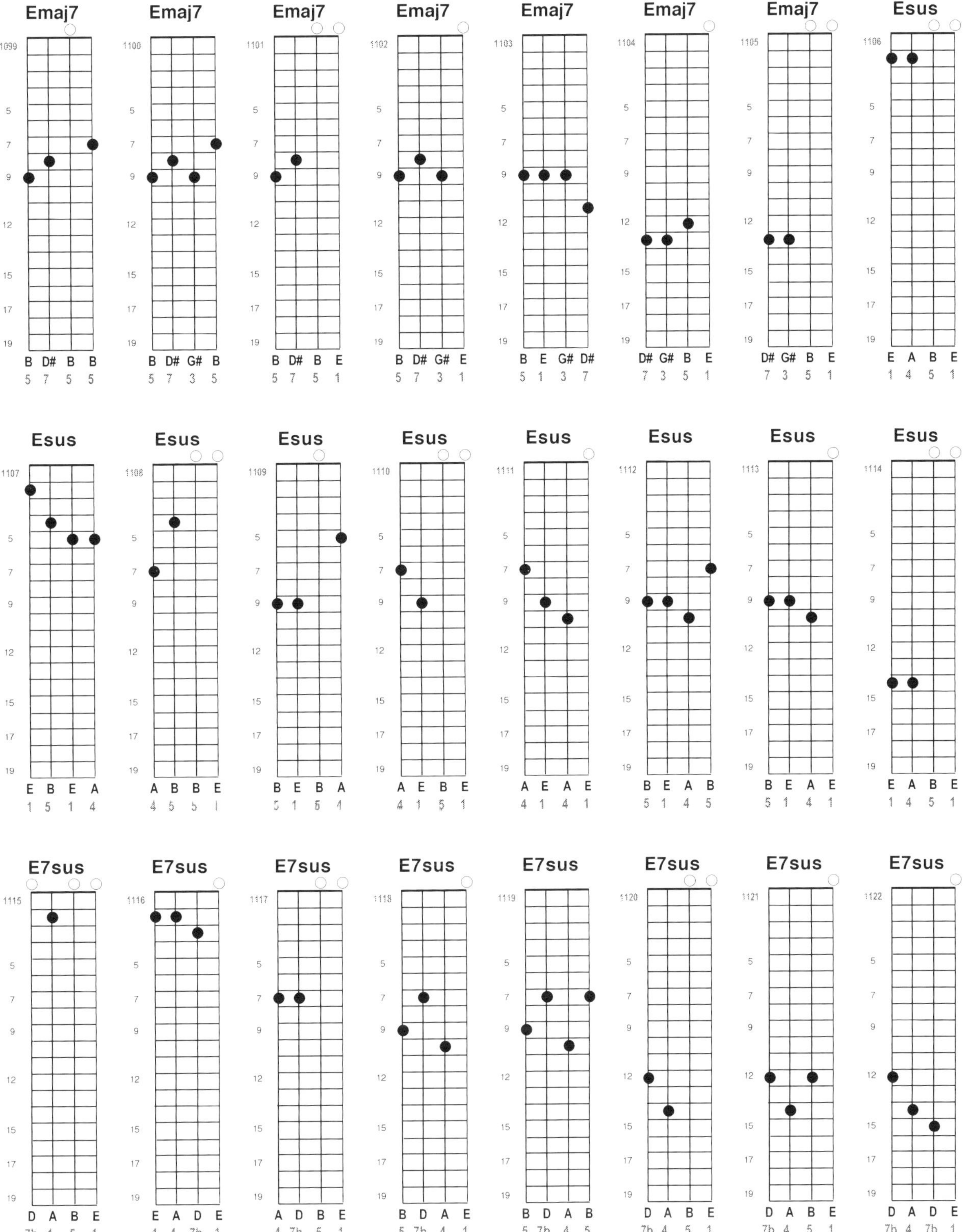

TUNING: D G B E

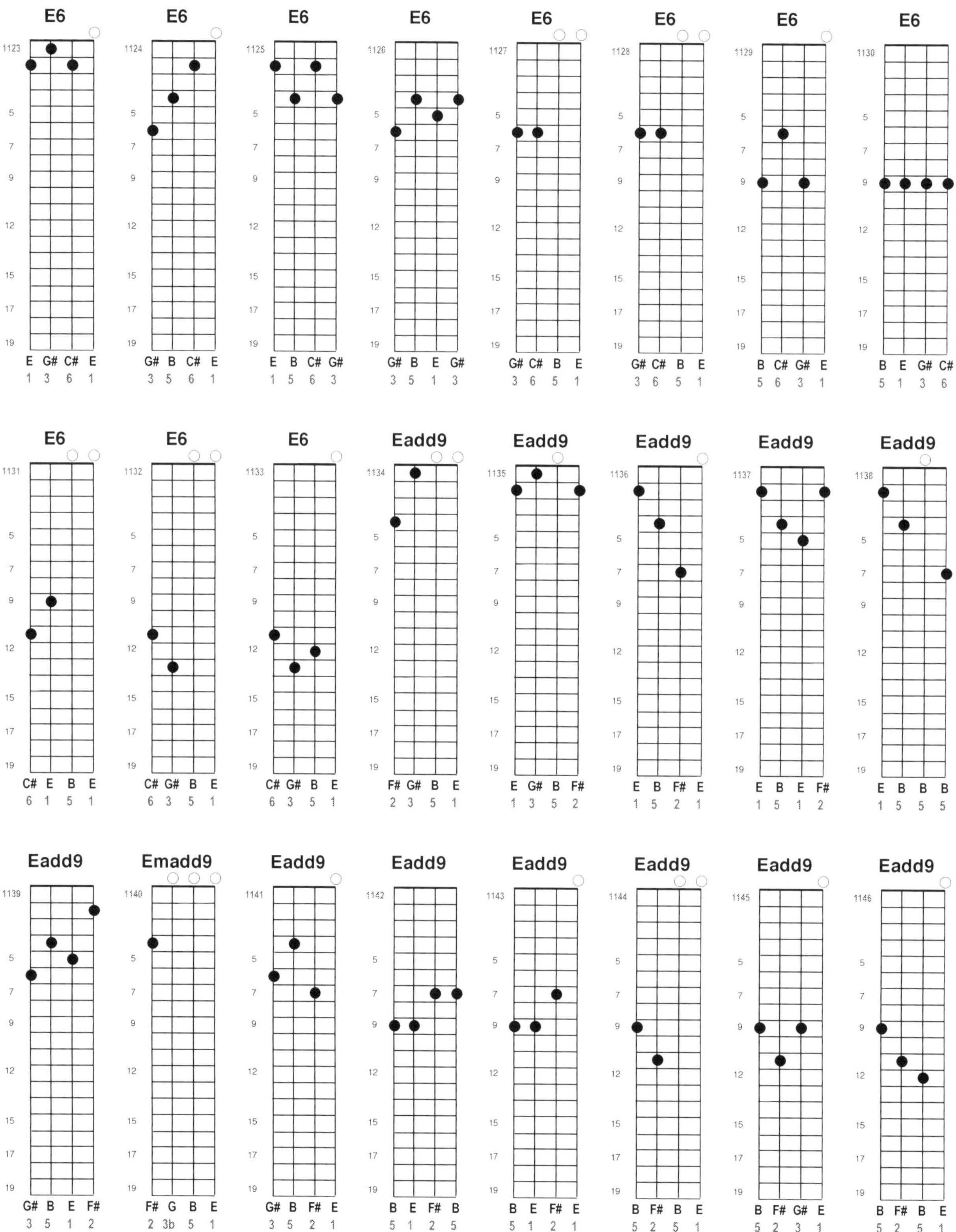

E6
1123
E G# C# E
1 3 6 1
E6
1124
G# B C# E
3 5 6 1
E6
1125
E B C# G#
1 5 6 3
E6
1126
G# B E G#
3 5 1 3
E6
1127
G# C# B E
3 6 5 1
E6
1128
G# C# B E
3 6 5 1
E6
1129
B C# G# E
5 6 3 1
E6
1130
B E G# C#
5 1 3 6
E6
1131
C# E B E
6 1 5 1
E6
1132
C# G# B E
6 3 5 1
E6
1133
C# G# B E
6 3 5 1
Eadd9
1134
F# G# B E
2 3 5 1
Eadd9
1135
E G# B F#
1 3 5 2
Eadd9
1136
E B F# E
1 5 2 1
Eadd9
1137
E B E F#
1 5 1 2
Eadd9
1138
E B B B
1 5 5 5
Eadd9
1139
G# B E F#
3 5 1 2
Emadd9
1140
F# G B E
2 3b 5 1
Eadd9
1141
G# B F# E
3 5 2 1
Eadd9
1142
B E F# B
5 1 2 5
Eadd9
1143
B E F# E
5 1 2 1
Eadd9
1144
B F# B E
5 2 5 1
Eadd9
1145
B F# G# E
5 2 3 1
Eadd9
1146
B F# B E
5 2 5 1

TUNING: D G B E

Eadd9
E9
E9
E9
E9
E9
E9
E9
E9
E9
E9
E9
E9
E9
E9
E11
E11
E11
E11
E6/7
E6/7
E6/7
E13
E13

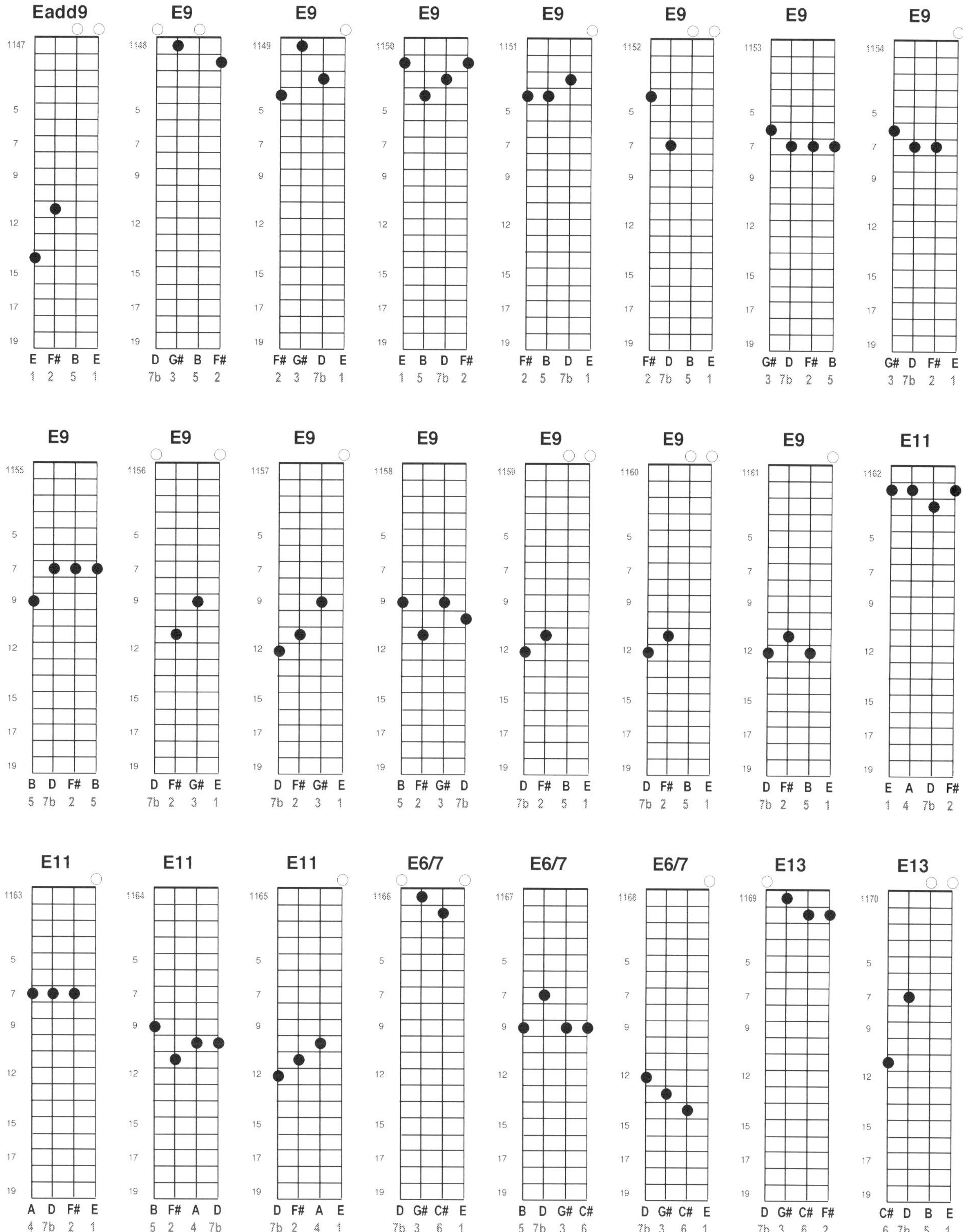

TUNING: D G B E

E13
1171
D F# C# E
7b 2 6 1
E6/9
1172
E G# C# F#
1 3 6 2
E6/9
1173
E B C# F#
1 5 6 2
E6/9
1174
G# C# F# E
3 6 2 1
E6/9
1175
C# F# B E
6 2 5 1
Edim
1176
E Bb C# E
1 5b 6 1
Edim
1177
G Bb C# E
3b 5b 6 1
Edim
1178
E Bb C# G
1 5b 6 3b
Edim
1179
G Bb E E
3b 5b 1 1
Edim
1180
G C# E Bb
3b 6 1 5b
Edim
1181
Bb C# G E
5b 6 3b 1
Edim
1182
Bb E G C#
5b 1 3b 6
Edim
1183
C# G Bb E
6 3b 5b 1
Edim
1184
C# G Bb E
6 3b 5b 1
Edim
1185
C# G Bb E
6 3b 5b 1
E+
1186
E G# C E
1 3 5# 1
E+
1187
G# C E G#
3 5# 1 3
E+
1188
G# C E E
3 5# 1 1
E+
1189
C E G# C
5# 1 3 5#
E+
1190
C E G# E
5# 1 3 1
E+
1191
E G# C E
1 3 5# 1
Em6
1192
E G C# E
1 3b 6 1
Em6
1193
E B C# G
1 5 6 3b
Em6
1194
G B C# E
3b 5 6 1

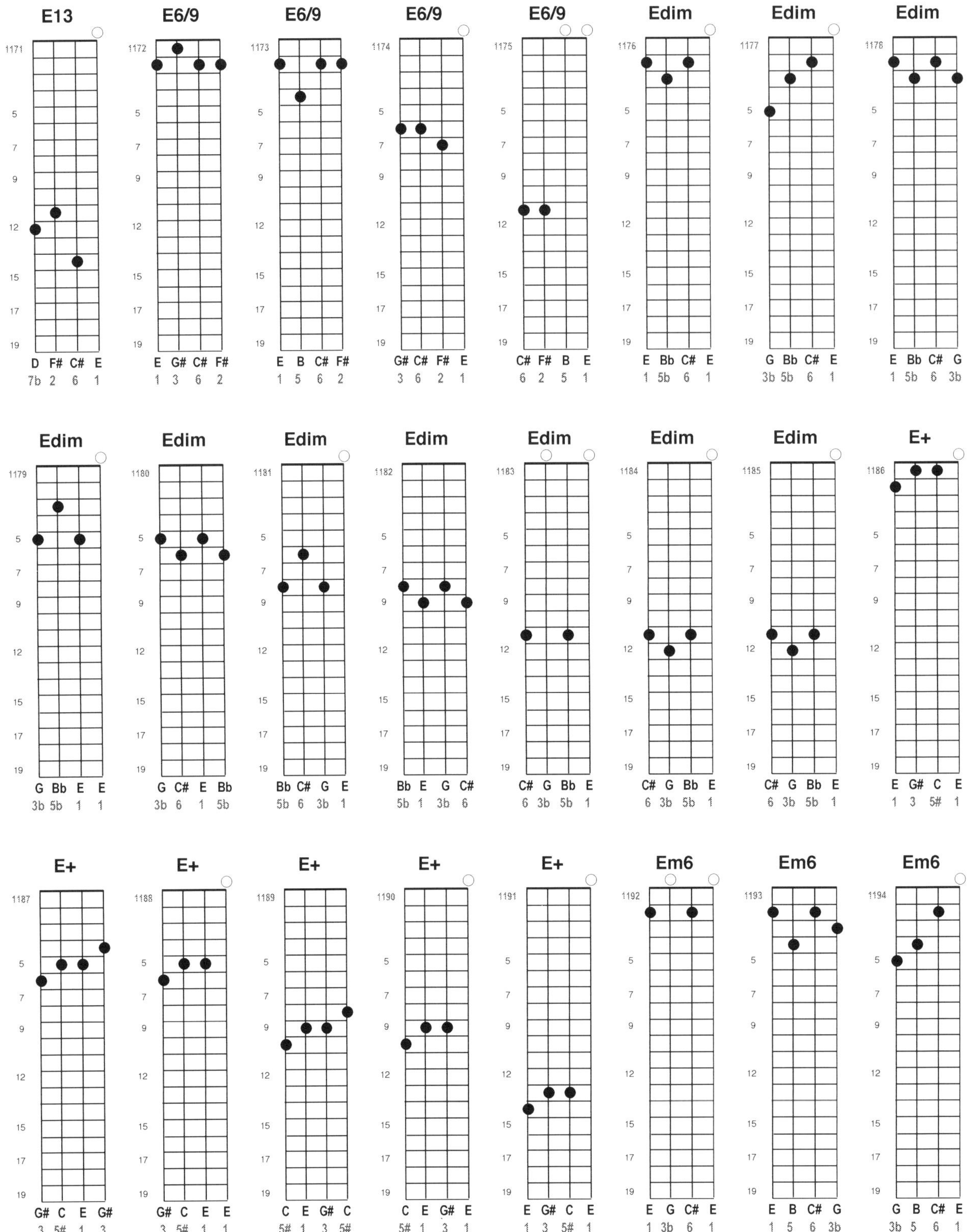

TUNING: D G B E

Em6
1195
G C# E G
3b 6 1 3b
Em6
1196
G C# B E
3b 6 5 1
Em6
1197
G C# E E
3b 6 1 1
Em6
1198
G C# G E
3b 6 3b 1
Em6
1199
G C# E B
3b 6 1 5
Em6
1200
B C# G E
5 6 3b 1
Em6
1201
C# G B E
6 3b 5 1
Em6
1202
C# G B E
6 3b 5 1
Em6
1203
C# G B E
6 3b 5 1
Em6/9
1204
E G C# F#
1 3b 6 2
Em6/9
1205
F# B C# G
2 5 6 3b
Em6/9
1206
G C# F# E
3b 6 2 1
Em6/9
1207
G C# F# B
3b 6 2 5
Em9
1208
D G B F#
7b 3b 5 2
Em9
1209
F# G D E
2 3b 7b 1
Em9
1210
G D F# E
3b 7b 2 1
Em9
1211
G D F# B
3b 7b 2 5
Em9
1212
D G F# E
7b 3b 2 1
Em9
1213
D F# G E
7b 2 3b 1
Emadd9
1214
E G B F#
1 3b 5 2
Emadd9
1215
G B E F#
3b 5 1 2
Emadd9
1216
G B F# E
3b 5 2 1
Emadd9
1217
B F# G E
5 2 3b 1
Emaj6
1218
G# C# D# E
3 6 7 1

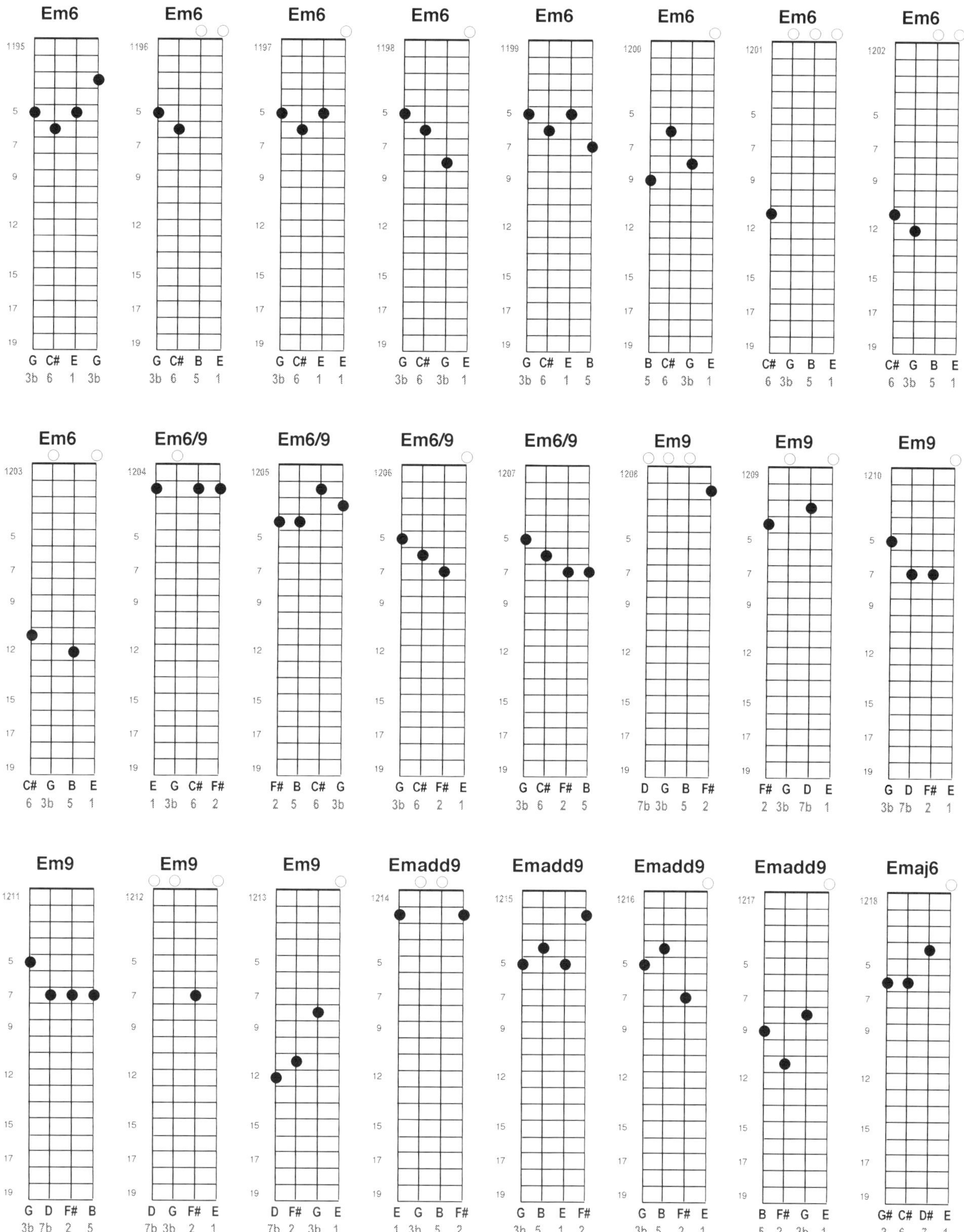

TUNING: D G B E

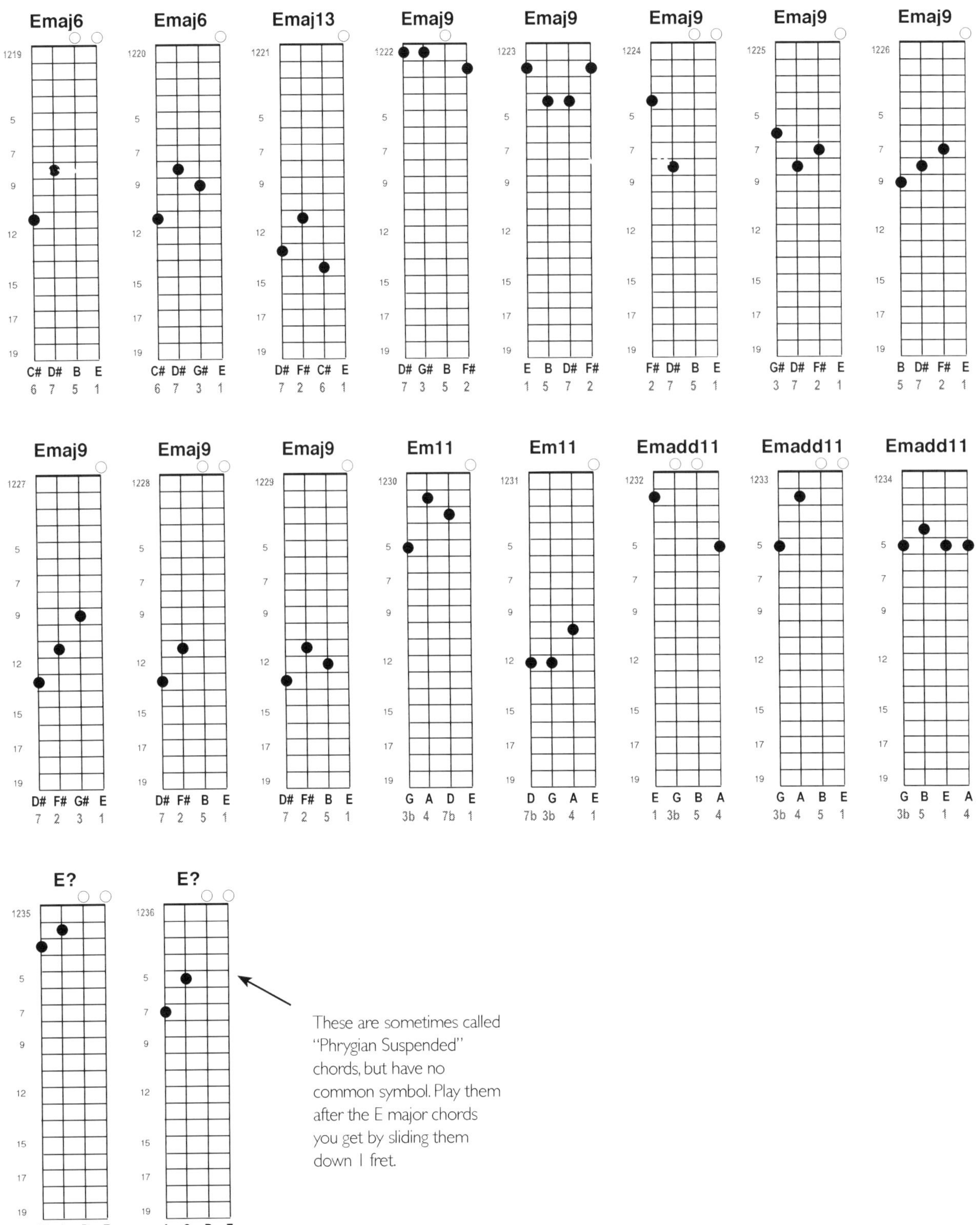

These are sometimes called "Phrygian Suspended" chords, but have no common symbol. Play them after the E major chords you get by sliding them down 1 fret.

TUNING: D G B E

F

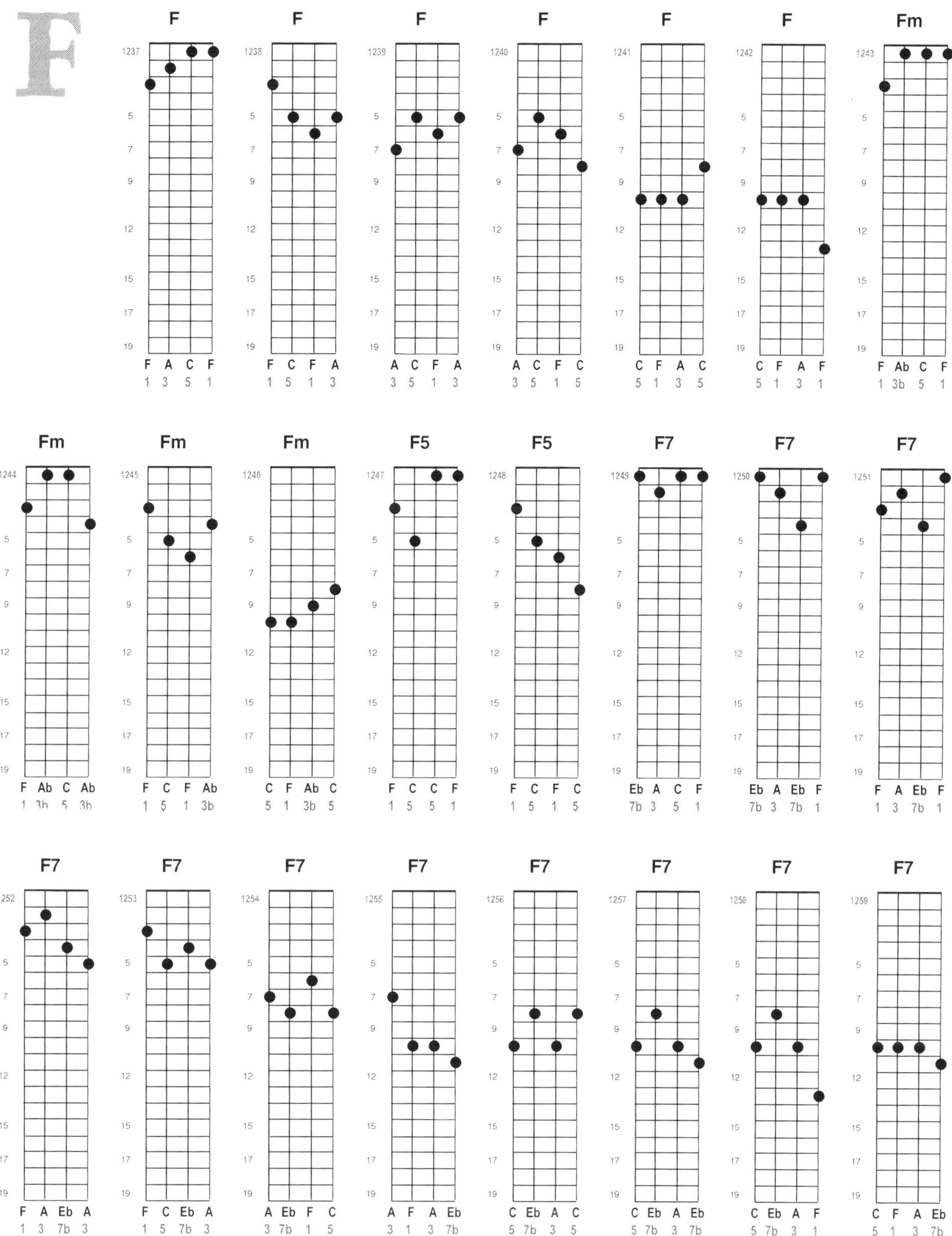

TUNING: D G B E

F7
1260
Eb F A F
7b 1 3 1
Fm7
1261
Eb Ab C F
7b 3b 5 1
Fm7
1262
Eb Ab Eb F
7b 3b 7b 1
Fm7
1263
F Ab Eb F
1 3b 7b 1
Fm7
1264
F Ab Eb Ab
1 3b 7b 3b
Fm7
1265
F C Eb Ab
1 5 7b 3b
Fm7
1266
C Eb Ab C
5 7b 3b 5
Fmaj7
1267
F A C E
1 3 5 7
Fmaj7
1268
E A C F
7 3 5 1
Fmaj7
1269
F A F E
1 3 1 7
Fmaj7
1270
F C E A
1 5 7 3
Fmaj7
1271
F C F E
1 5 1 7
Fmaj7
1272
A C E A
3 5 7 3
Fmaj7
1273
A C F E
3 5 1 7
Fmaj7
1274
C E A C
5 7 3 5
Fmaj7
1275
C F C E
5 1 5 7
Fmaj7
1276
C F A E
5 1 3 7
Fsus
1277
F Bb C F
1 4 5 1
Fsus
1278
F C F Bb
1 5 1 4
Fsus
1279
C F Bb C
5 1 4 5
F7sus
1280
Eb Bb C F
7b 4 5 1
F7sus
1281
C Eb Bb C
5 7b 4 5
F6
1282
D A D F
6 3 6 1
F6
1283
F A D F
1 3 6 1

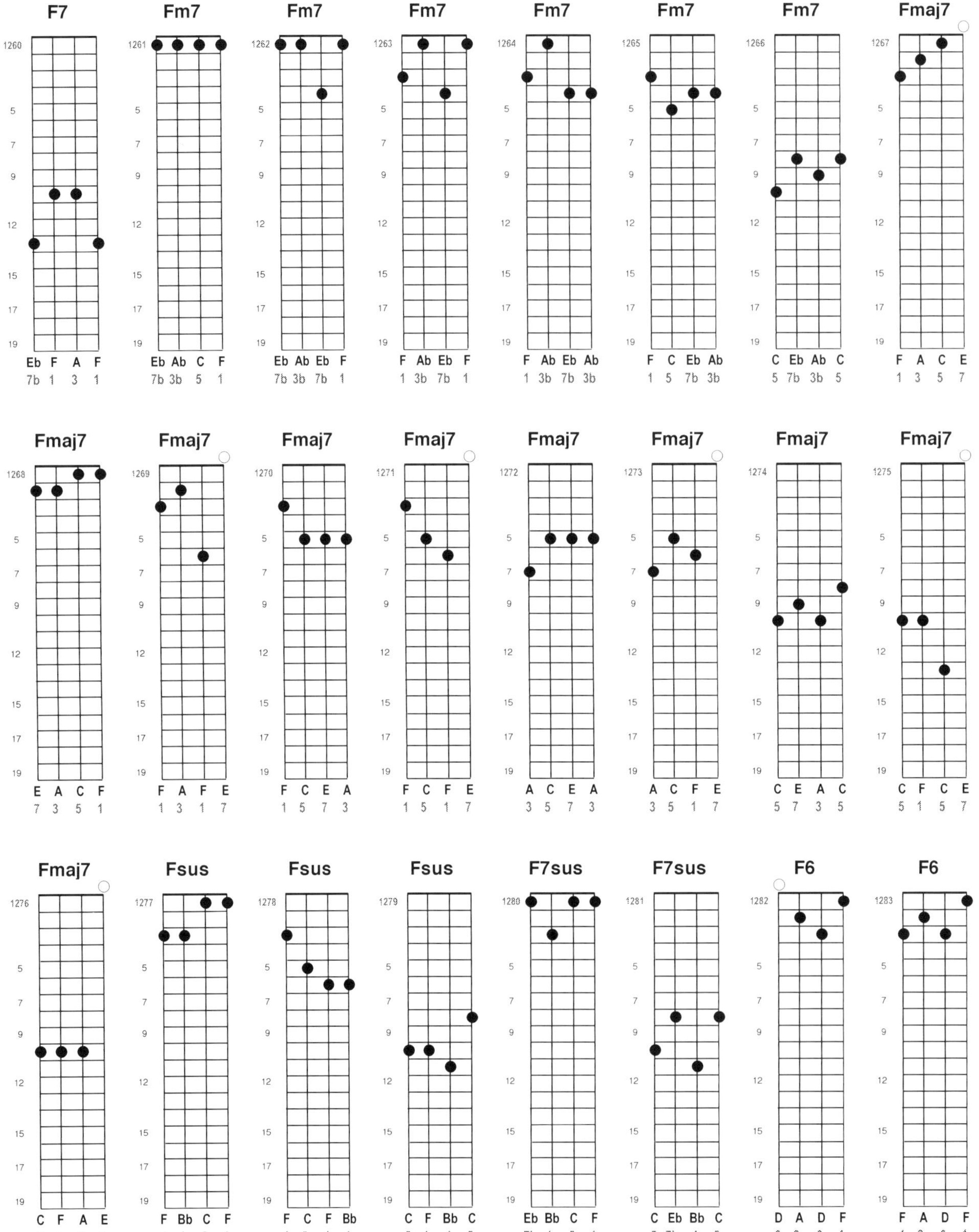

TUNING: D G B E

F6
1284
F C D A
1 5 6 3
F6
1285
C F A D
5 1 3 6
Fadd9
1286
F G C F
1 2 5 1
Fadd9
1287
F G C G
1 2 5 2
Fadd9
1288
F A C G
1 3 5 2
Fadd9
1289
F C F G
1 5 1 2
Fadd9
1290
A C F G
3 5 1 2
Fadd9
1291
A G F A
3 2 1 3
Fadd9
1292
A G F C
3 2 1 5
Fadd9
1293
C F G C
5 1 2 5
Fadd11
1294
Bb F A C
4 1 3 5
F9
1295
Eb A C G
7b 3 5 2
F9
1296
F G Eb A
1 2 7b 3
F9
1297
F C Eb G
1 5 7b 2
F9
1298
G C Eb A
2 5 7b 3
F9
1299
A Eb G C
3 7b 2 5
F9
1300
C Eb G C
5 7b 2 5
F11
1301
F Bb Eb G
1 4 7b 2
F6/7
1302
Eb A D F
7b 3 6 1
F6/7
1303
C Eb A D
5 7b 3 6
F6/9
1304
F G D F
1 2 6 1
F6/9
1305
F G D A
1 2 6 3
F6/9
1306
F G D G
1 2 6 2
F6/9
1307
C F G D
5 1 2 6

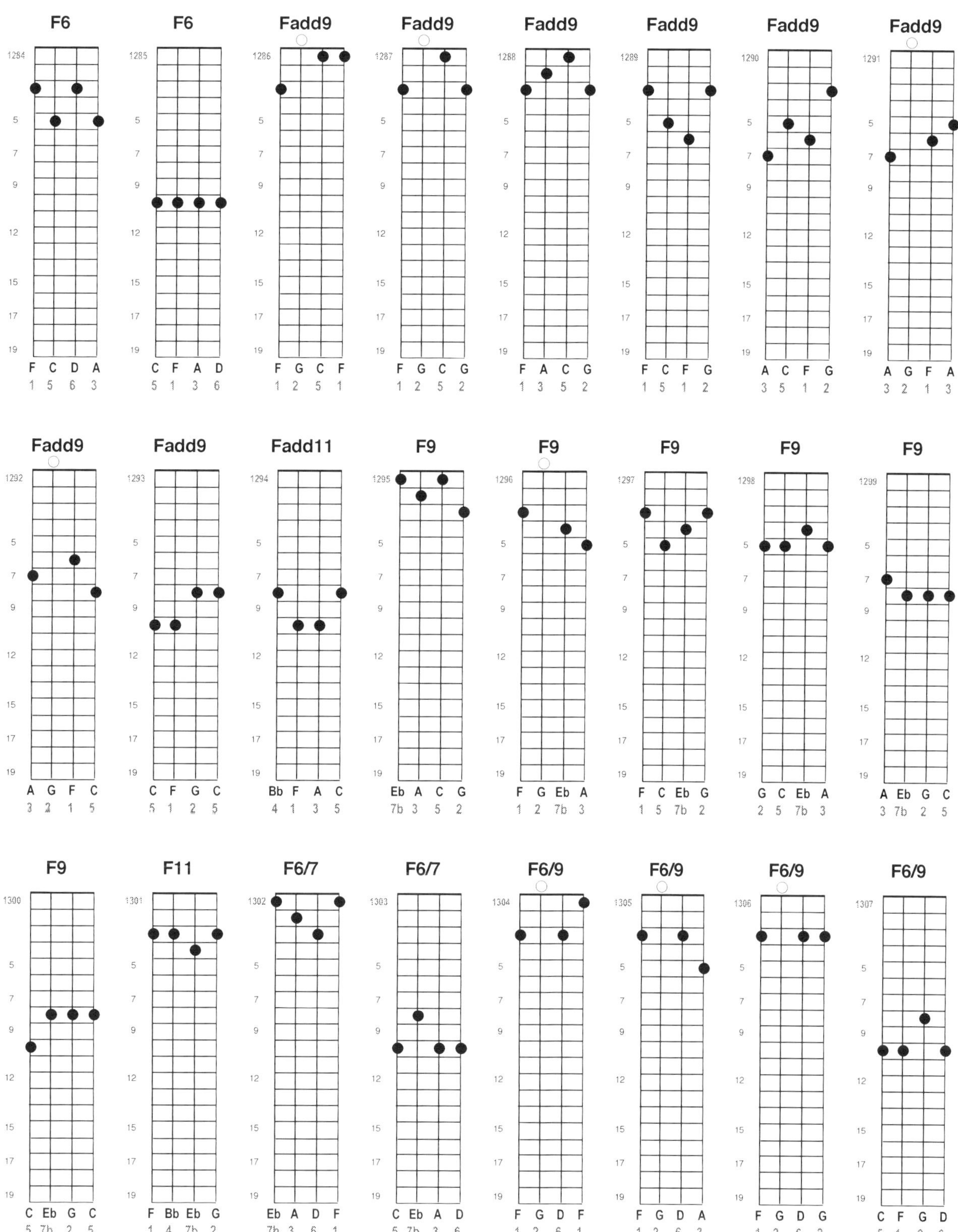

TUNING: D G B E

Fdim 1308 D Ab B F 6 3b 5b 1
Fdim 1309 F B D Ab 1 5b 6 3b
Fdim 1310 D B F Ab 6 5b 1 3b
Fdim 1311 Ab D F B 3b 6 1 5b
Fdim 1312 D F Ab B 6 1 3b 5b
Fdim 1313 B F Ab D 5b 1 3b 6
F+ 1314 F A C# F 1 3 5# 1
F+ 1315 A C# F A 3 5# 1 3
F+ 1316 A C# F x 3 5# 1 x
F+ 1317 C# F A C# 5# 1 3 5#
F+ 1318 C# F A x 5# 1 3 x
Fm6 1319 D Ab C F 6 3b 5 1
Fm6 1320 F Ab D F 1 3b 6 1
Fm6 1321 F C D Ab 1 5 6 3b
Fm6 1322 D C F Ab 6 5 1 3b
Fm6 1323 Ab D F C 3b 6 1 5
Fm6 1324 D F Ab C 6 1 3b 5
Fm6/9 1325 F G D Ab 1 2 6 3b
Fm6/9 1326 C G Ab D 5 2 3b 6
Fm9 1327 Eb Ab C G 7b 3b 5 2
Fm9 1328 Eb Ab Eb G 7b 3b 7b 2
Fm9 1329 F G Eb Ab 1 2 7b 3b
Fm9 1330 Ab C Eb G 3b 5 7b 2
Fm9 1331 C G Ab Eb 5 2 3b 7b

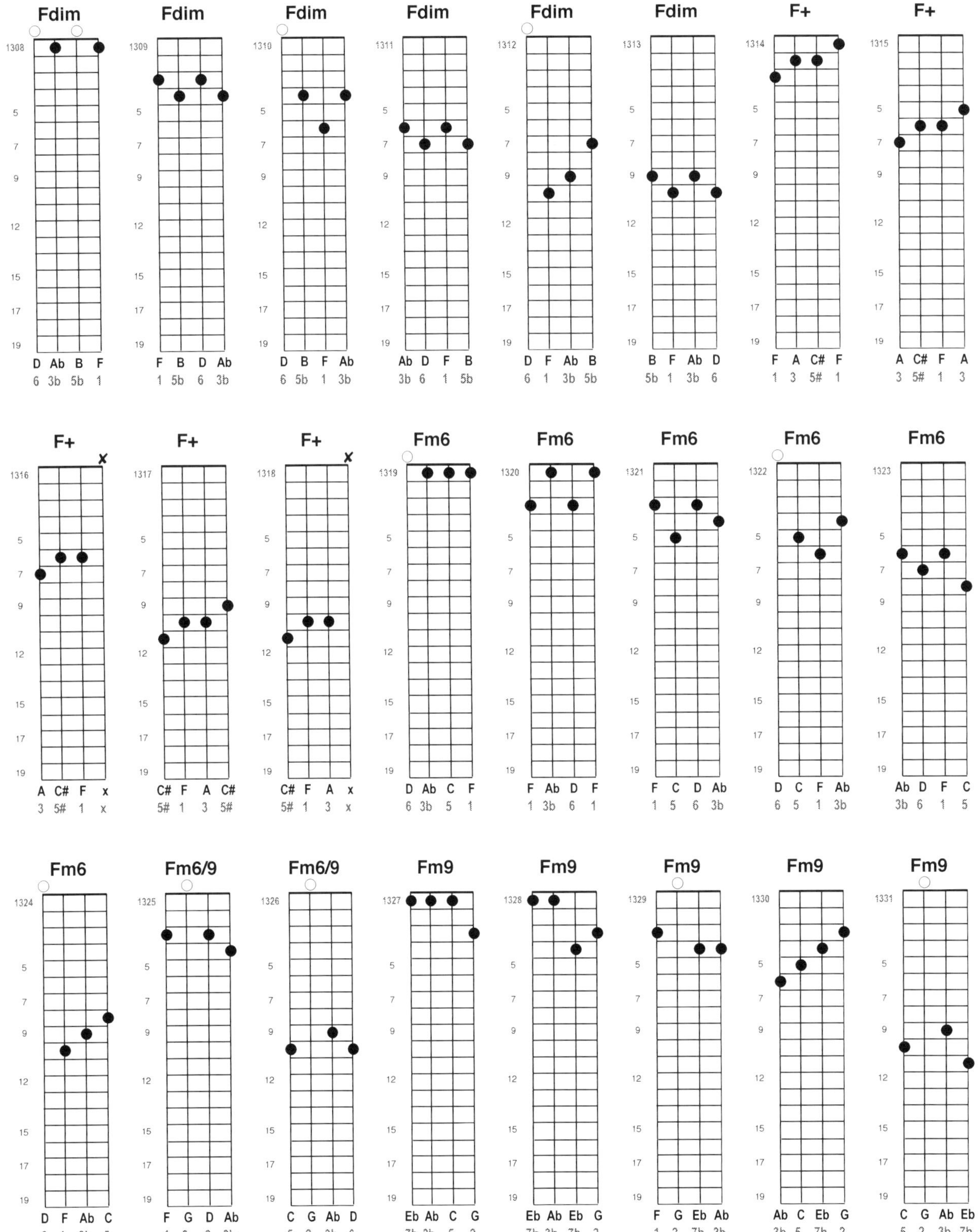

TUNING: D G B E

Fmadd9 1332
F Ab C G
1 3b 5 2

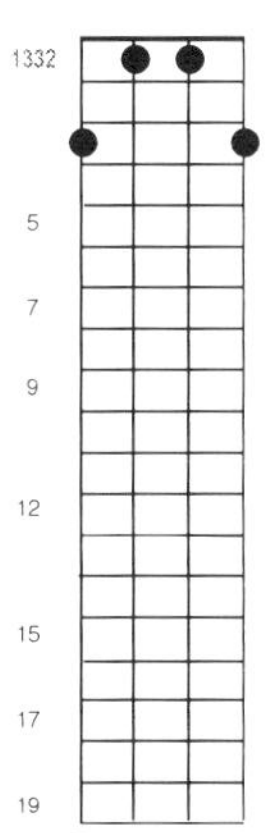

Fmadd9 1333
Ab C F G
3b 5 1 2

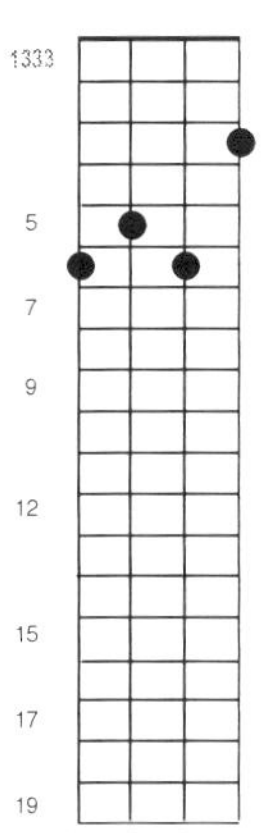

Fmaj6 1334
D A C E
6 3 5 7

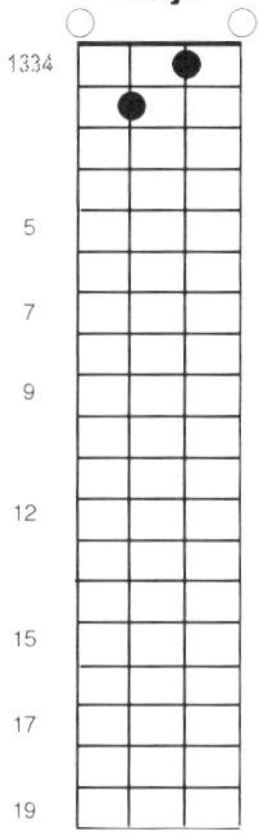

Fmaj6 1335
F A D E
1 3 6 7

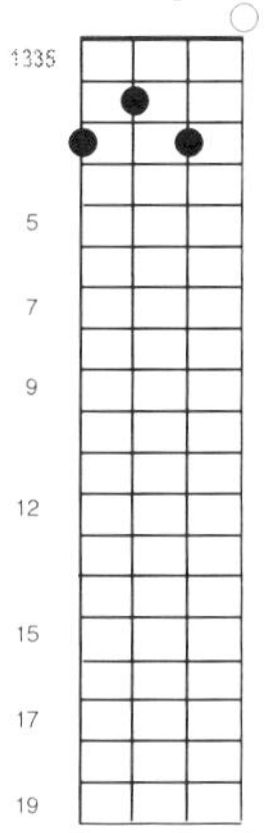

Fmaj6 1336
D C F E
6 5 1 7

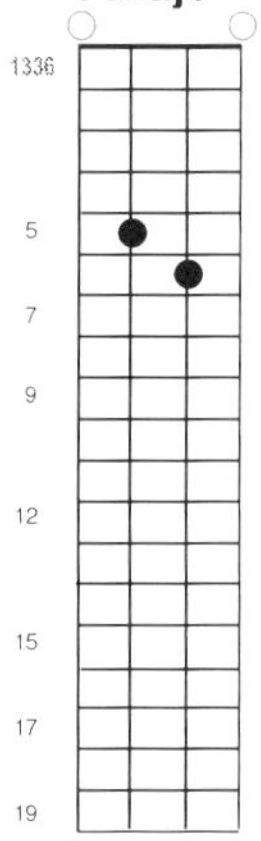

Fmaj6 1337
A D F E
3 6 1 7

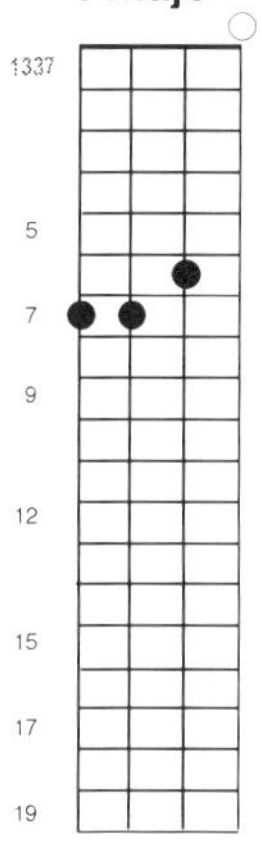

Fmaj6 1338
C D A E
5 6 3 7

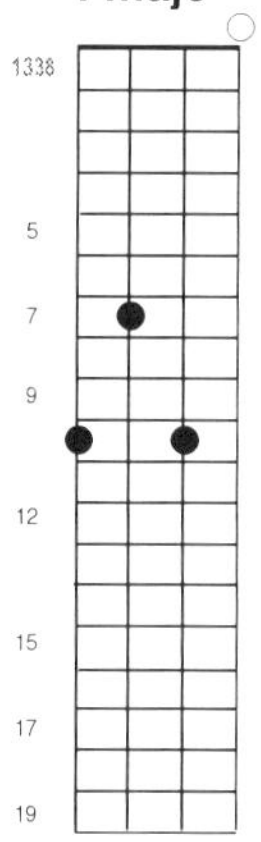

Fmaj6 1339
D F C E
6 1 5 7

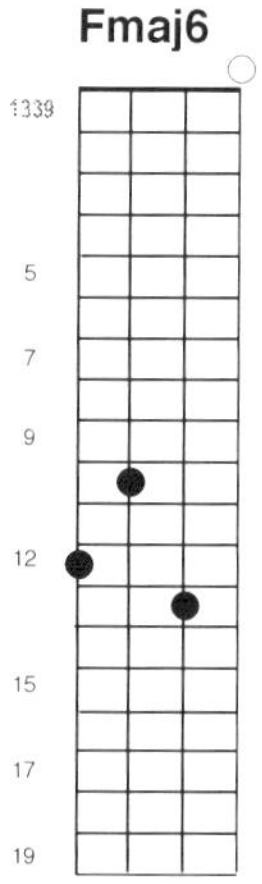

Fmaj6/9 1340
F G D E
1 2 6 7

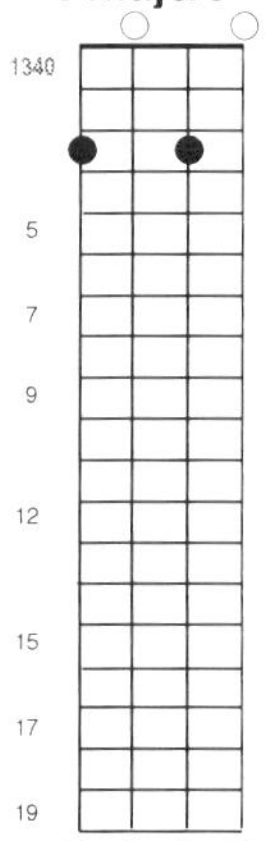

Fmaj9 1341
F G C E
1 2 5 7

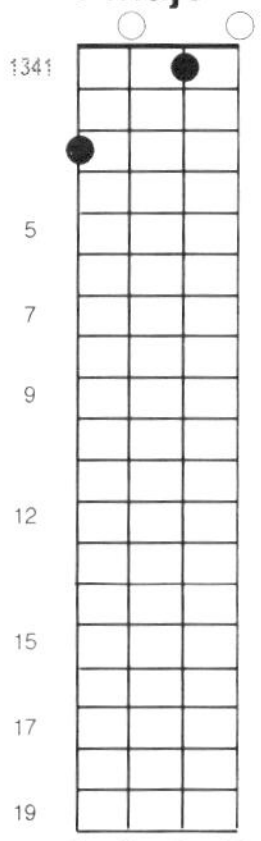

Fmaj9 1342
F C E G
1 5 7 2

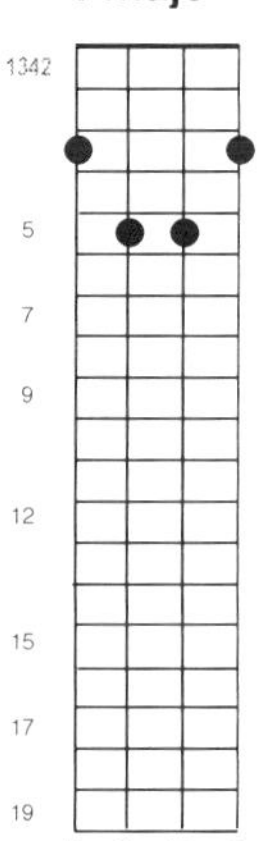

Fmaj9 1343
A C G E
3 5 2 7

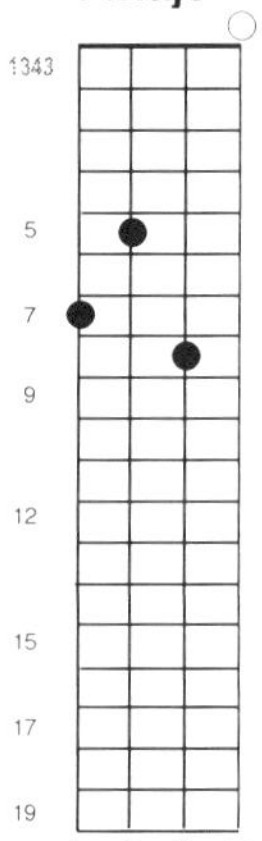

Fmaj9 1344
A G F E
3 2 1 7

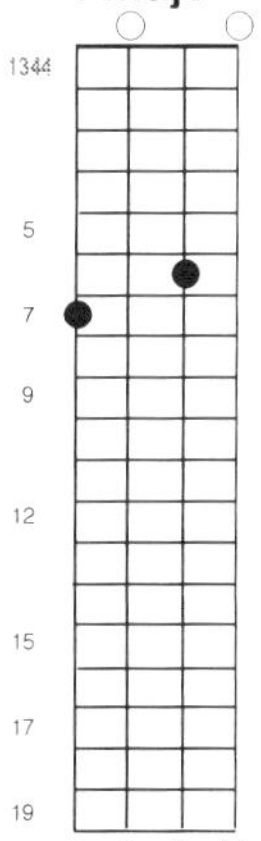

Fmaj9 1345
A G G E
3 2 2 7

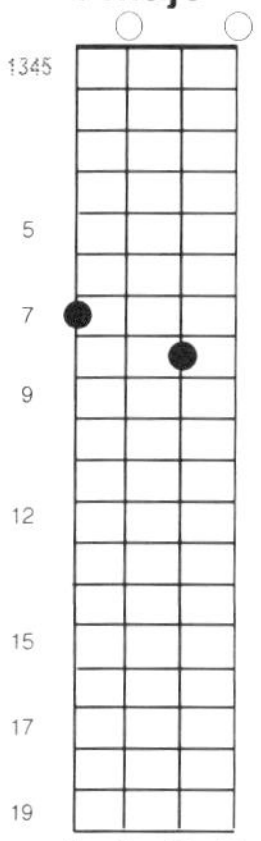

Fmaj9 1346
A F G E
3 1 2 7

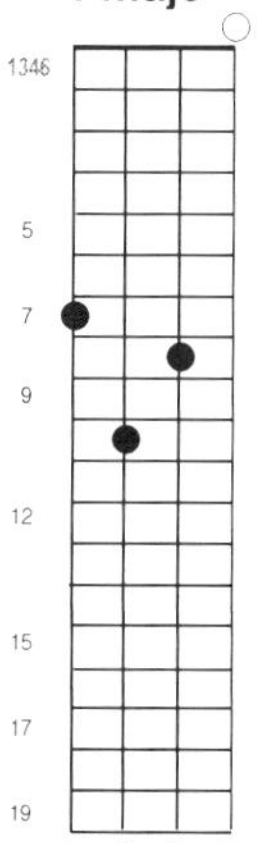

Fmaj9 1347
C F G E
5 1 2 7

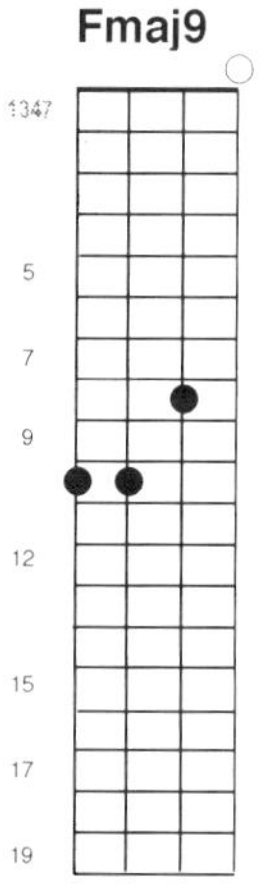

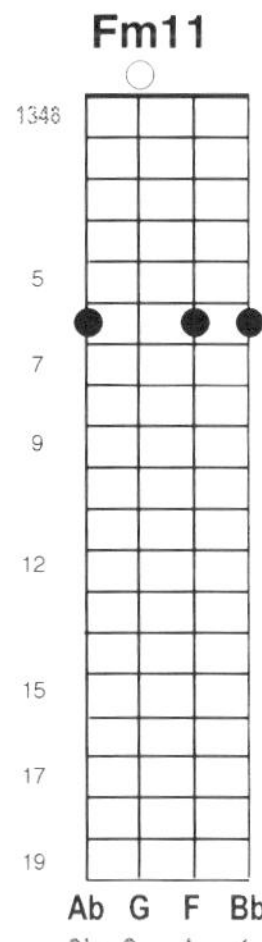

Baritone Ukulele Chords

TUNING: D G B E

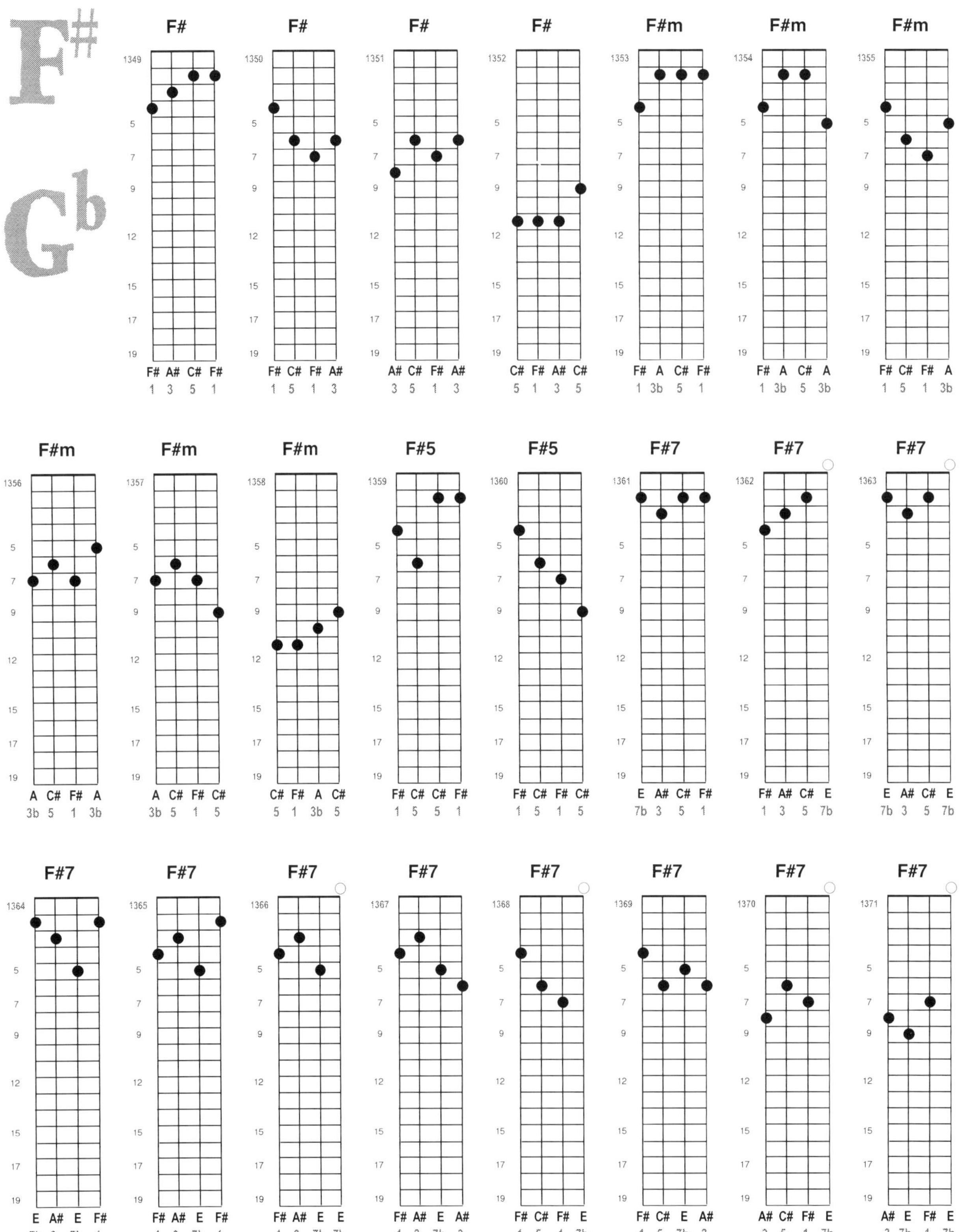

TUNING: D G B E

F#7
1372
C# E F# C#
5 7b 1 5
F#7
1373
A# F# A# E
3 1 3 7b
F#7
1374
C# E A# C#
5 7b 3 5
F#7
1375
C# E A# E
5 7b 3 7b
F#7
1376
C# E A# E
5 7b 3 7b
F#7
1377
C# E A# F#
5 7b 3 1
F#7
1378
C# F# A# E
5 1 3 7b
F#7
1379
C# F# A# E
5 1 3 7b
F#m7
1380
E A C# F#
7b 3b 5 1
F#m7
1381
F# A C# E
1 3b 5 7b
F#m7
1382
E A E F#
7b 3b 7b 1
F#m7
1383
F# A E F#
1 3b 7b 1
F#m7
1384
F# A E F#
1 3b 7b 1
F#m7
1385
F# C# E F#
1 5 7b 1
F#m7
1386
F# A E A
1 3b 7b 3b
F#m7
1387
F# C# E A
1 5 7b 3b
F#m7
1388
A F# A E
3b 1 3b 7b
F#m7
1389
C# E A C#
5 7b 3b 5
F#m7
1390
C# F# A E
5 1 3b 7b
F#maj7
1391
F# A# C# E#
1 3 5 7
F#maj7
1392
E# A# C# F#
7 3 5 1
F#7
1393
F# A# F# E
1 3 1 7b
F#maj7
1394
A# C# E# A#
3 5 7 3
F#maj7
1395
C# E# A# C#
5 7 3 5

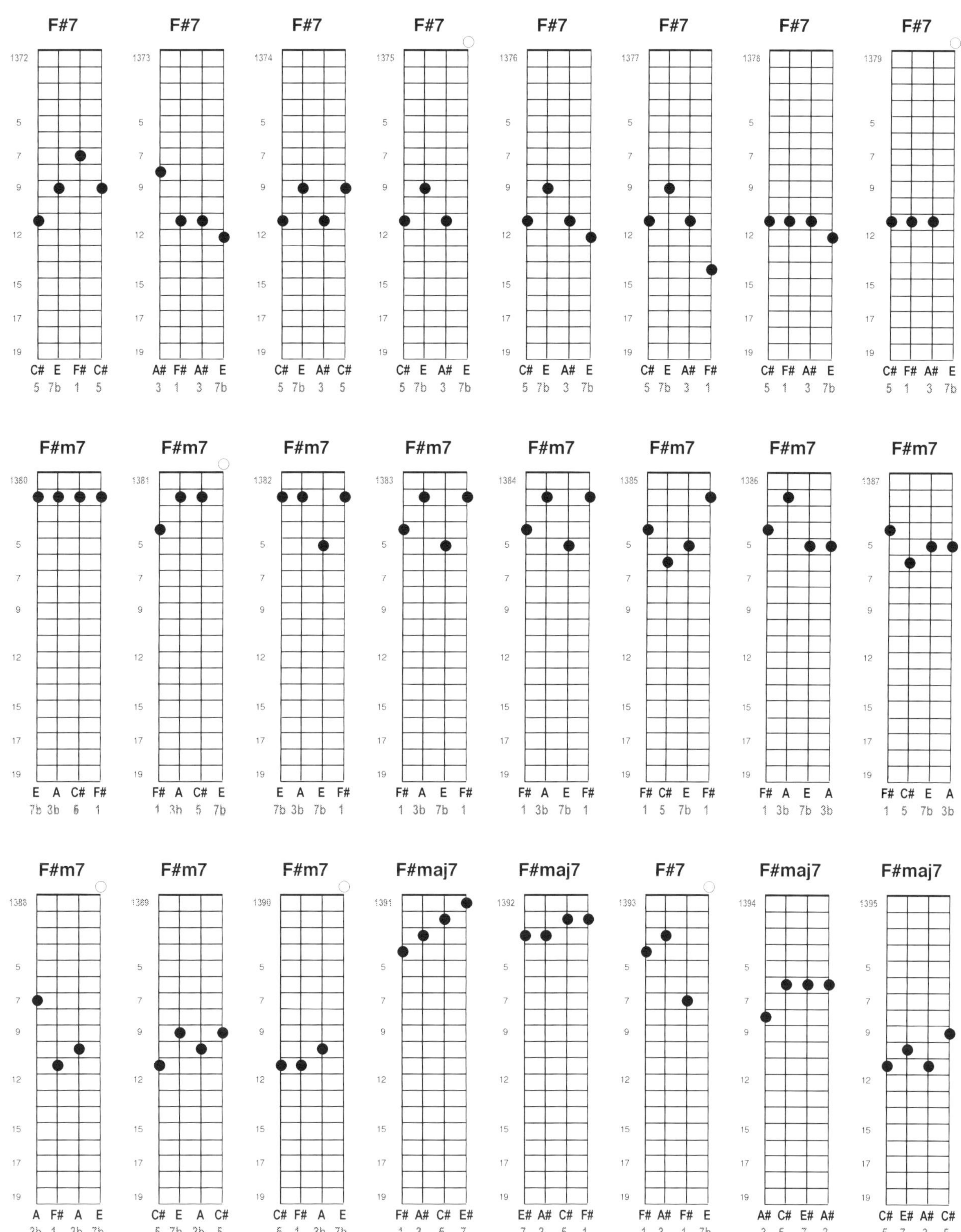

TUNING: D G B E

F#sus
1396
F# B C# F#
1 4 5 1
F#sus
1397
F# C# F# B
1 5 1 4
F#sus
1398
C# F# B C#
5 1 4 5
F#7sus
1399
E B C# F#
7b 4 5 1
F#7sus
1400
F# B C# E
1 4 5 7b
F#7sus
1401
F# C# B E
1 5 4 7b
F#7sus
1402
B C# F# E
4 5 1 7b
F#7sus
1403
C# E B C#
5 7b 4 5
F#7sus
1404
C# F# B E
5 1 4 7b
F#6
1405
F# C# D# A#
1 5 6 3
F#6
1406
C# F# A# D#
5 1 3 6
F#add9
1407
F# C# F# G#
1 5 1 2
F#add9
1408
A# C# F# G#
3 5 1 2
F#add9
1409
C# F# G# C#
5 1 2 5
F#add9
1410
C# G# C# F#
5 2 5 1
F#7add11
1411
F# A# B E
1 3 4 7b
F#9
1412
E G# C# E
7b 2 5 7b
F#9
1413
E G# C# F#
7b 2 5 1
F#9
1414
E A# C# G#
7b 3 5 2
F#9
1415
F# C# E G#
1 5 7b 2
F#9
1416
G# C# F# E
2 5 1 7b
F#9
1417
A# E G# C#
3 7b 2 5
F#9
1418
A# F# G# E
3 1 2 7b
F#9
1419
C# E G# C#
5 7b 2 5

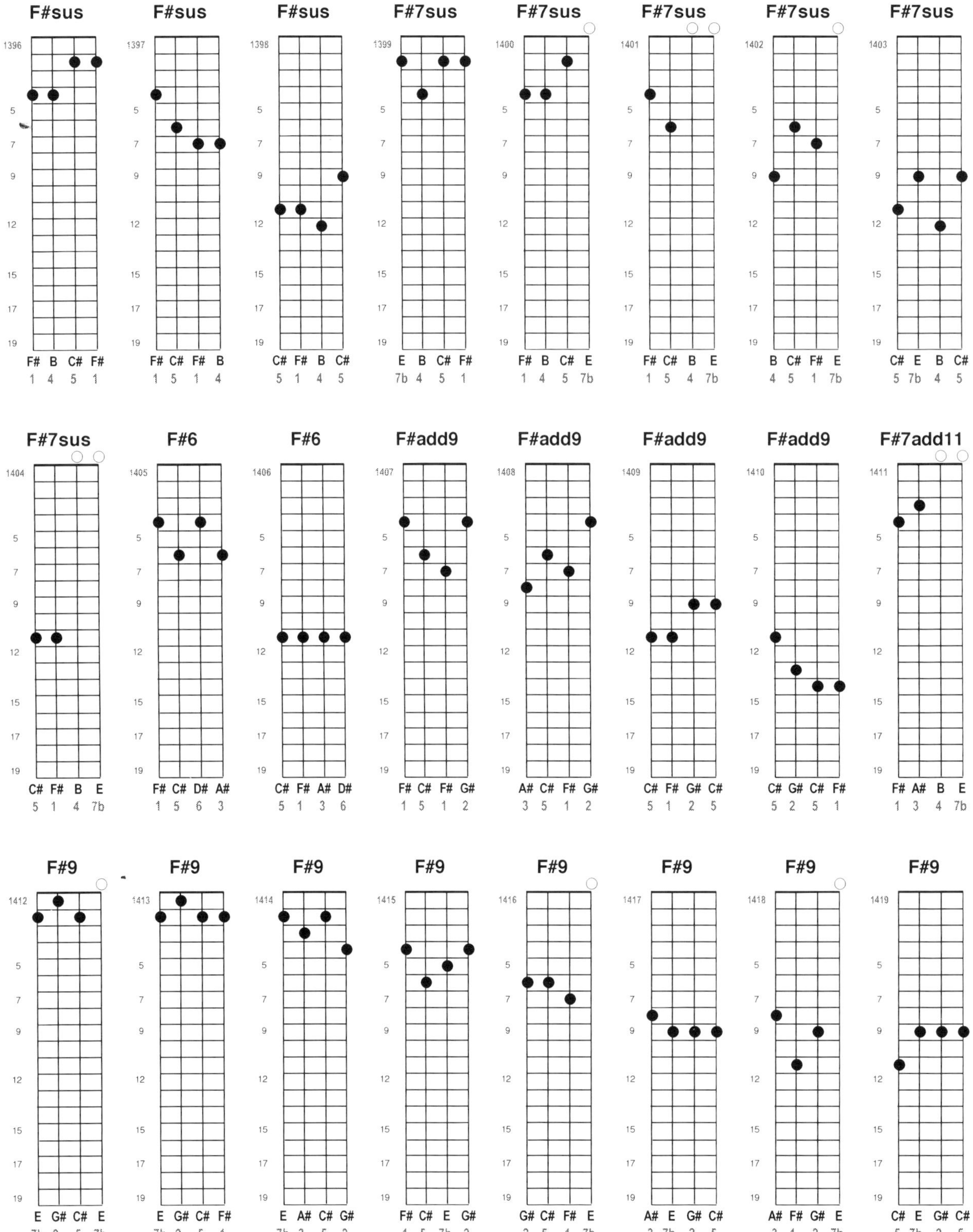

TUNING: D G B E

F#9
1420
C# F# G# E
5 1 2 7b
F#9
1421
C# G# A# E
5 2 3 7b
F#9
1422
E G# C# E
7b 2 5 7b
F#11
1423
F# G# B E
1 2 4 7b
F#6/7
1424
E A# D# F#
7b 3 6 1
F#6/7
1425
C# E A# D#
5 7b 3 6
F#6/9
1426
D# G# C# F#
6 2 5 1
F#6/9
1427
C# F# G# D#
5 1 2 6
F#6/9
1428
D# F# G# C#
6 1 2 5
F#6/9
1429
D# G# C# F#
6 2 5 1
F#dim
1430
F# A C x
1 3b 5b x
F#dim
1431
D# A C F#
6 3b 5b 1
F#dim
1432
F# C D# F#
1 5b 6 1
F#dim
1433
F# C D# A
1 5b 6 3b
F#dim
1434
A C F# x
3b 5b 1 x
F#dim
1435
A D# F# C
3b 6 1 5b
F#dim
1436
C F# A C
5b 1 3b 5b
F#dim
1437
C F# A x
5b 1 3b x
F#dim
1438
C F# A D#
5b 1 3b 6
F#+
1439
D A# D F#
5# 3 5# 1
F#+
1440
F# A# D F#
1 3 5# 1
F#+
1441
F# A# D x
1 3 5# x
F#+
1442
D D F# A#
5# 5# 1 3
F#+
1443
A# D F# A#
3 5# 1 3

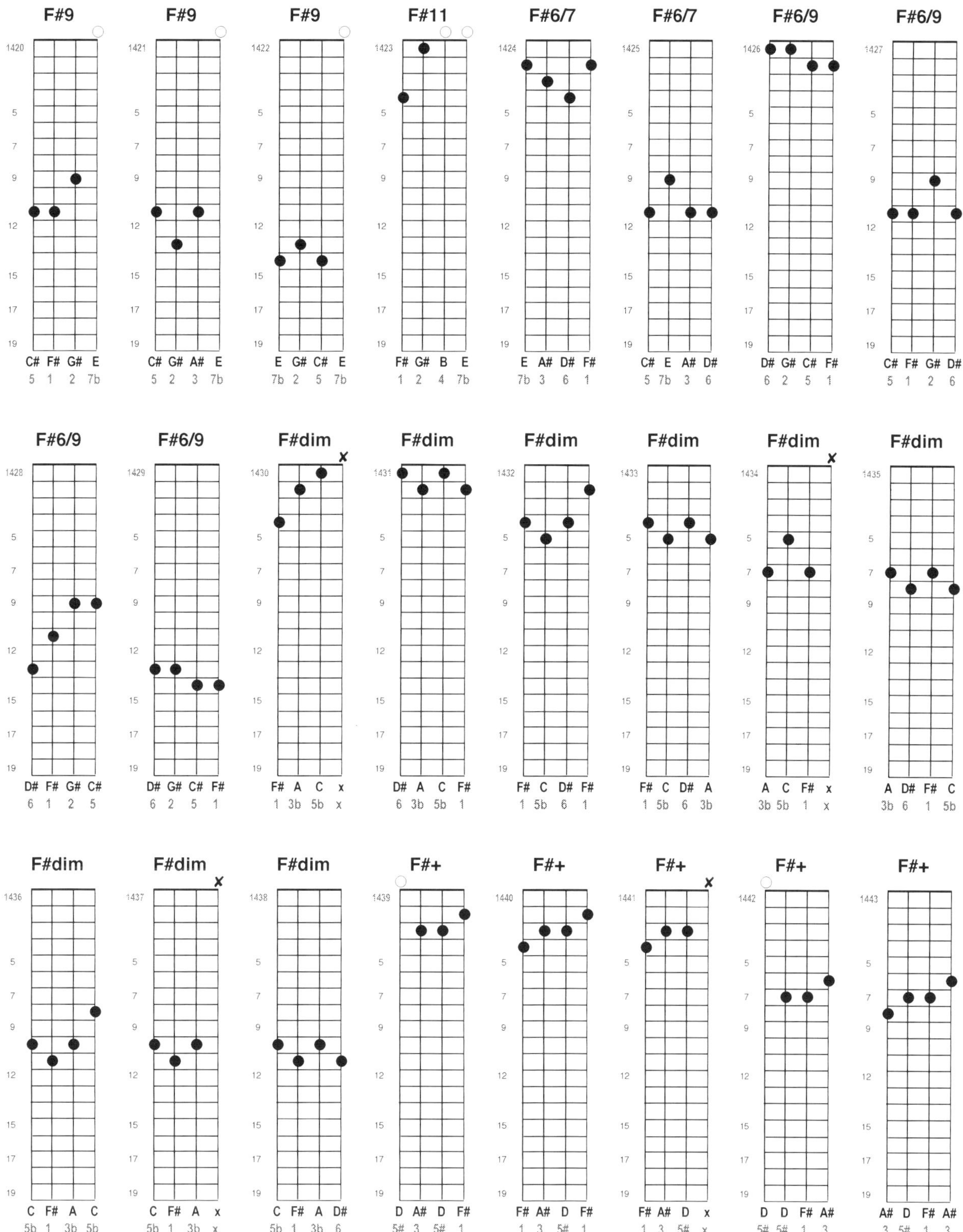

TUNING: D G B E

F#+
1444
A# D F# x
3 5# 1 x
F#+
1445
D F# A# D
5# 1 3 5#
F#+
1446
D F# A# D
5# 1 3 5#
F#+
1447
D F# A# x
5# 1 3 x
F#m6
1448
D# A C# F#
6 3b 5 1
F#m6
1449
F# A D# F#
1 3b 6 1
F#m6
1450
F# C# D# A
1 5 6 3b
F#m6
1451
A D# F# A
3b 6 1 3b
F#m6
1452
A D# F# C#
3b 6 1 5
F#m6
1453
C# F# A D#
5 1 3b 6
F#m6
1454
D# A C# F#
6 3b 5 1
F#m6/9
1455
C# F# G# D#
5 1 2 6
F#m9
1456
F# G# C# E
1 2 5 7b
F#m9
1457
A C# E G#
3b 5 7b 2
F#m9
1458
A C# G# E
3b 5 2 7b
F#m9
1459
A F# G# E
3b 1 2 7b
F#m9
1460
C# G# A E
5 2 3b 7b
F#madd9
1461
F# A C# G#
1 3b 5 2
F#maj9
1462
F# C# E# G#
1 5 7 2
F#m11
1463
F# A B E
1 3b 4 7b
F#9/11
1464
A# C# B G#
3 5 4 2

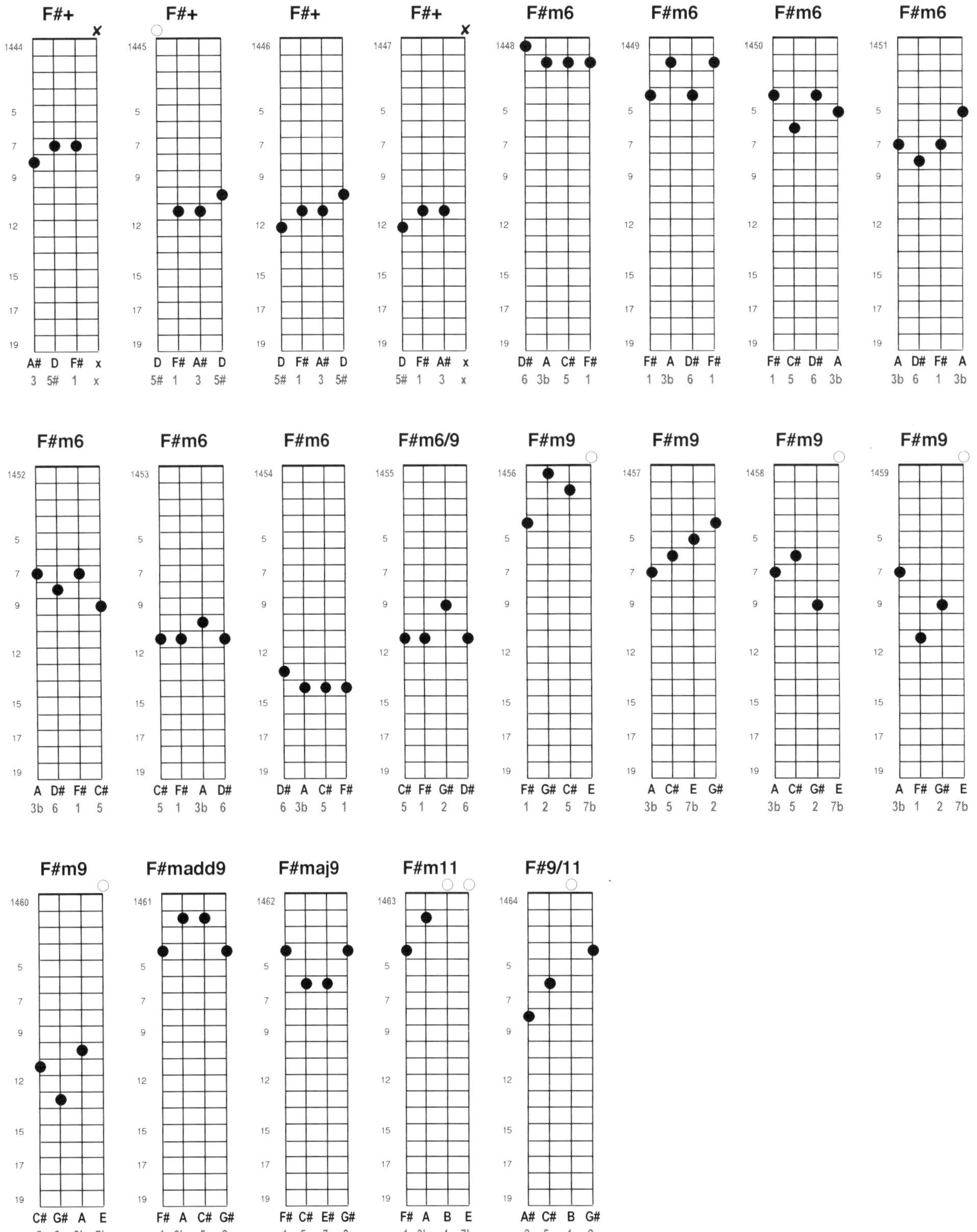

TUNING: D G B E

G

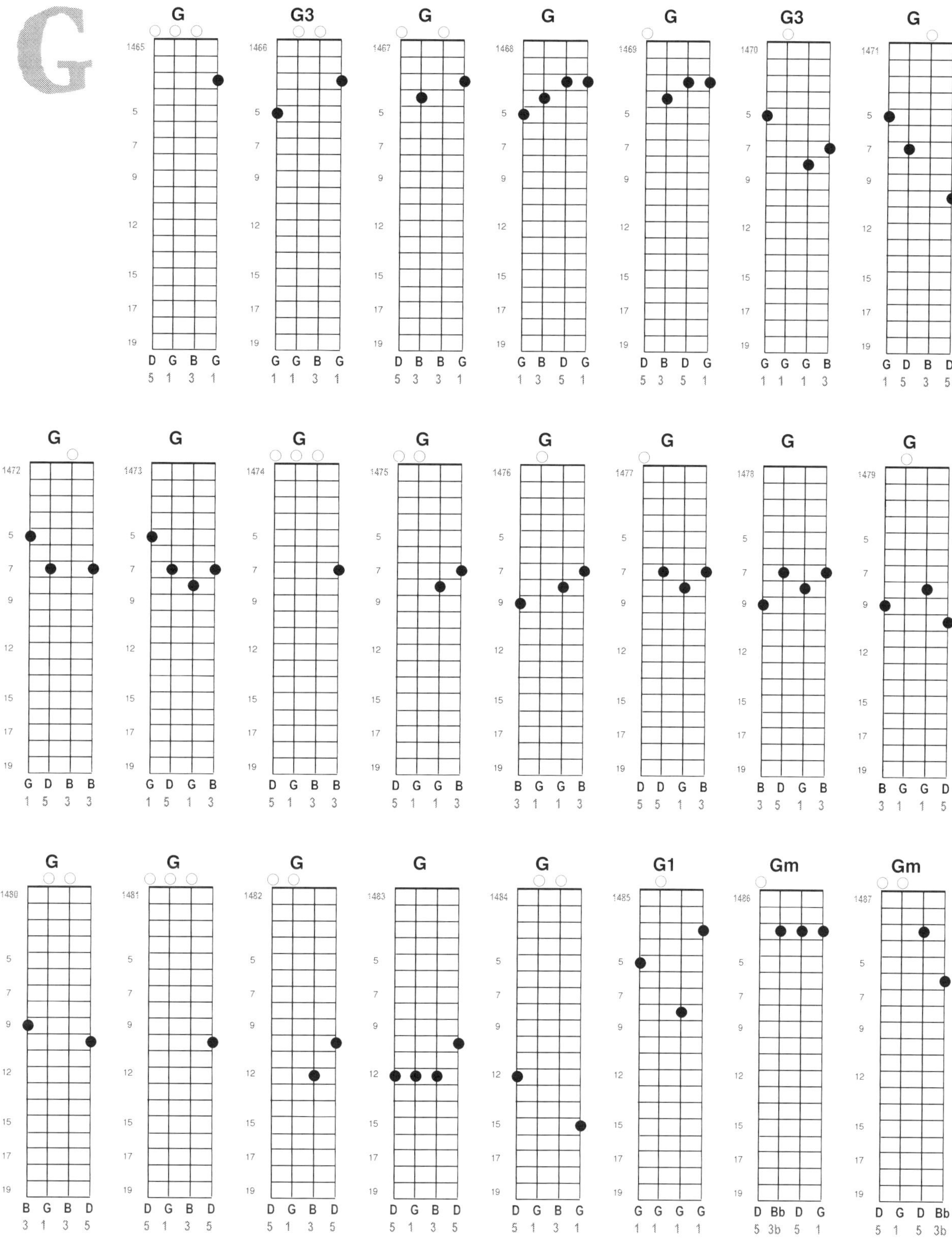

TUNING: D G B E

Gm 1488 G Bb D G 1 3b 5 1
Gm 1489 G Bb D Bb 1 3b 5 3b
Gm 1490 G D G Bb 1 5 1 3b
Gm 1491 D G G Bb 5 1 1 3b
Gm 1492 D D G Bb 5 5 1 3b
Gm 1493 Bb G G D 3b 1 1 5
Gm 1494 D G Bb D 5 1 3b 5
Gm 1495 D G Bb D 5 1 3b 5
Gm 1496 D G Bb G 5 1 3b 1
G5 1497 D G D G 5 1 5 1
G5 1498 G G D G 1 1 5 1
G5 1499 G D D G 1 5 5 1
G5 1500 G D G D 1 5 1 5
G5 1501 D G G D 5 1 1 5
G5 1502 D G D G 5 1 5 1
G7 1503 D G B F 5 1 3 7b
G7 1504 D G D F 5 1 5 7b
G7 1505 D B D F 5 3 5 7b
G7 1506 G B D F 1 3 5 7b
G7 1507 F G B G 7b 1 3 1
G7 1508 D G F G 5 1 7b 1
G7 1509 F B D G 7b 3 5 1
G7 1510 G G F G 1 1 7b 1
G7 1511 D B F G 5 3 7b 1

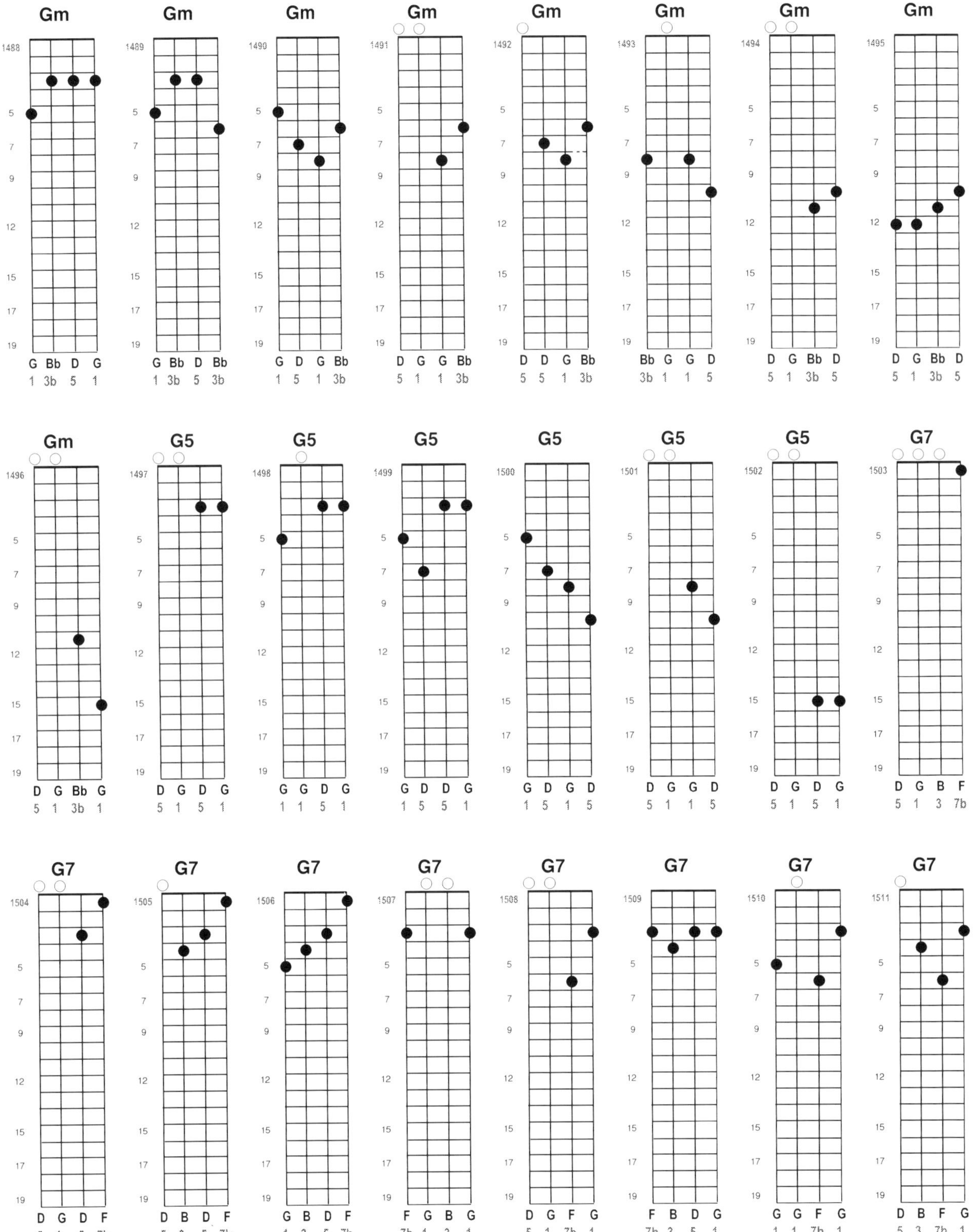

TUNING: D G B E

G7
1512
F B F G
7b 3 7b 1
G7
1513
F G D G
7b 1 5 1
G7
1514
G B F G
1 3 7b 1
G7
1515
G B F B
1 3 7b 3
G7
1516
G G F B
1 1 7b 3
G7
1517
G D F B
1 5 7b 3
G7
1518
D G F B
5 1 7b 3
G7
1519
D F G D
5 7b 1 5
G7
1520
B G B F
3 1 3 7b
G7
1521
D F B D
5 7b 3 5
G7
1522
D F B D
5 7b 3 5
G7
1523
D F B F
5 7b 3 7b
G7
1524
D G B F
5 1 3 7b
G7
1525
D G B F
5 1 3 7b
G7
1526
D G B F
5 1 3 7b
Gm7
1527
F Bb D G
7b 3b 5 1
Gm7
1528
F Bb F G
7b 3b 7b 1
Gm7
1529
D Bb F G
5 3b 7b 1
Gm7
1530
G Bb F G
1 3b 7b 1
Gm7
1531
G Bb F Bb
1 3b 7b 3b
Gm7
1532
G D F Bb
1 5 7b 3b
Gm7
1533
D G F Bb
5 1 7b 3b
Gm7
1534
Bb F G D
3b 7b 1 5
Gm7
1535
D G Bb F
5 1 3b 7b

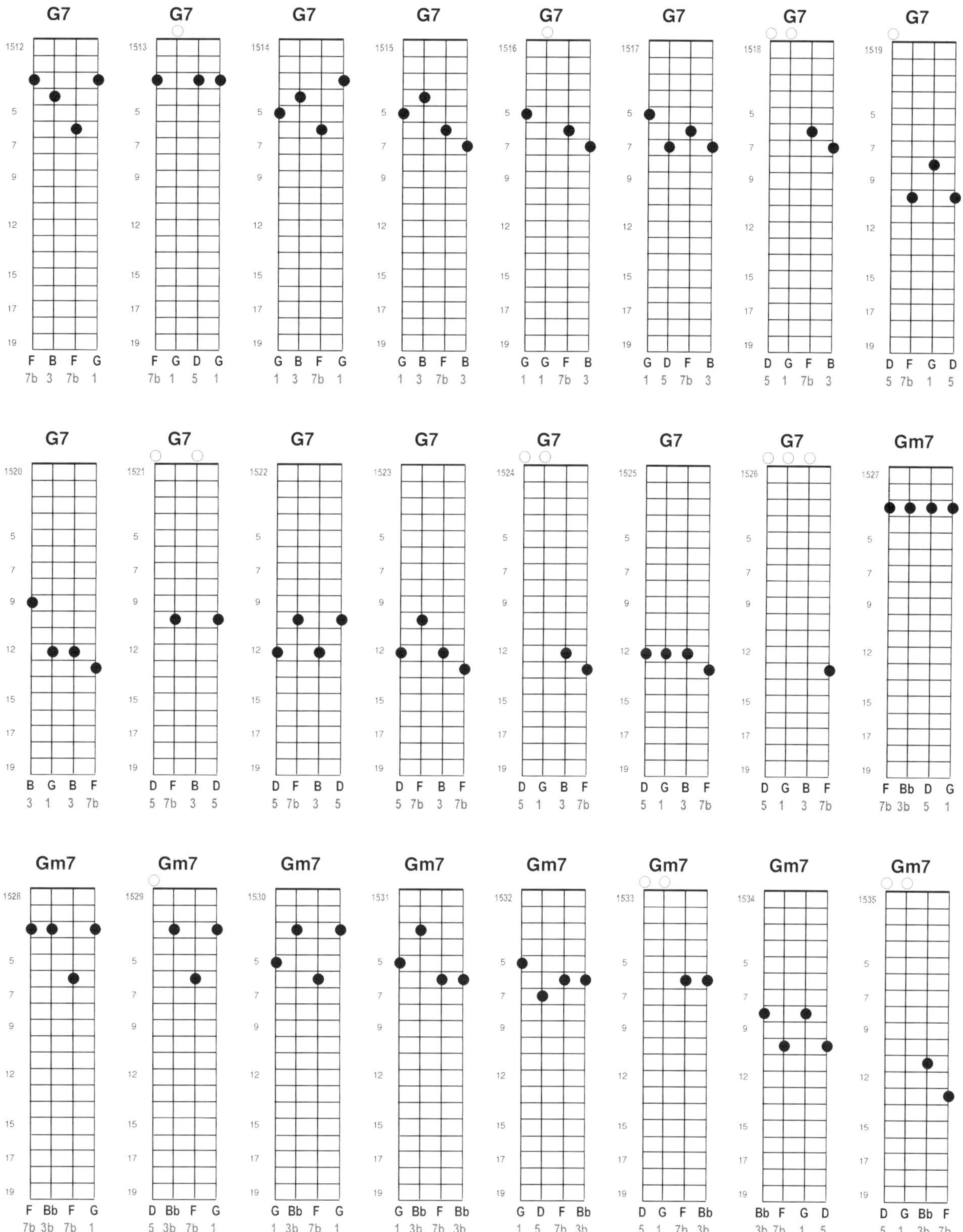

TUNING: D G B E

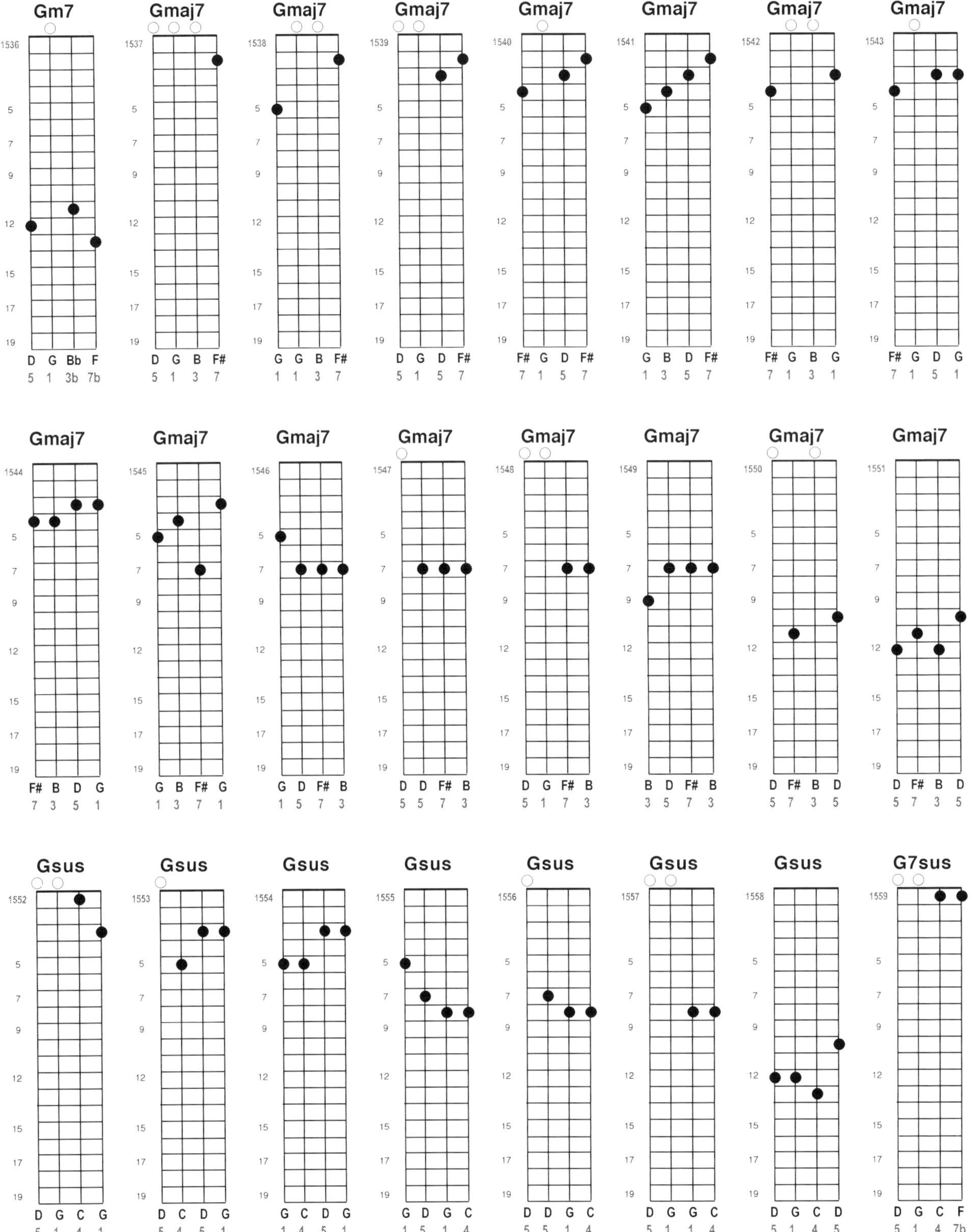

TUNING: D G B E

G7sus
1560
F C D G
7b 4 5 1
G7sus
1561
D G F C
5 1 7b 4
G7sus
1562
D F G C
5 7b 1 4
G6
1563
E G D E
6 1 5 6
G6
1564
E B D G
6 3 5 1
G6
1565
D G D E
5 1 5 6
G6
1566
G G D E
1 1 5 6
G6
1567
G B D E
1 3 5 6
G6
1568
G B B E
1 3 3 6
G6
1569
D G E B
5 1 6 3
G6
1570
G D B E
1 5 3 6
G6
1571
G D E B
1 5 6 3
G6
1572
G D G E
1 5 1 6
G6
1573
B D G E
3 5 1 6
G6
1574
D E G B
5 6 1 3
G6
1575
D G G E
5 1 1 6
G6
1576
B G G E
3 1 1 6
G6
1577
B G B E
3 1 3 6
G6
1578
E G B D
6 1 3 5
G6
1579
D G B E
5 1 3 6
G6
1580
D G B E
5 1 3 6
G6
1581
D G B E
5 1 3 6
G6
1582
D G B E
5 1 3 6
G6
1583
D G B E
5 1 3 6

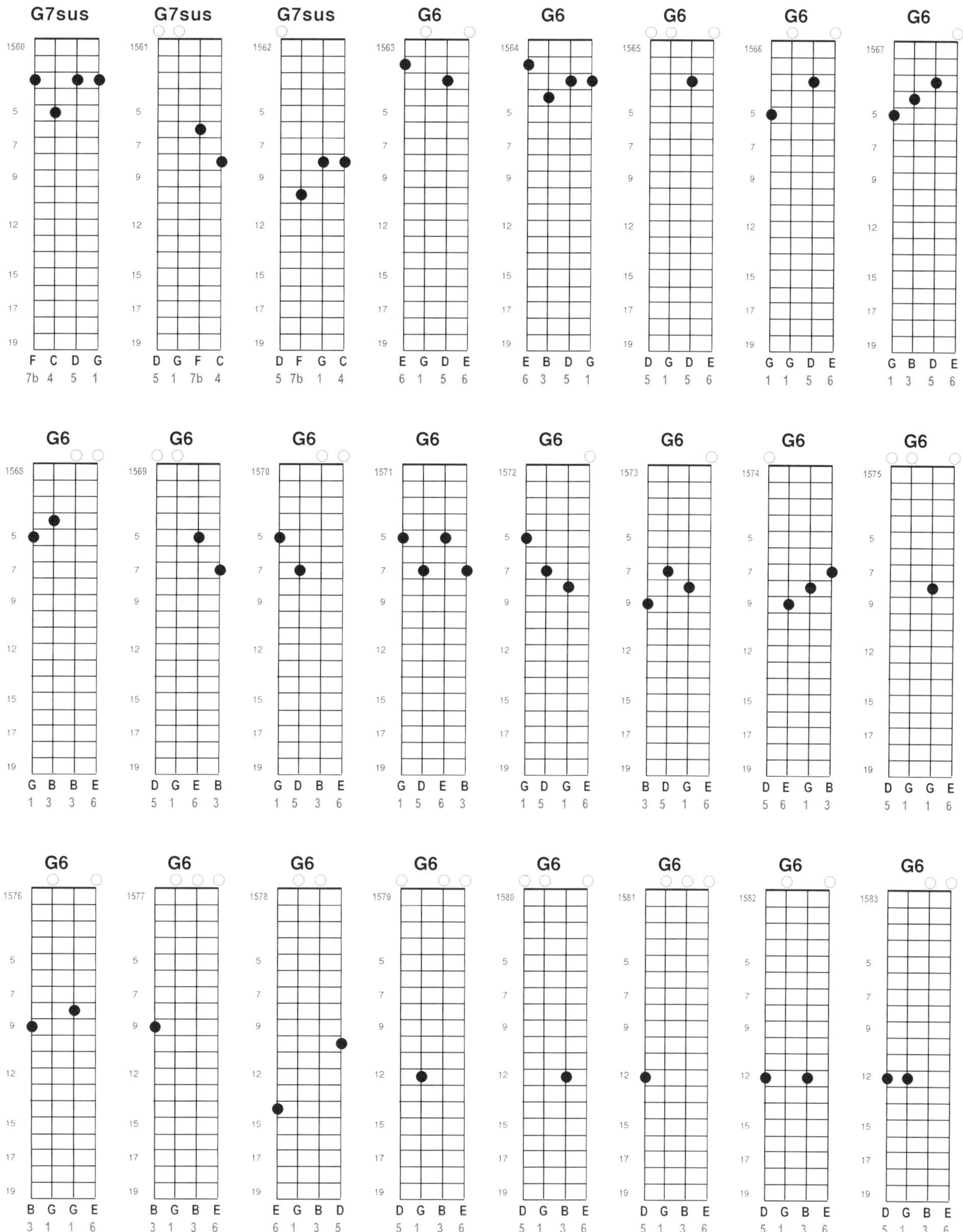

TUNING: D G B E

G6
1584
D G B E
5 1 3 6
G6
1585
D G B E
5 1 3 6
Gadd9
1586
D A B G
5 2 3 1
Gadd9
1587
D A D G
5 2 5 1
Gadd9
1588
D G D A
5 1 5 2
Gadd9
1589
D G B A
5 1 3 2
Gadd9
1590
B D G A
3 5 1 2
Gadd9
1591
D G A B
5 1 2 3
Gadd9
1592
D G A B
5 1 2 3
Gadd9
1593
B G A D
3 1 2 5
Gadd9
1594
D G A D
5 1 2 5
Gadd11
1595
C D G B
4 5 1 3
G9
1596
D A B F
5 2 3 7b
G9
1597
F A D G
7b 2 5 1
G9
1598
F G B A
7b 1 3 2
G9
1599
F G D A
7b 1 5 2
G9
1600
F B D A
7b 3 5 2
G9
1601
D B F A
5 3 7b 2
G9
1602
D G F A
5 1 7b 2
G9
1603
G D F A
1 5 7b 2
G9
1604
B F A D
3 7b 2 5
G9
1605
D F A D
5 7b 2 5
G9
1606
D F A D
5 7b 2 5
G9
1607
D A B F
5 2 3 7b

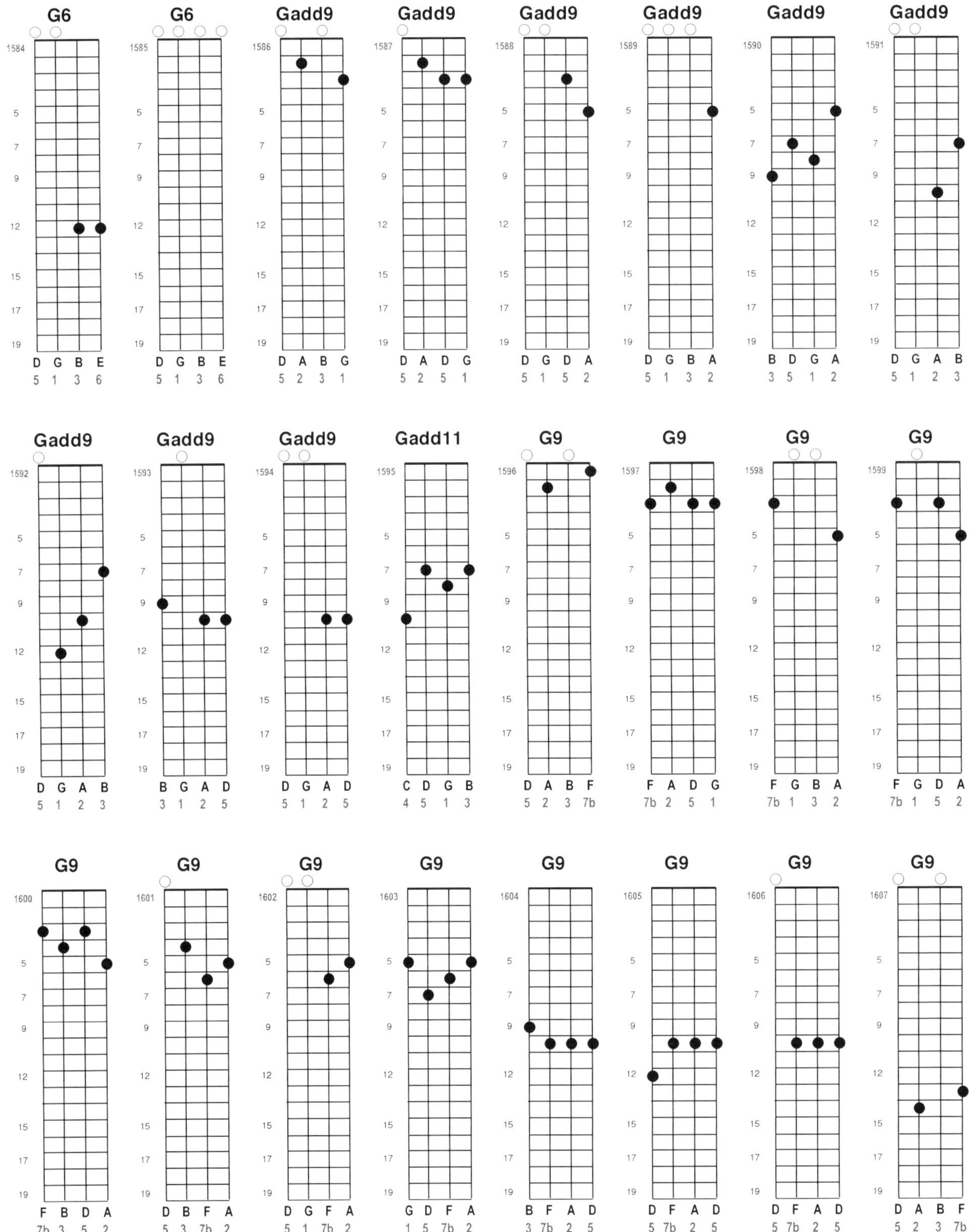

TUNING: D G B E

G11
1608
D A C F
5 2 4 7b
G11
1609
D C F A
5 4 7b 2
G6/7
1610
F G B E
7b 1 3 6
G6/7
1611
F G D E
7b 1 5 6
G6/7
1612
F B E G
7b 3 6 1
G6/7
1613
G B F E
1 3 7b 6
G6/7
1614
D G F E
5 1 7b 6
G6/7
1615
B F G E
3 7b 1 6
G6/7
1616
D F B E
5 7b 3 6
G6/9
1617
G A B E
1 2 3 6
G6/9
1618
E A D G
6 2 5 1
G6/9
1619
D G E A
5 1 6 2
G6/9
1620
A G E B
2 1 6 3
G6/9
1621
A G B E
2 1 3 6
G6/9
1622
B G A E
3 1 2 6
G6/9
1623
D G A E
5 1 2 6
Gdim
1624
E G Db E
6 1 5b 6
Gdim
1625
G Bb Db E
1 3b 5b 6
Gdim
1626
E Bb Db E
6 3b 5b 6
Gdim
1627
E Bb Db G
6 3b 5b 1
Gdim
1628
G Db E Bb
1 5b 6 3b
Gdim
1629
Bb Db G E
3b 5b 1 6
Gdim
1630
Bb E G Db
3b 6 1 5b
Gdim
1631
Db G Bb E
5b 1 3b 6

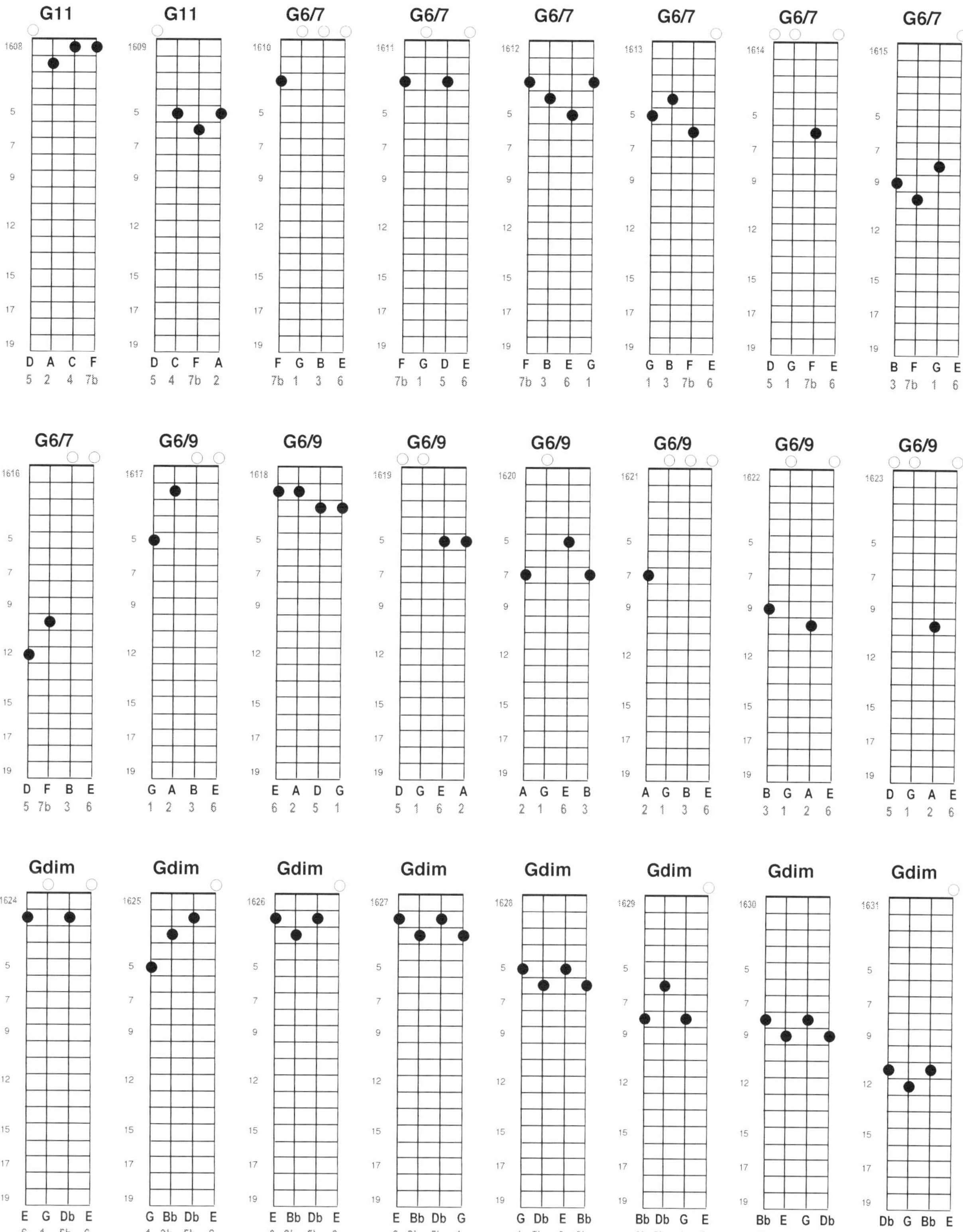

TUNING: D G B E

Gdim
1632
Db G Bb E
5b 1 3b 6
Gdim
1633
Db G Bb E
5b 1 3b 6
G+
1634
D# G B x
5# 1 3 x
G+
1635
G B D# G
1 3 5# 1
G+
1636
G B D# x
1 3 5# x
G+
1637
B D# G B
3 5# 1 3
G+
1638
B D# G x
3 5# 1 x
G+
1639
D# G B D#
5# 1 3 5#
G+
1640
D# G B x
5# 1 3 x
Gm6
1641
G Bb D E
1 3b 5 6
Gm6
1642
G Bb E G
1 3b 6 1
Gm6
1643
D G E Bb
5 1 6 3b
Gm6
1644
G D E Bb
1 5 6 3b
Gm6
1645
D E G Bb
5 6 1 3b
Gm6
1646
Bb D G E
3b 5 1 6
Gm6
1647
Bb E G D
3b 6 1 5
Gm6
1648
D G Bb E
5 1 3b 6
Gm6
1649
D G Bb E
5 1 3b 6
Gm6
1650
D G Bb E
5 1 3b 6
Gm6
1651
D G Bb E
5 1 3b 6
Gm9
1652
F Bb D A
7b 3b 5 2
Gm9
1653
F Bb F A
7b 3b 7b 2
Gm9
1654
Bb G F A
3b 1 7b 2
Gm9
1655
Bb D F A
3b 5 7b 2

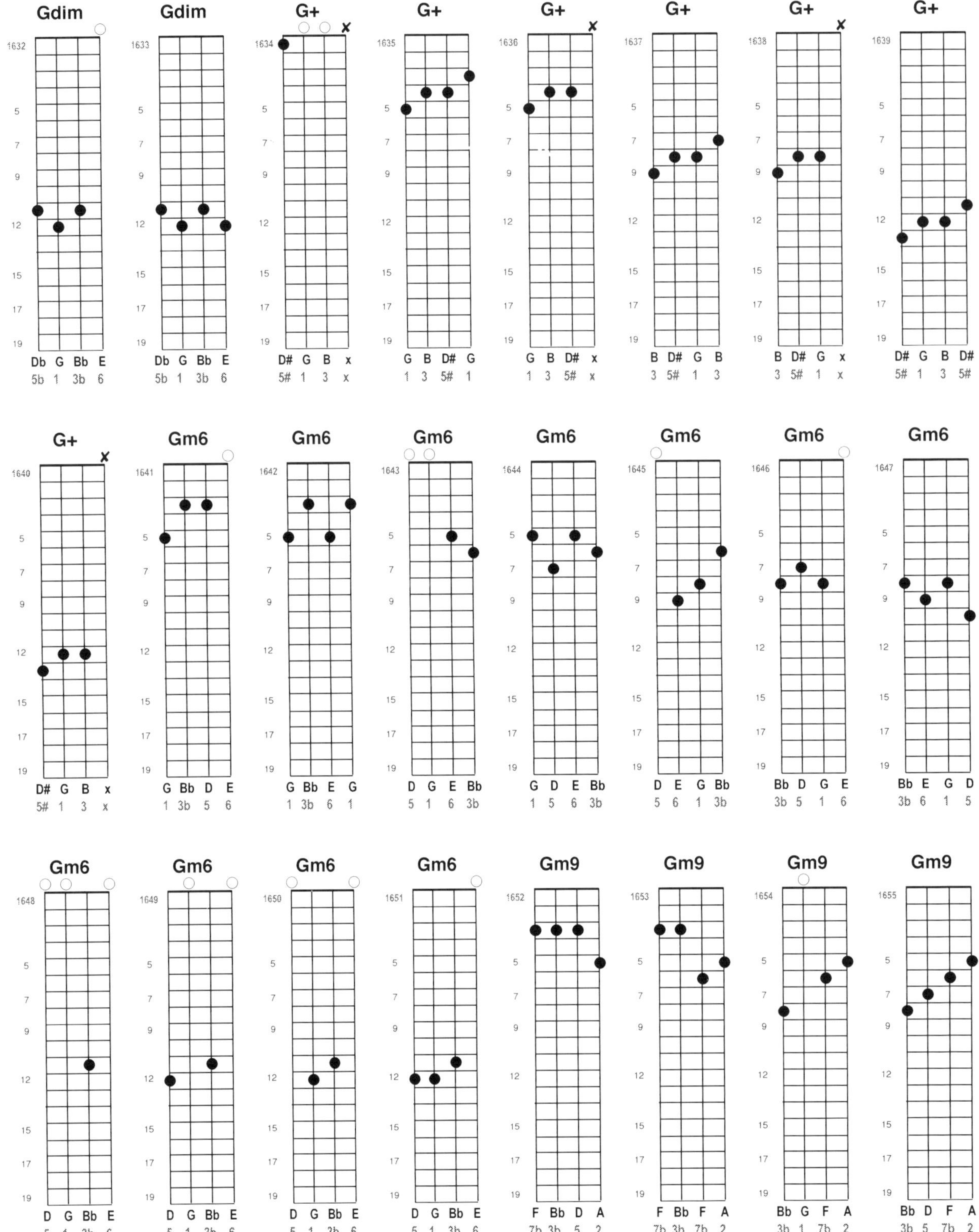

TUNING: D G B E

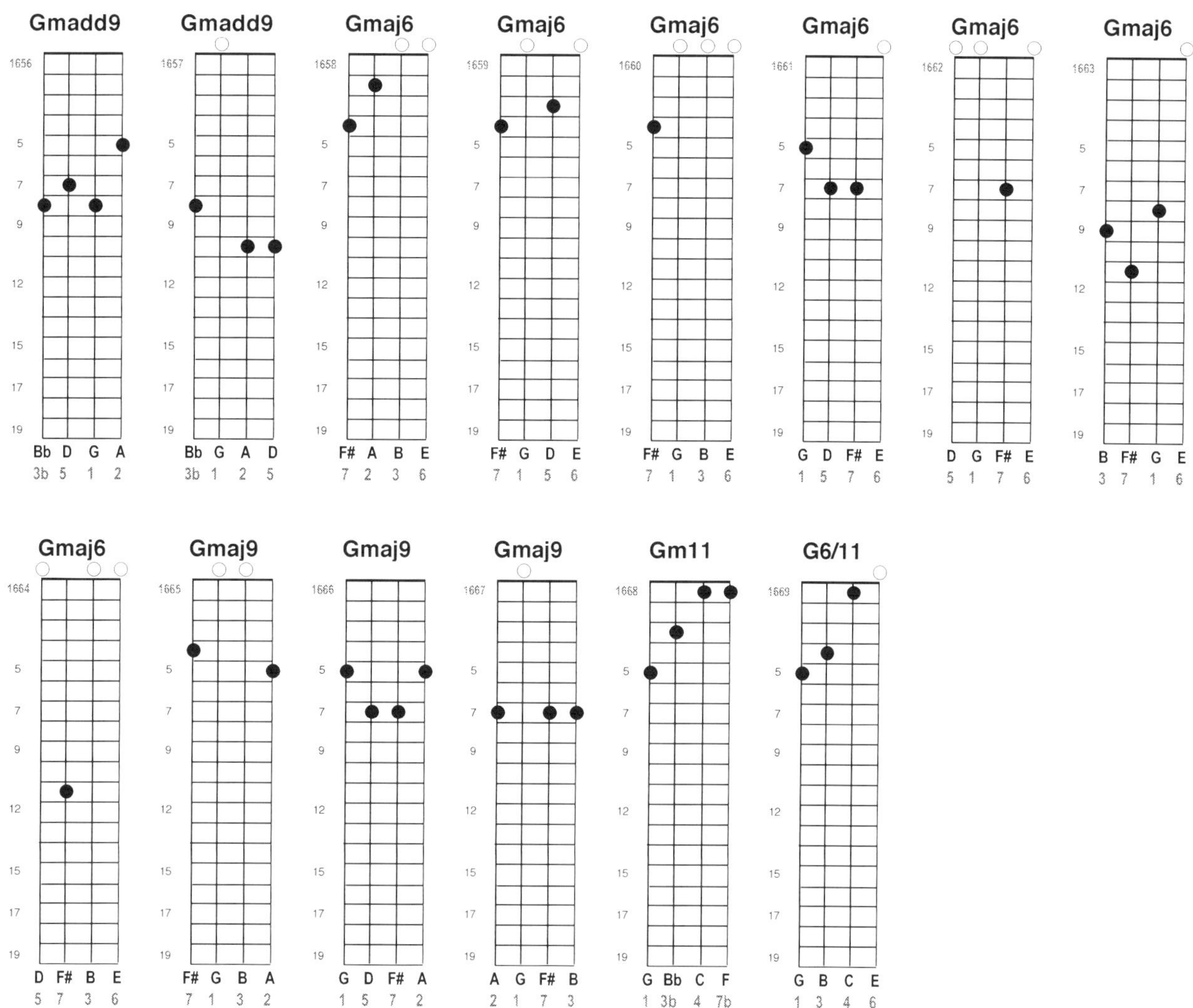

*The uke is often seen as an easier alternative to guitar, though without some different tunings or partial capos (or both!), you still need to deal with 3-finger chords, as well as many of the common chord shapes that have always made beginning guitar difficult for children and beginners. In the back of this book and in my book "*Baritone Ukulele Simplified,*" I show a number of other ground-breaking new ways to play easy chord shapes that sound great but are much easier to play than standard fingerings.*

TUNING: D G B E

G#
Ab
Ab
1670
Eb Ab C Ab
5 1 3 1
Ab
1671
Eb Ab C x
5 1 3 x
Ab
1672
Ab C Eb Ab
1 3 5 1
Ab
1673
Ab Eb Ab C
1 5 1 3
Ab
1674
C Eb Ab C
3 5 1 3
Abm
1675
Eb Ab Cb x
5 1 3b x
Abm
1676
Ab Cb Eb Ab
1 3b 5 1
Abm
1677
Ab Cb Eb Cb
1 3b 5 3b
Abm
1678
Ab Eb Cb x
1 5 3b x
Abm
1679
Ab Eb Cb Cb
1 5 3b 3b
Abm
1680
Ab Eb Cb Eb
1 5 3b 5
Abm
1681
Ab Eb Ab Cb
1 5 1 3b
Abm
1682
Eb Ab Cb x
5 1 3b x
Ab5
1683
Ab Eb Eb Ab
1 5 5 1
Ab5
1684
Ab Eb Ab Eb
1 5 1 5
Ab7
1685
Eb Ab C Gb
5 1 3 7b
Ab7
1686
Gb Ab C Ab
7b 1 3 1
Ab7
1687
Ab C Eb Gb
1 3 5 7b
Ab7
1688
Gb C Eb Ab
7b 3 5 1
Ab7
1689
Gb C Gb Ab
7b 3 7b 1
Ab7
1690
Ab C Gb Ab
1 3 7b 1
Ab7
1691
Ab C Gb C
1 3 7b 3
Ab7
1692
Ab Eb Gb C
1 5 7b 3

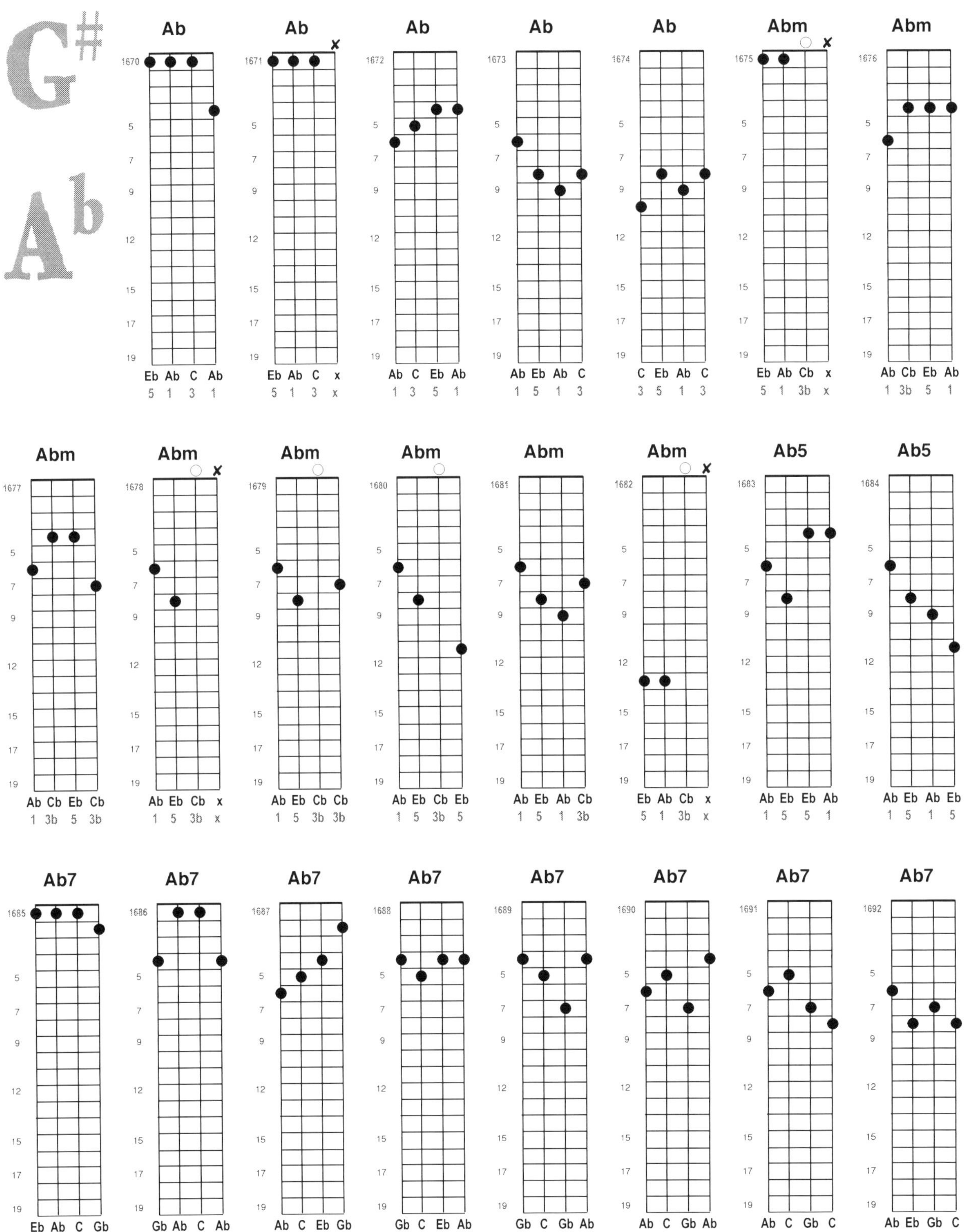

TUNING: D G B E

Ab7
1693
C Ab C Gb
3 1 3 7b
Abm7
1694
Eb Ab Cb Gb
5 1 3b 7b
Abm7
1695
Ab Cb Cb Gb
1 3b 3b 7b
Abm7
1696
Gb Cb Eb Ab
7b 3b 5 1
Abm7
1697
Gb Cb Gb Ab
7b 3b 7b 1
Abm7
1698
Ab Cb Gb Ab
1 3b 7b 1
Abm7
1699
Ab Cb Gb Cb
1 3b 7b 3b
Abm7
1700
Ab Eb Gb Cb
1 5 7b 3b
Abmaj7
1701
Eb Ab C G
5 1 3 7
Abmaj7
1702
Ab C Eb G
1 3 5 7
Abmaj7
1703
G C Eb Ab
7 3 5 1
Abmaj7
1704
Ab C G Ab
1 3 7 1
Abmaj7
1705
C Eb G C
3 5 7 3
Absus
1706
Ab Db Eb Ab
1 4 5 1
Absus
1707
Ab Eb Ab Db
1 5 1 4
Ab7sus
1708
Gb Db Eb Ab
7b 4 5 1
Ab6
1709
Eb Ab C F
5 1 3 6
Ab6
1710
Ab C Eb F
1 3 5 6
Ab6
1711
Ab Eb F C
1 5 6 3
Abadd9
1712
Ab Eb Ab Bb
1 5 1 2
Abadd9
1713
C Eb Ab Bb
3 5 1 2
Ab9
1714
Gb Bb Eb Ab
7b 2 5 1
Ab9
1715
Gb C Eb Bb
7b 3 5 2
Ab9
1716
Ab Eb Gb Bb
1 5 7b 2

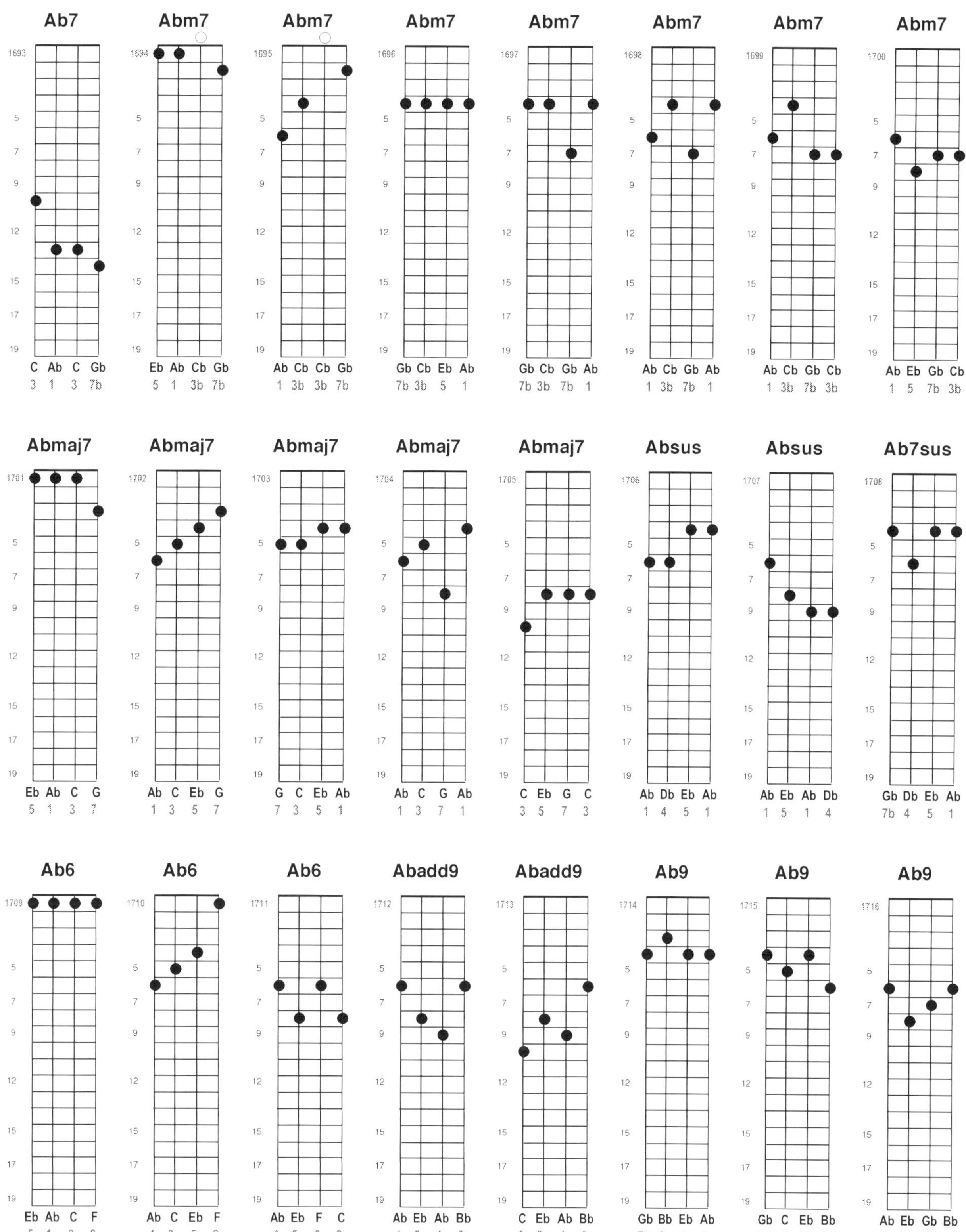

Baritone Ukulele Chords

TUNING: D G B E

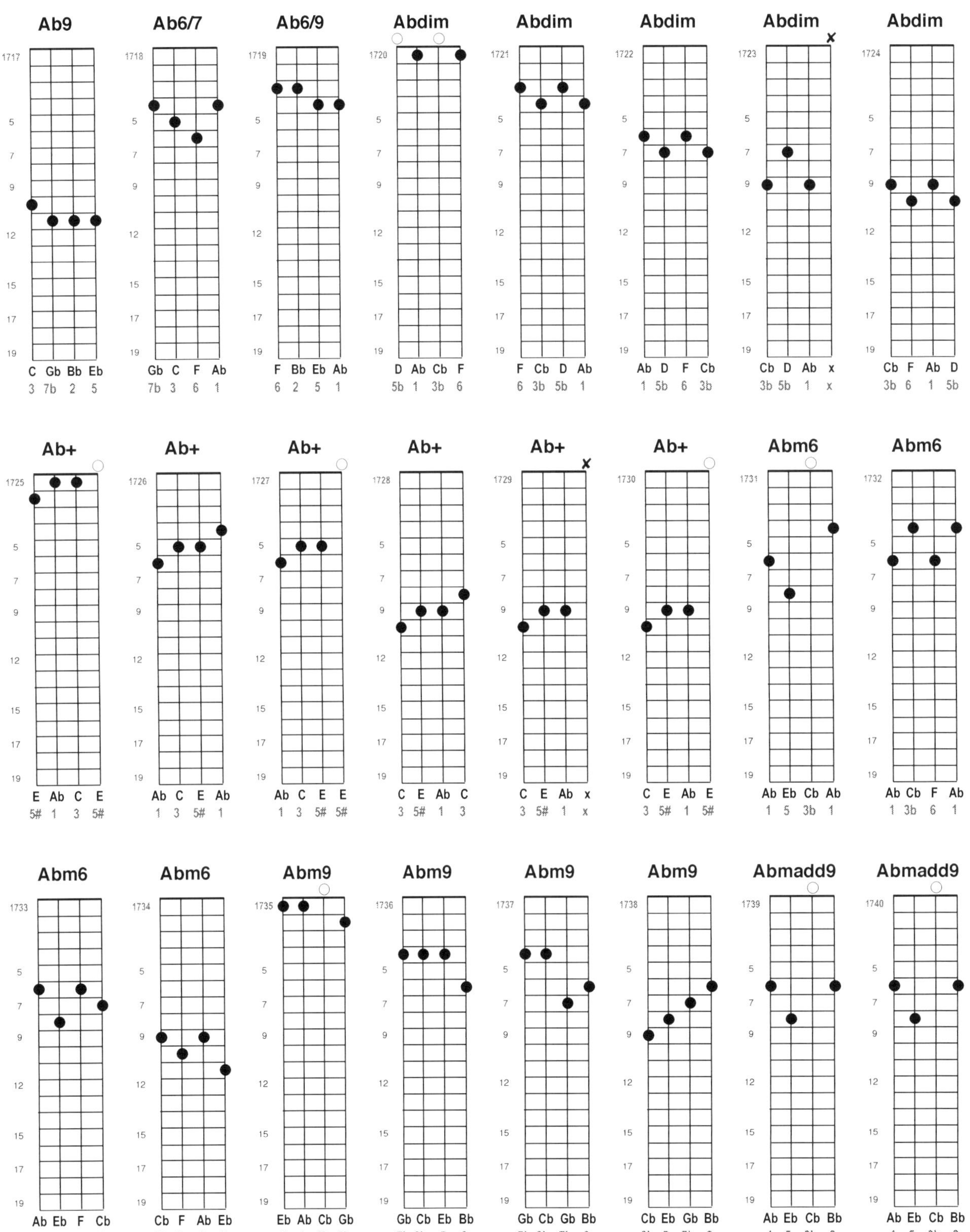

TUNING: D G B E

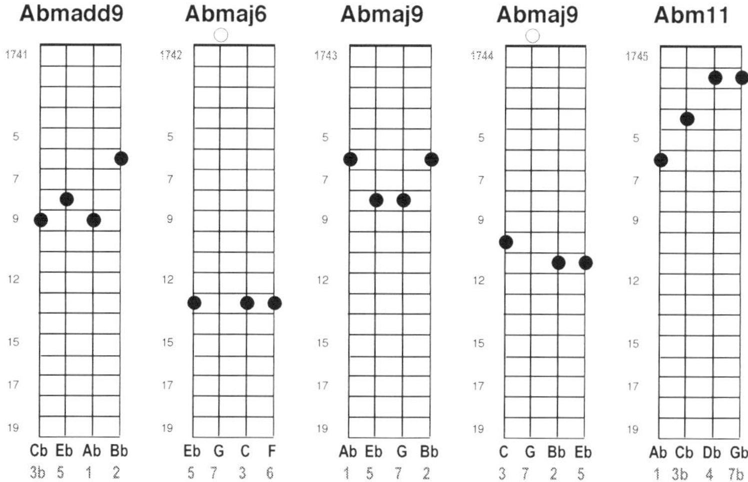

My books on Liberty Tuning for guitar show that it can be easier for beginners to play guitar chords in that tuning than standard chords on ukulele. The guitar has a much bigger sound, fuller voicings.

Liberty Tuning on the uke (later in this book) allows you to play easily in 3 keys instead of just 2, and offers another level more simplicity. In my book "Baritone Ukulele Simplified," I show a number of other new ways to play easy chord shapes that sound great but are much easier to play than standard guitar or uke fingerings.

Using Partial Capos

Partial capos have existed in a small corner of the guitar world for a few decades, but their use in the ukulele family is unknown.

The chords in this section are not a complete map of all possible chords, but are intended to illustrate how the partial capos work, and to get you started playing the new music they allow. Partial capos can be very confusing, and it can take a while to get oriented.

Some ideas here use standard tuning and some use a slightly altered tuning. They are pictured with *Liberty FLIP* Model 43 capos, though some other types of partial capos might work on your instrument.

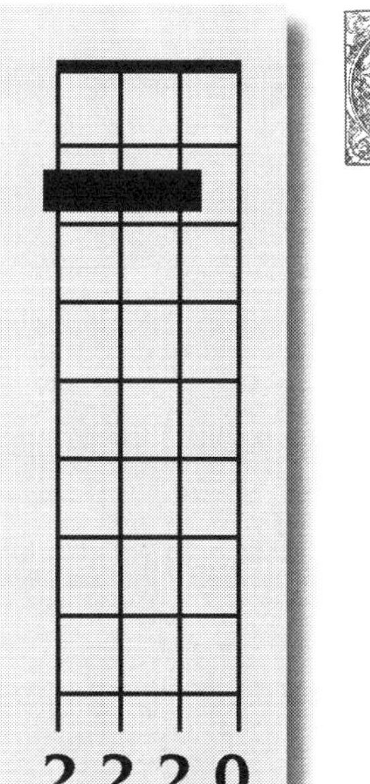

2 2 2 0

1- Open A [2220]

Partial capos change the landscape of what can be done on a fretboard in a way that is similar to using an altered tuning, though fundamentally the two ideas are different. When you change the tuning, the scale and chord geometry of the instrument change, while a partial capo gives new open-string voicings and resonances without moving the positions of the notes and changing the fretboard geometry.

The uke is now sounding an open A chord, so it makes by far the most sense to play in that key. This is similar but not the same as "Slack-Key" tuning, where the 1st string is lowered 2 frets to D. Here we instead capo the other 3 strings up to create a similar environment.

The advantages are that you can play the 1-4-5 chords in E with very easy fingerings (chords #1, #26 and #37 or #39), and also you get a 6 minor (F#m) and a 3 minor (C#m) that are playable with just 2 fingers. You don't have an easy flat 7 (G) or 2 minor (Bm) and you can't get good-sounding A7, D7 (or D9) chords for blues chord progressions. There are some easy and good chords like the Dmadd9 (#35) and the F#7 (#51) that you might be able to put to use.

Watch for the notes next to the capo, such as chords #16 and #18.

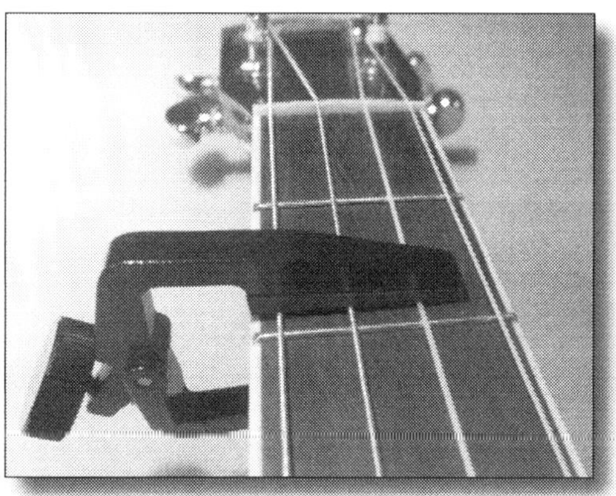

A Liberty "Flip" Model 43 at fret 2 making the 2220 configuration.

I have published the Capo Voodoo series of books that map out almost 200 ways to use partial capos on the guitar. The concept works for any stringed instrument, though the ideas shown here are to my knowledge the first ones published for a ukulele. The positions of the capos and fingers will also translate to any similar instrument, such as tenor banjo or tenor guitar, as long as the strings are tuned to these pitches.

"Open A" Configuration Chords p.1 [Capo2220]

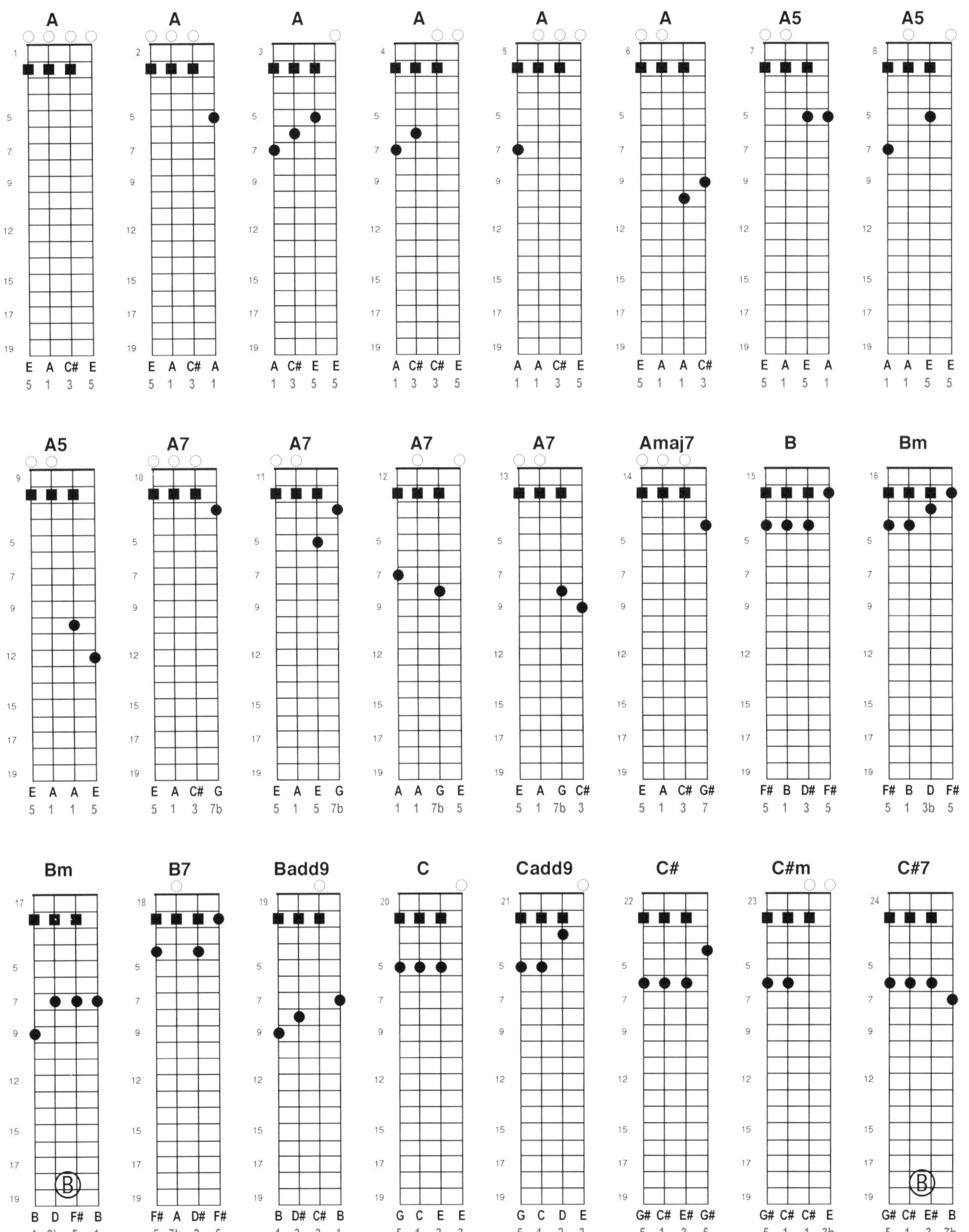

"Open A" Configuration Chords p.2 [Capo2220]

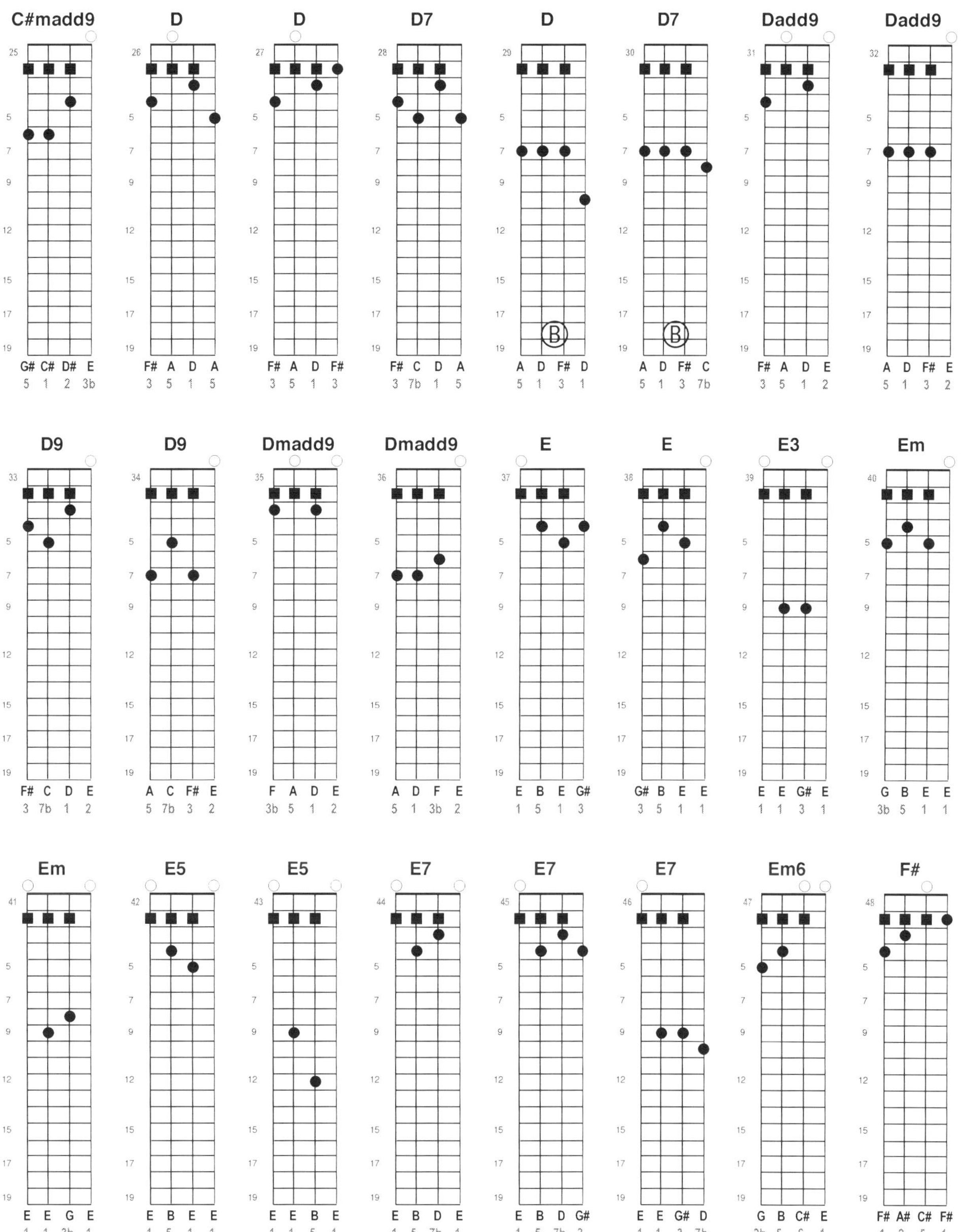

"Open A" Configuration Chords p.3 [Capo2220]

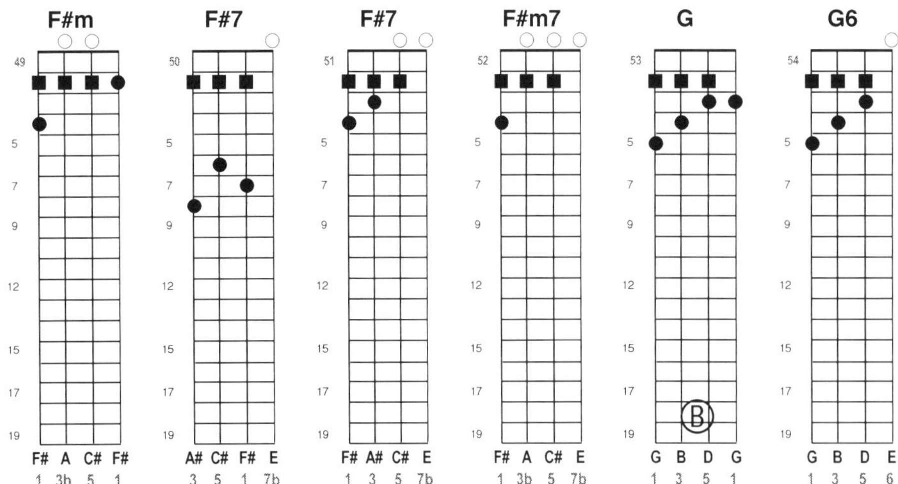

2- "Liberty Tuning" [44400]

I discovered the guitar version of "*Liberty Tuning*" in 2011, and have published many books detailing how it changes the guitar fingerboard and offers a wealth of exciting new musical possibilities. It upended my life, and caused me to develop and manufacture the *Liberty FLIP* capos and create a new beginning guitar method. The *Model 43,* that was designed to clamp 3 or 4 strings on the guitar, and the *Model 65*, that clamps 6 or 5 guitar strings, are perfect as both a full and partial capo on a number of other instruments, including the baritone uke. On my uke, the longer side of the model 43 is perfect for clamping 3 outer strings. The shorter side of the *Model 65* also works.

Like any tuning or partial capo environment, this one offers new possibilities to advanced players, but its greatest value is probably in the very exciting opportunities it offers for simplified chording. On guitar, there are 2 "versions" of *Liberty Tuning*, with different numbers of strings clamped, and it allows extremely easy but very good-sounding fingerings for strummed chords or instrumental playing in the keys of E or A.

On uke, everything is another level simpler than guitar, and all fingerings are easier to play, with these advantages:

A Liberty "Flip" Model 43 capo at fret 4 making the 4440 "Liberty Tuning" configuration.

1- There is only one version of the tuning/capo combination
2- There are just 4 strings
3- A shorter neck and nylon strings make chording easier
4- It allows easy chording in 3 keys (not just 2): E, A and B.

This means that by adding a full capo below the partial capo, you gain the ability to play extremely easy but great-sounding chords in the keys of A, Bb, B, C, C#/Db, D,E, F,F#,G and G#/Ab. (This pretty much means everything but Eb.) There are also easy and good-sounding fingerings for other chord changes, including the 2 chord, 6 minor, and the modal flat 7th.

For anyone who wants an immediate musical success experience, there is nothing like this, and it also offers the ability to play good-sounding music to very young children, and to a huge number of people who otherwise might have trouble forming chords.

The next 3 pages map out the easy chord fingerings in *Liberty Tuning* to illustrate its musical power for children or beginners. It's the closest thing to "instant music" ever found.

shows a barre (bar) chord

Liberty Tuning: [D G C E / capo 4440]

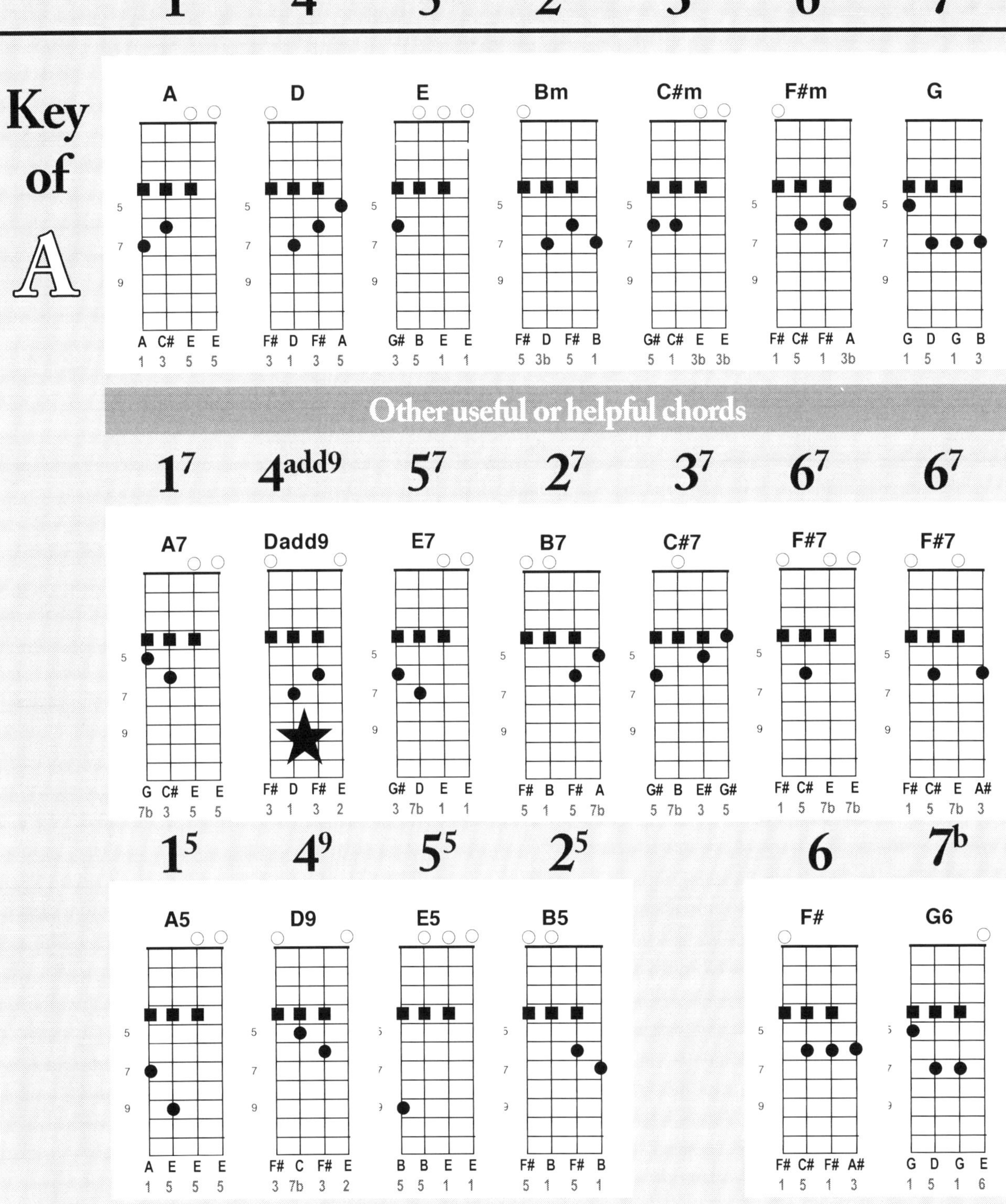

Liberty Tuning: [D G C E / capo 4440]

	1	5	2m4	3m	6m	7b

Key of E

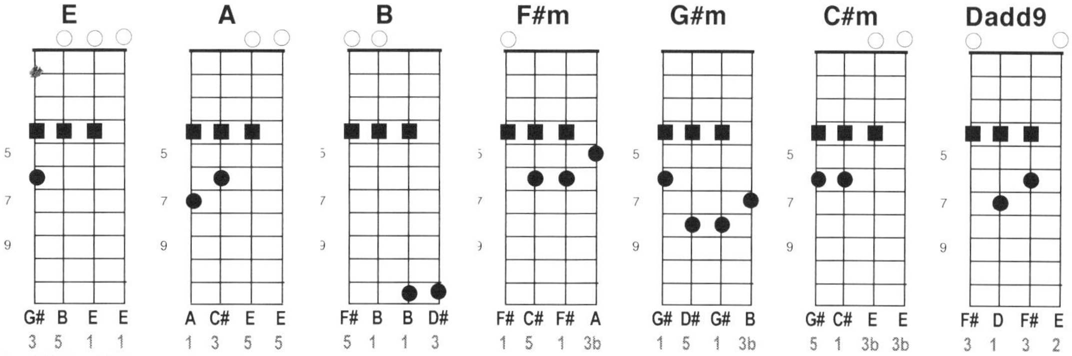

E	A	B	F#m	G#m	C#m	Dadd9
G# B E E	A C# E E	F# B B D#	F# C# F# A	G# D# G# B	G# C# E E	F# D F# E
3 5 1 1	1 3 5 5	5 1 1 3	1 5 1 3b	1 5 1 3b	5 1 3b 3b	3 1 3 2

Other useful or helpful chords

1⁷	4⁷	5⁷	2⁷	3⁷	6⁷	7b
E7	A7	B7	F#7	G#7	C#7	D
G# D E E	G C# E E	F# B F# A	F# C# E E	G# C F# x	G# B E# G#	F# D F# A
3 7b 1 1	7b 3 5 5	5 1 5 7b	1 5 7b 7b	1 3 7b x	5 7b 3 5	3 1 3 5

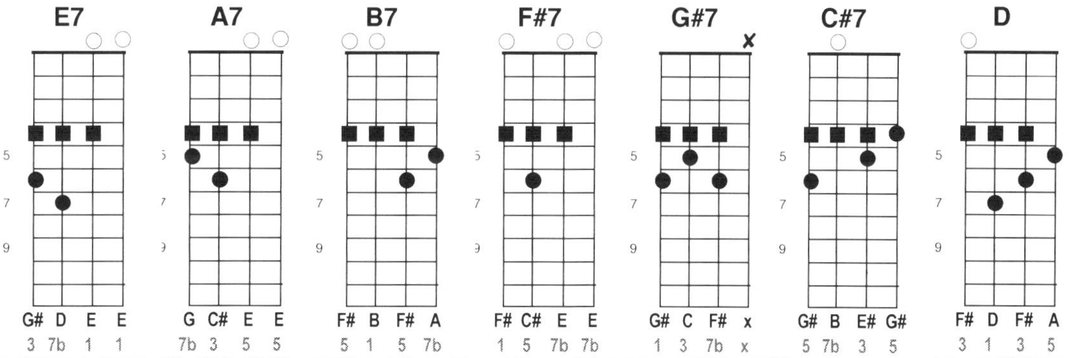

1⁵	4⁹	5⁵	2	3	6	6⁷
E5	A7	B5	F#	G#	C#	F#7
B B E E	C# G E E	F# B F# B	F# C# F# A#	G# D# G# C	G# C# E# G#	F# C# E A#
5 5 1 1	3 7b 5 5	5 1 5 1	1 5 1 3	1 5 1 3	5 1 3 5	1 5 7b 3

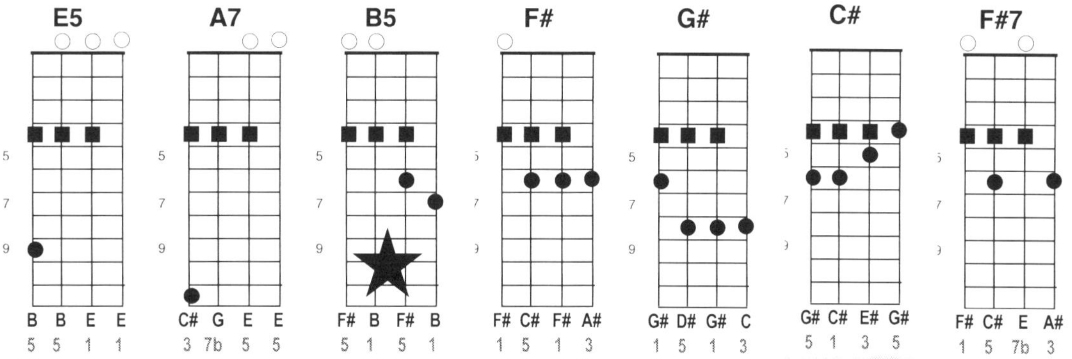

Liberty Tuning: [D G C E / capo 4440]

Key of B

	1	5	2^m 4	3^m	6^m	7^b
Chord	B5	E	F#	C#m	D#m	G#m	A
Notes	F# B F# B	G# B E E	F# C# F# A#	G# C# E E	A# D# F# A#	G# D# G# B	A C# E E
Intervals	5 1 5 1	3 5 1 1	1 5 1 3	5 1 3b 3b	5 1 3b 5	1 5 1 3b	1 3 5 5

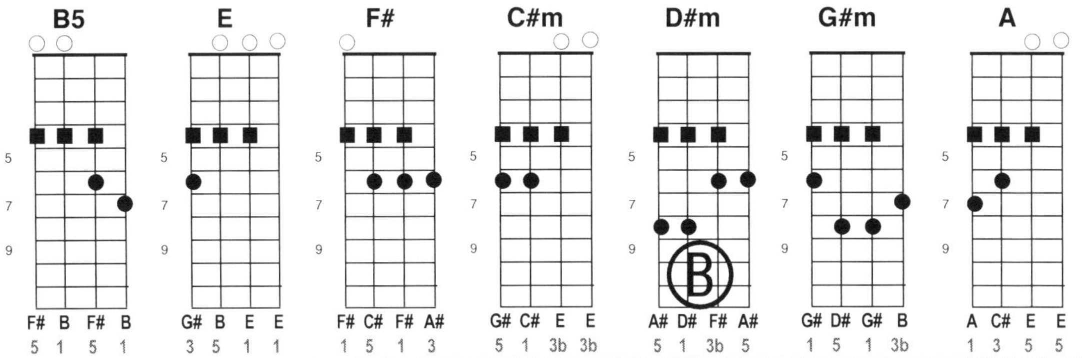

Other useful or helpful chords

	1^7	4^7	5^7	2^7	3^7	6^7	7^b5
Chord	B7	E7	F#7	C#7	D#7	G#7	A5
Notes	F# B F# A	G# D E E	F# C# E E	G# B E# G#	A# C# G A#	G# C F# x	A E E E
Intervals	5 1 5 7b	3 7b 1 1	1 5 7b 7b	5 7b 3 5	5 7b 3 5	1 3 7b x	1 5 5 5

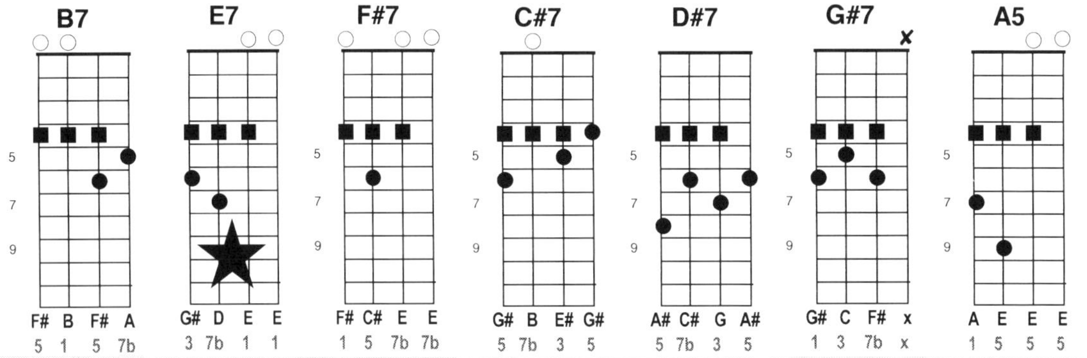

	1	4^5	5^7	2	3	6	7^b
Chord	B	E5	F#7	C#	D#	G#	A7
Notes	F# B B D#	B B E E	F# C# E A#	G# C# E# G#	A# D# G A#	G# D# G# C	G C# E E
Intervals	5 1 1 3	5 5 1 1	1 5 7b 3	5 1 3 5	5 1 3 5	1 5 1 3	7b 3 5 5

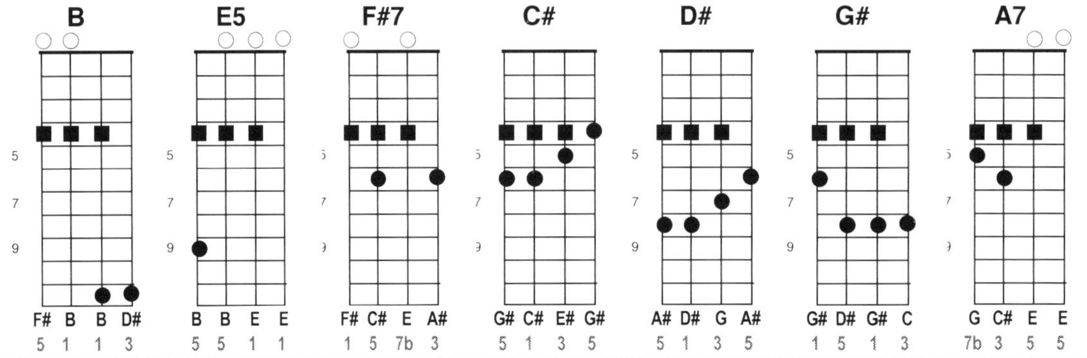

"Liberty Tuning" Chords p.1 (D G C E)

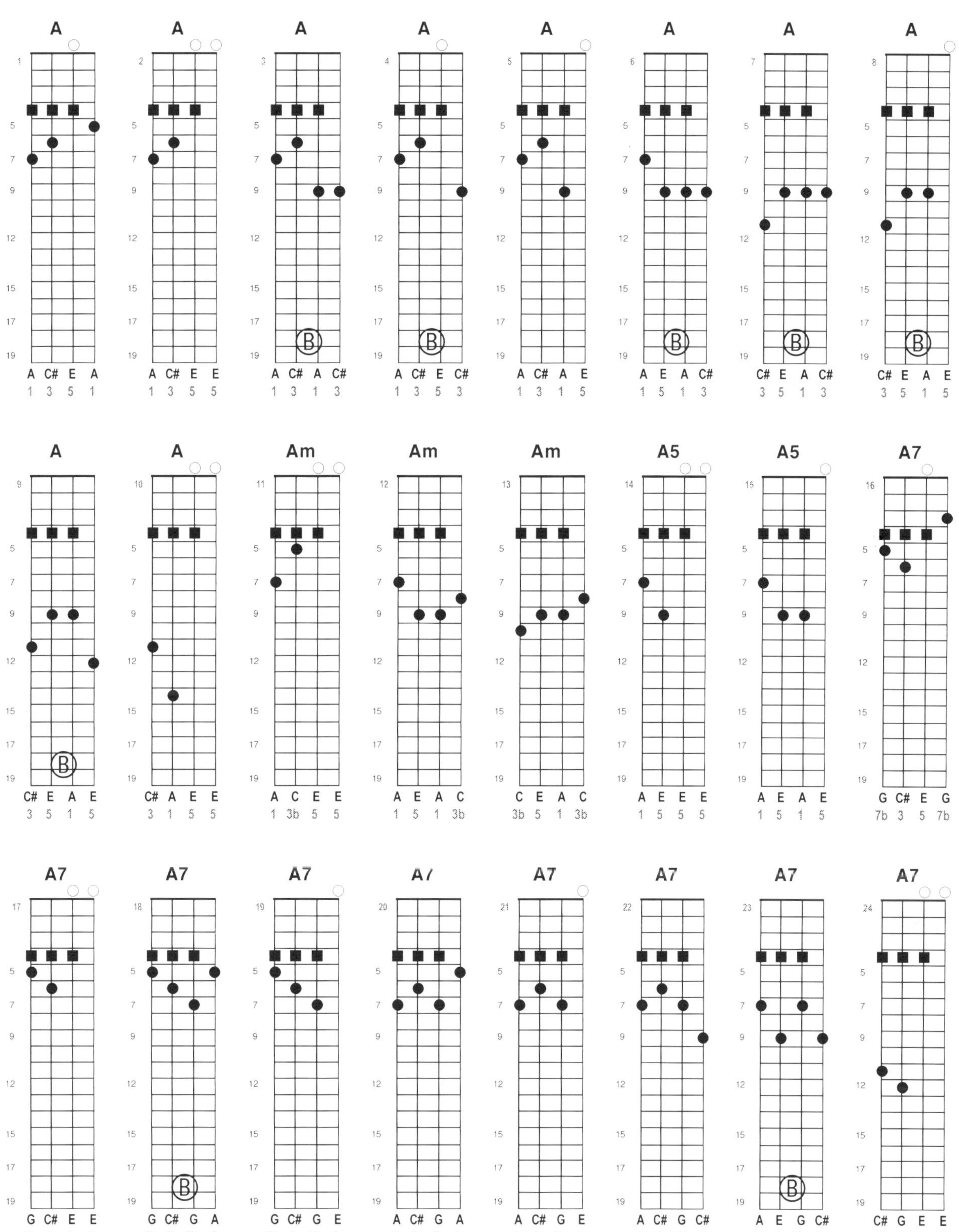

"Liberty Tuning" Chords p.2 (D G C E)

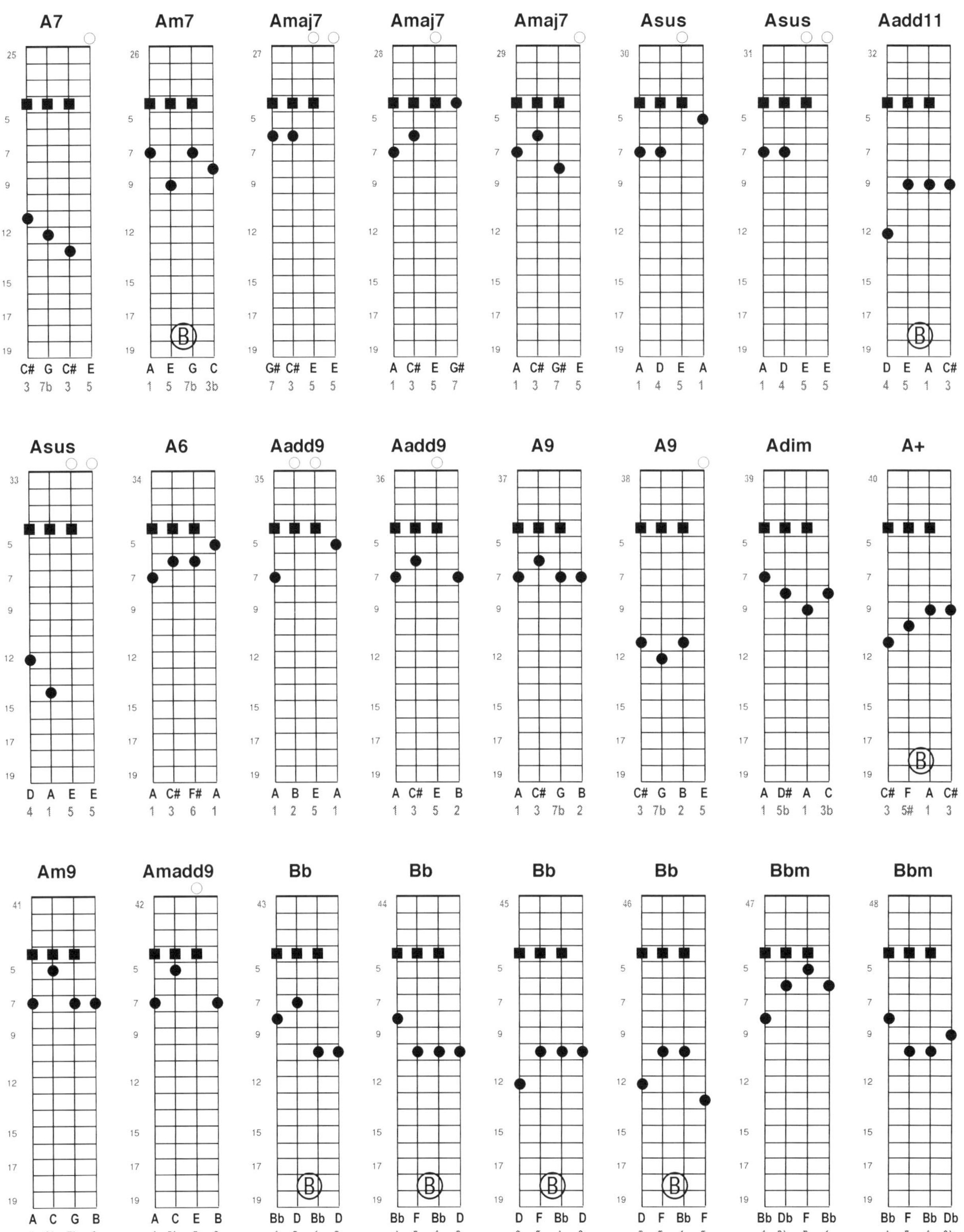

"Liberty Tuning" Chords p.3 (D G C E)

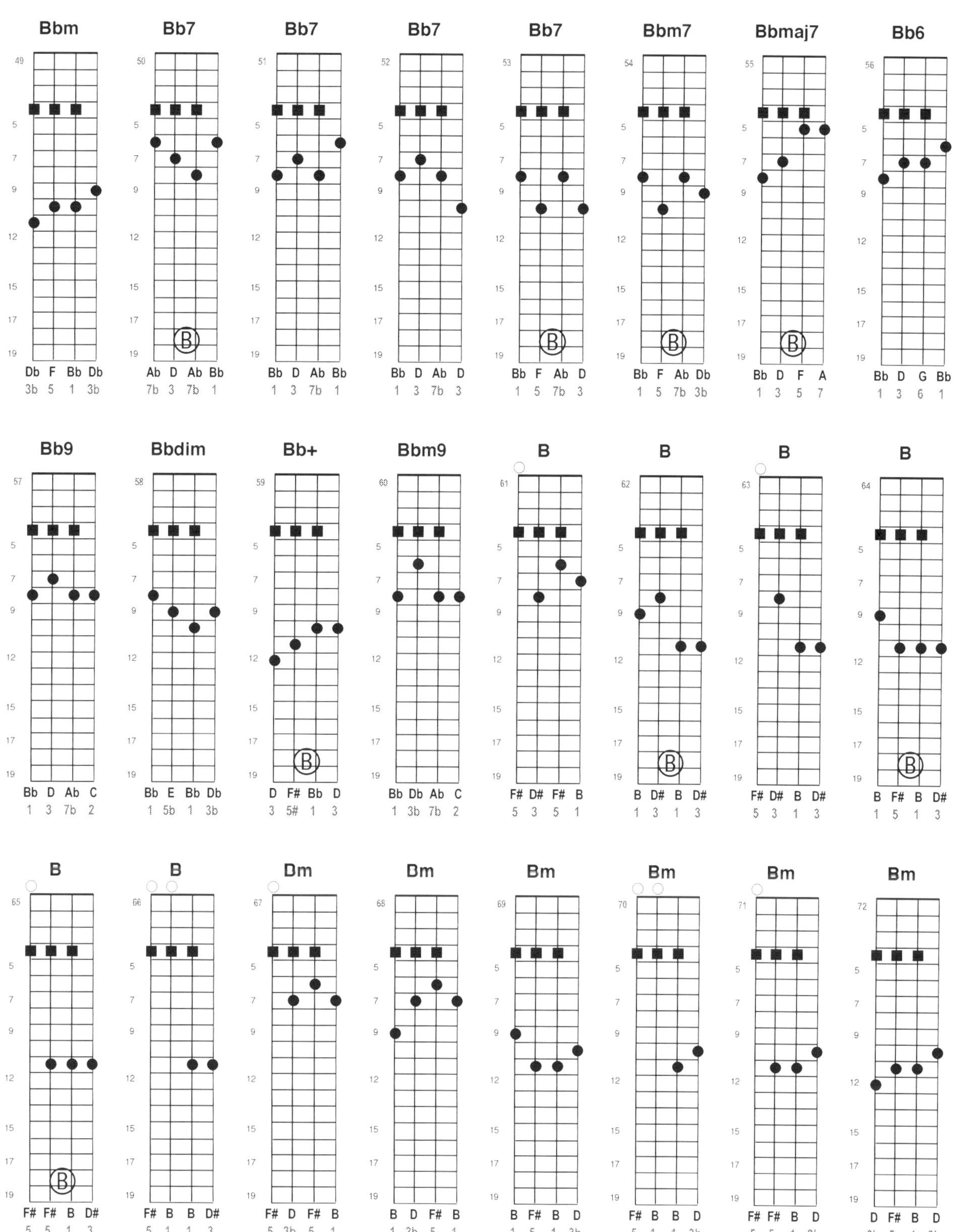

"Liberty Tuning" Chords p.4 (D G C E)

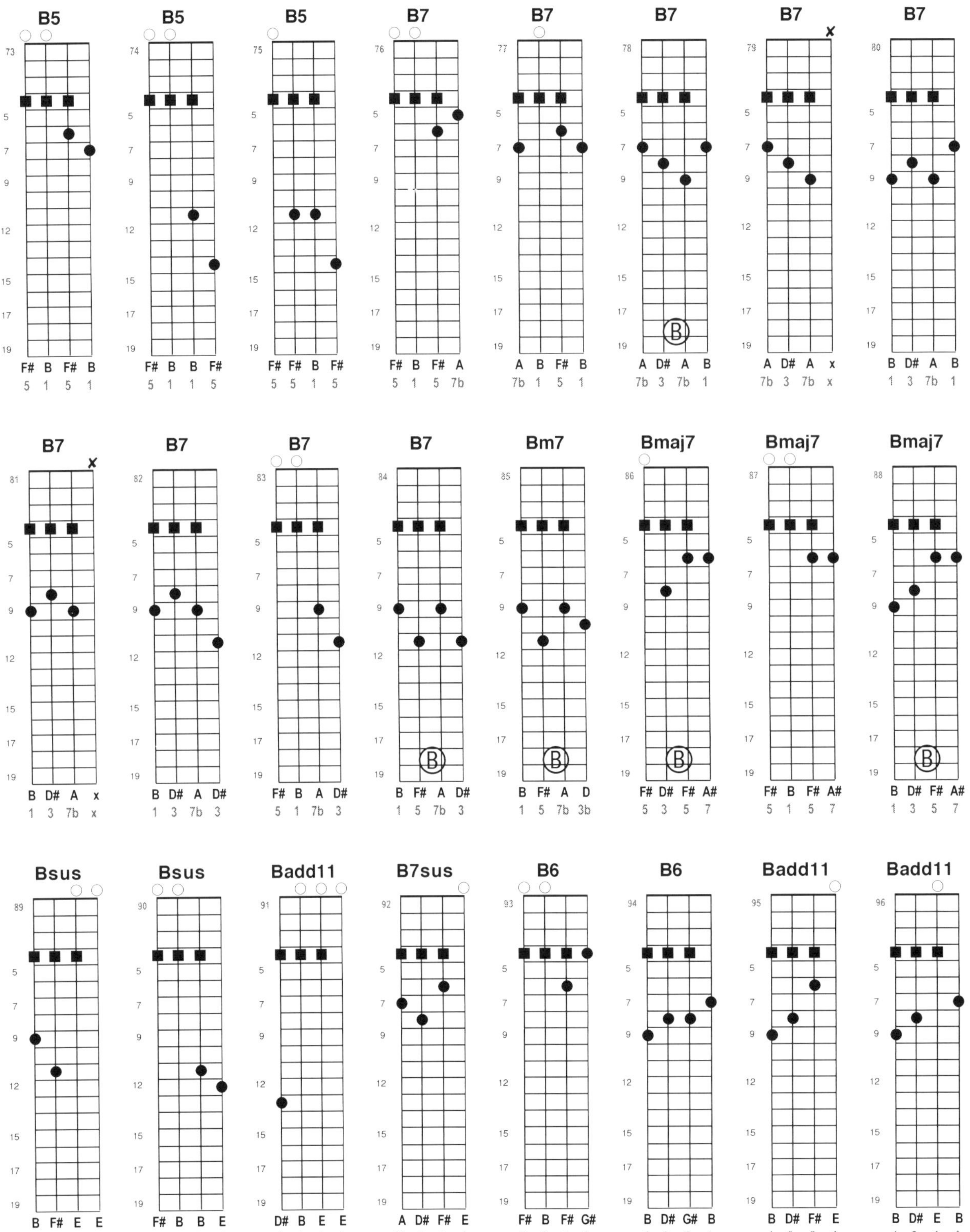

"Liberty Tuning" Chords p.5 (D G C E)

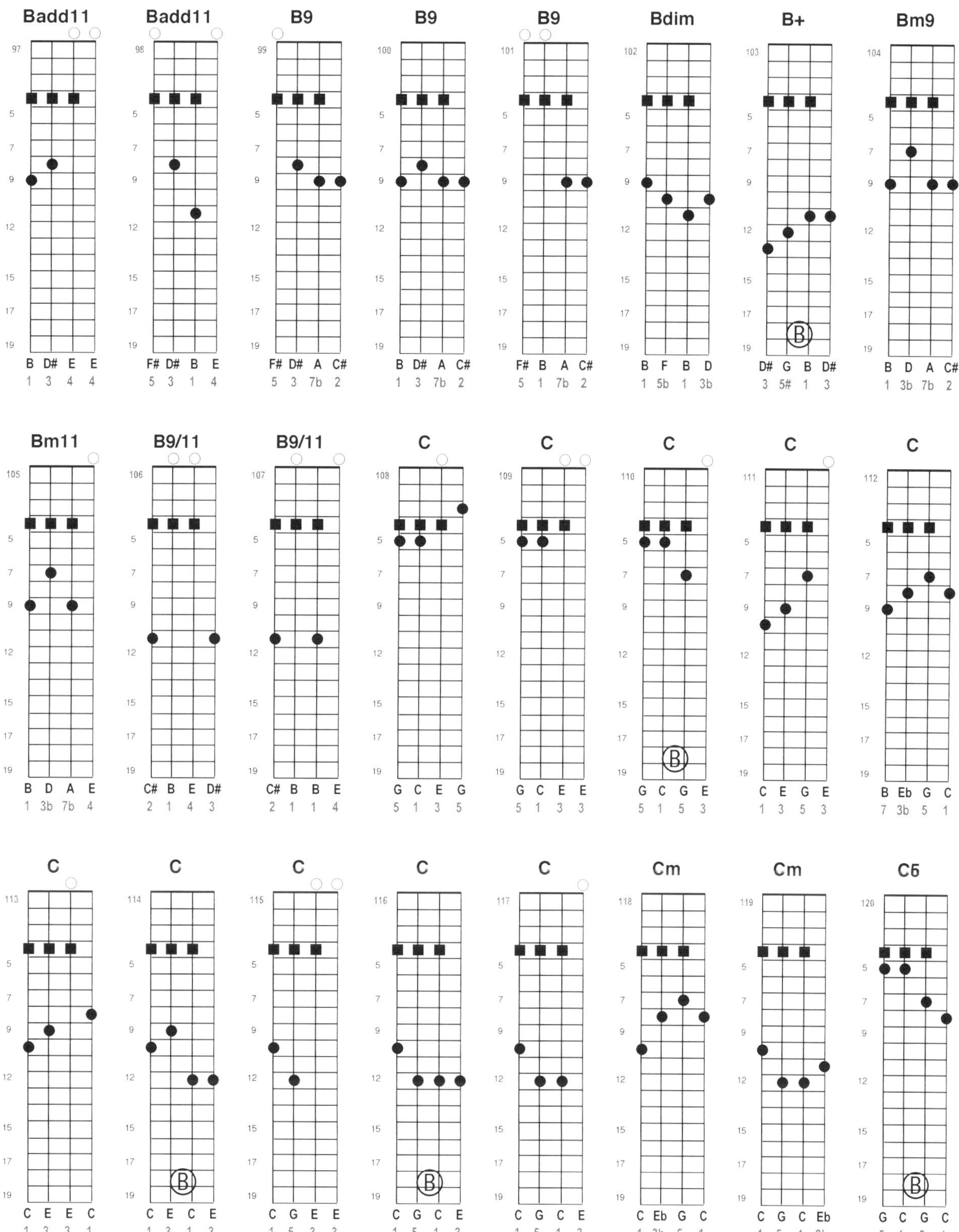

"Liberty Tuning" Chords p.6 (D G C E)

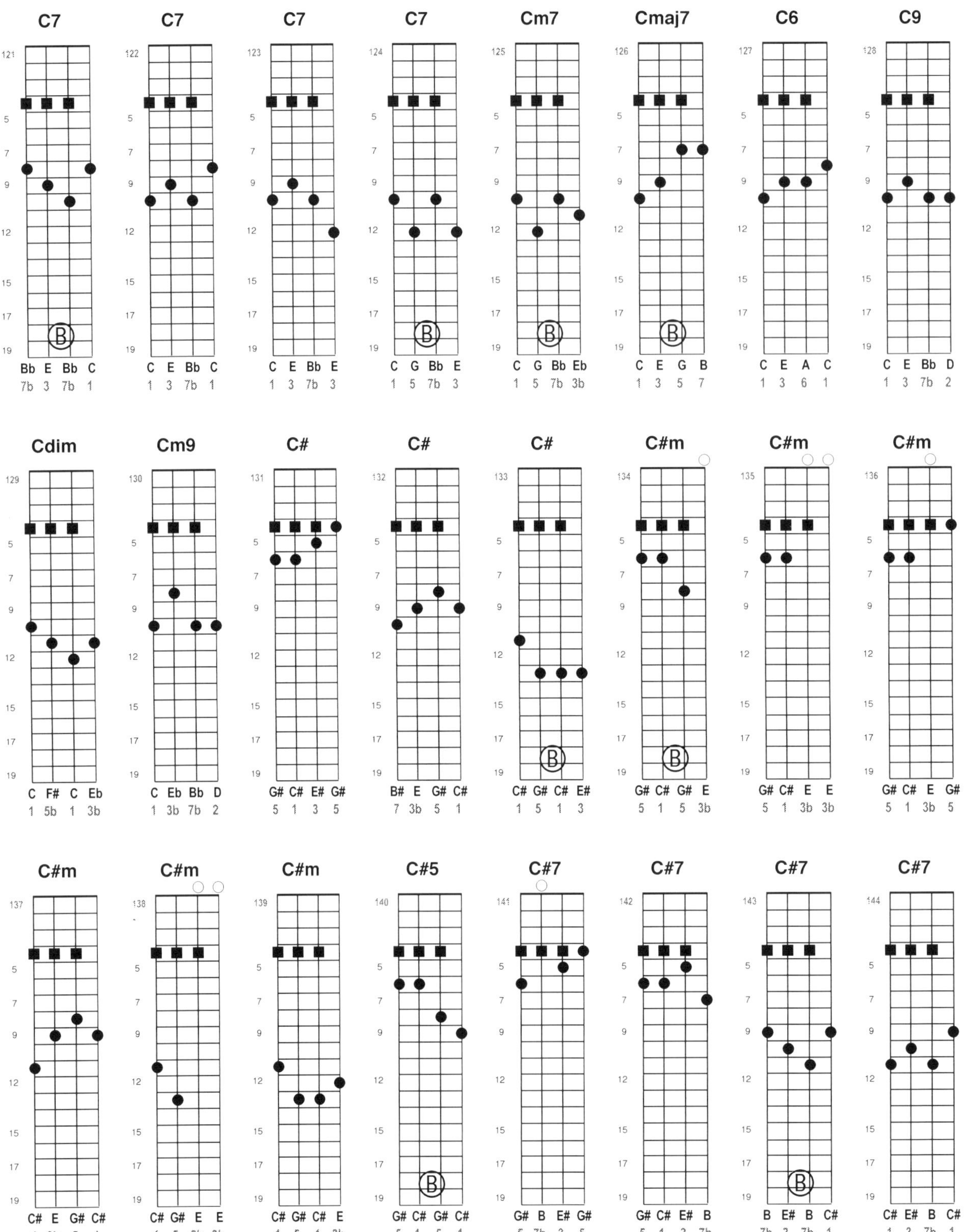

"Liberty Tuning" Chords p.7 (D G C E)

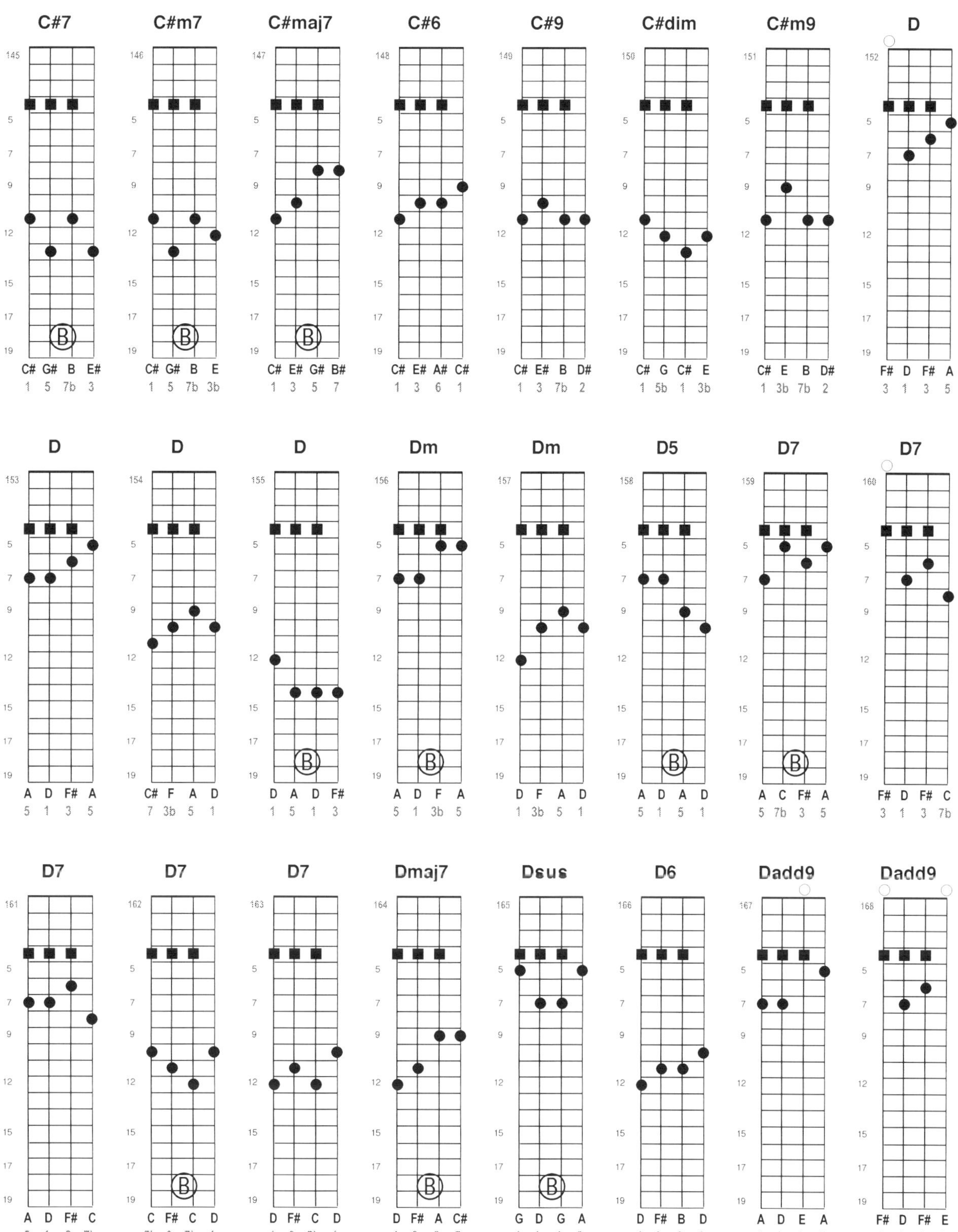

"Liberty Tuning" Chords p.8 (D G C E)

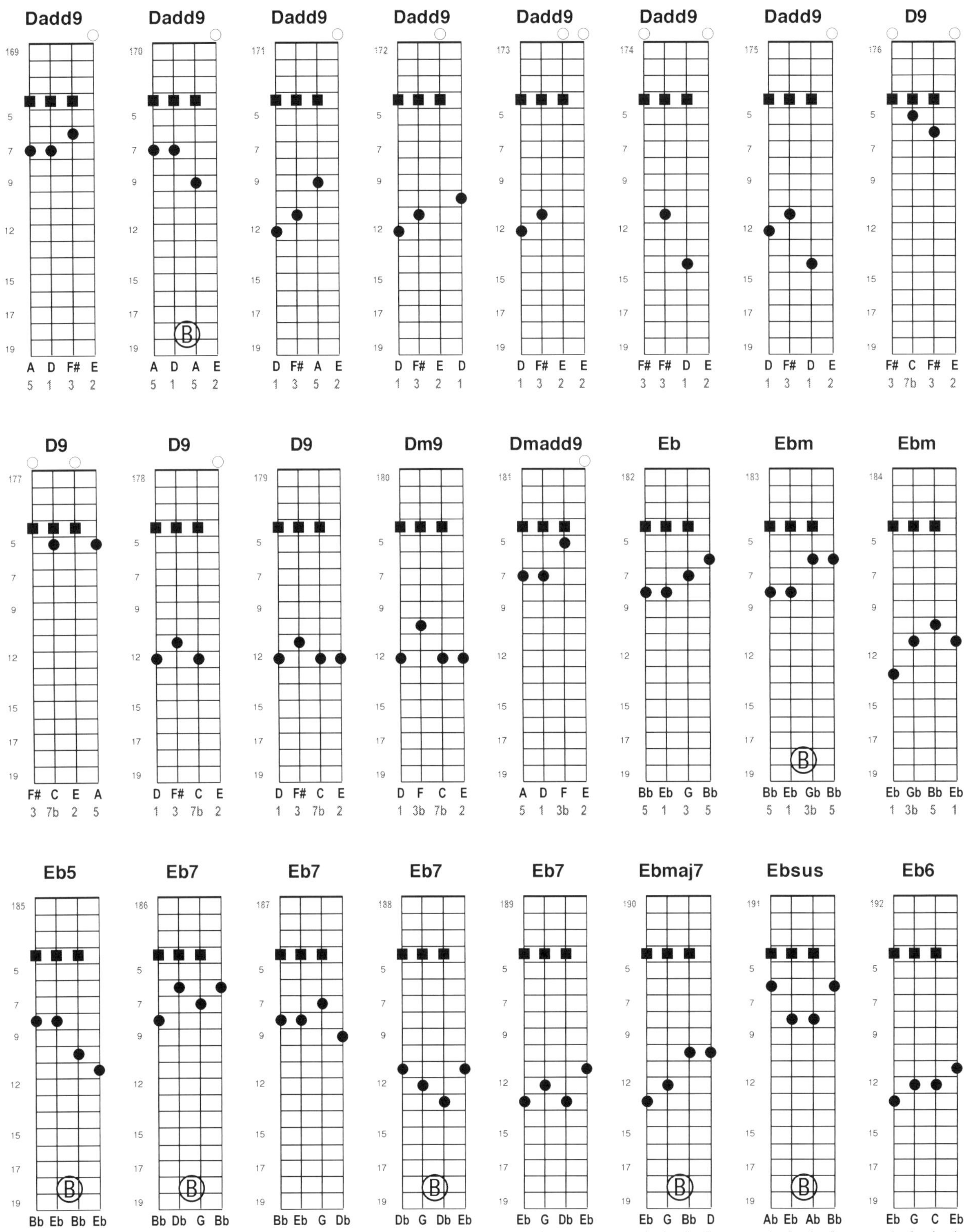

"Liberty Tuning" Chords p.9 (D G C E)

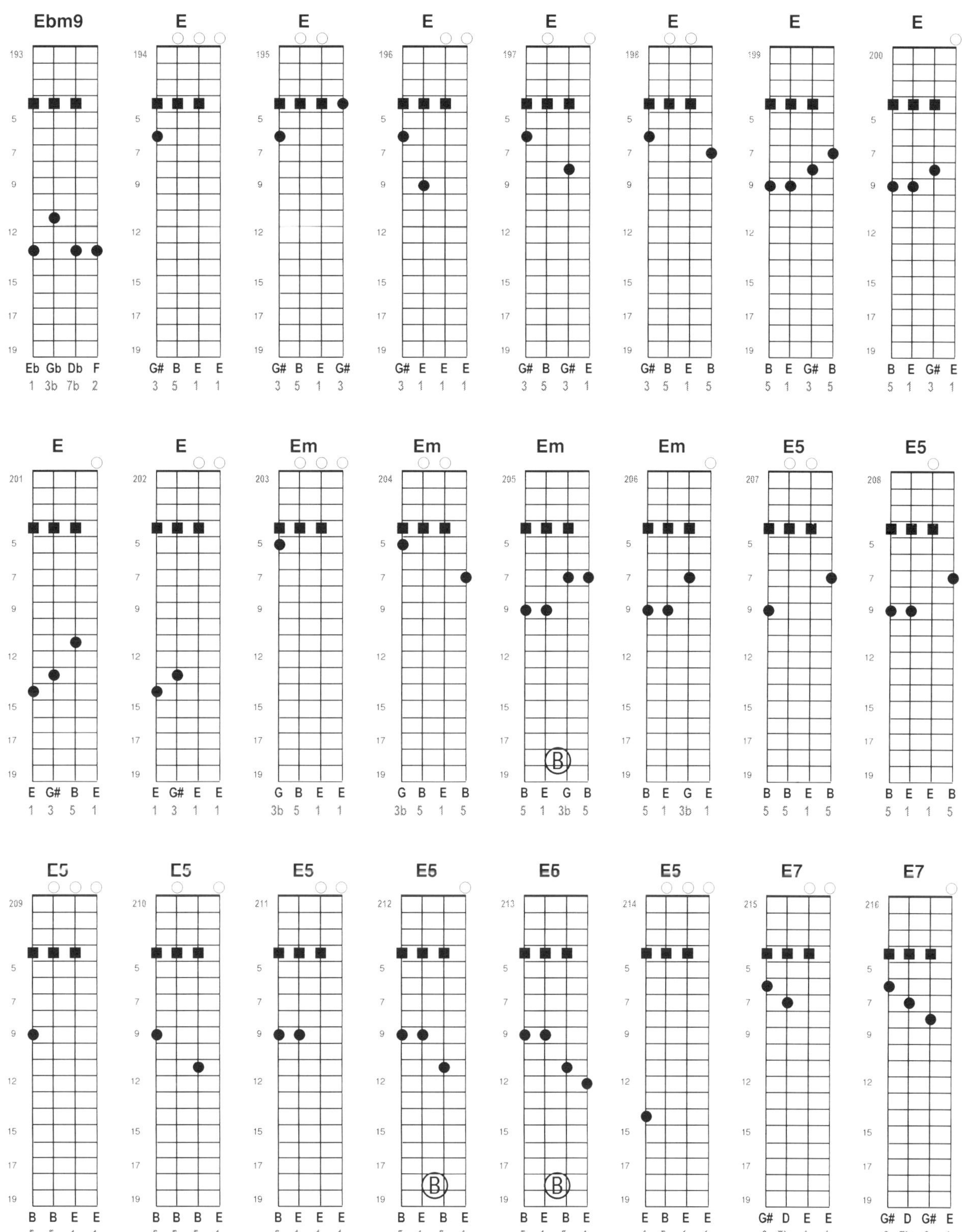

"Liberty Tuning" Chords p.10 (D G C E)

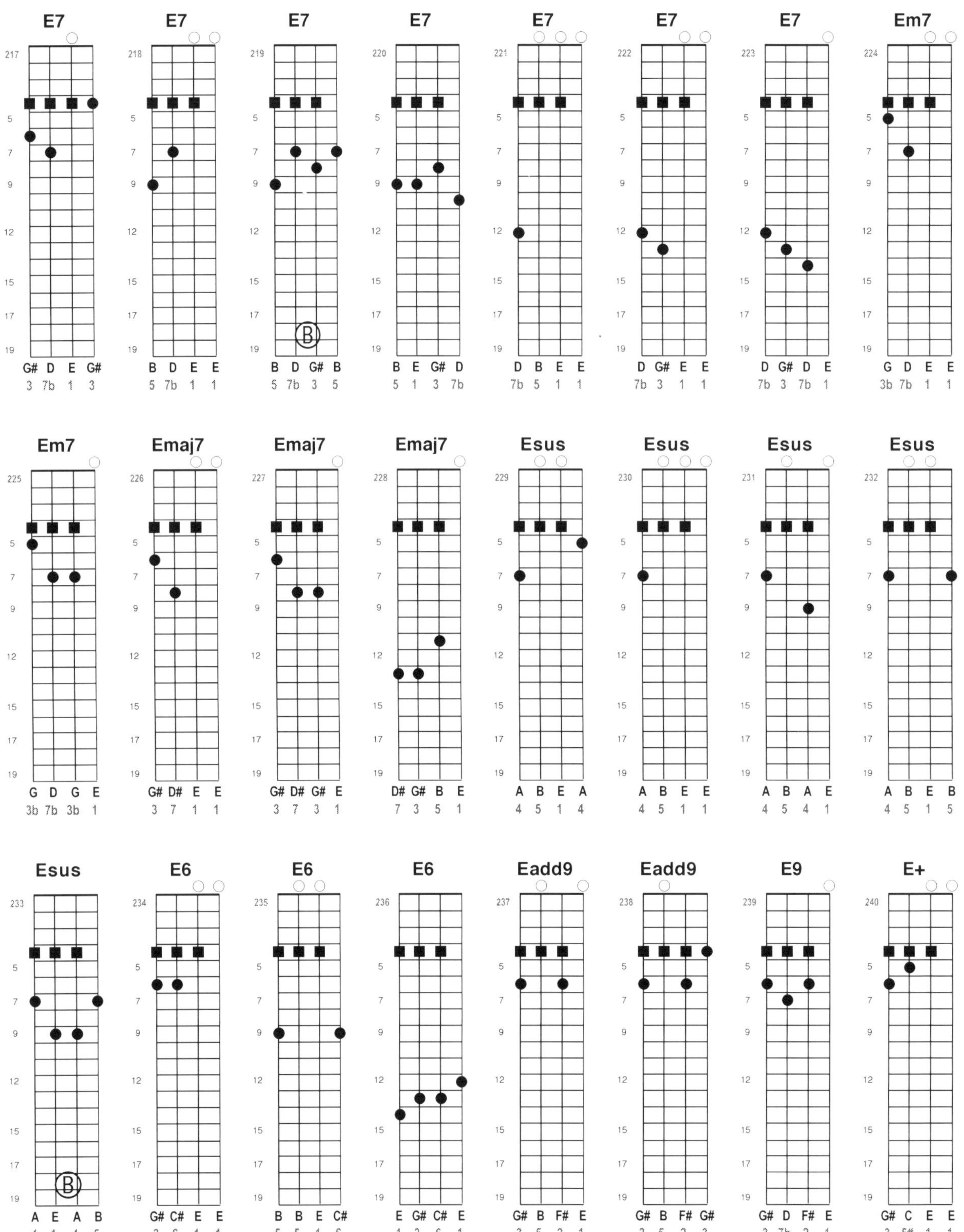

"Liberty Tuning" Chords p.11 (D G C E)

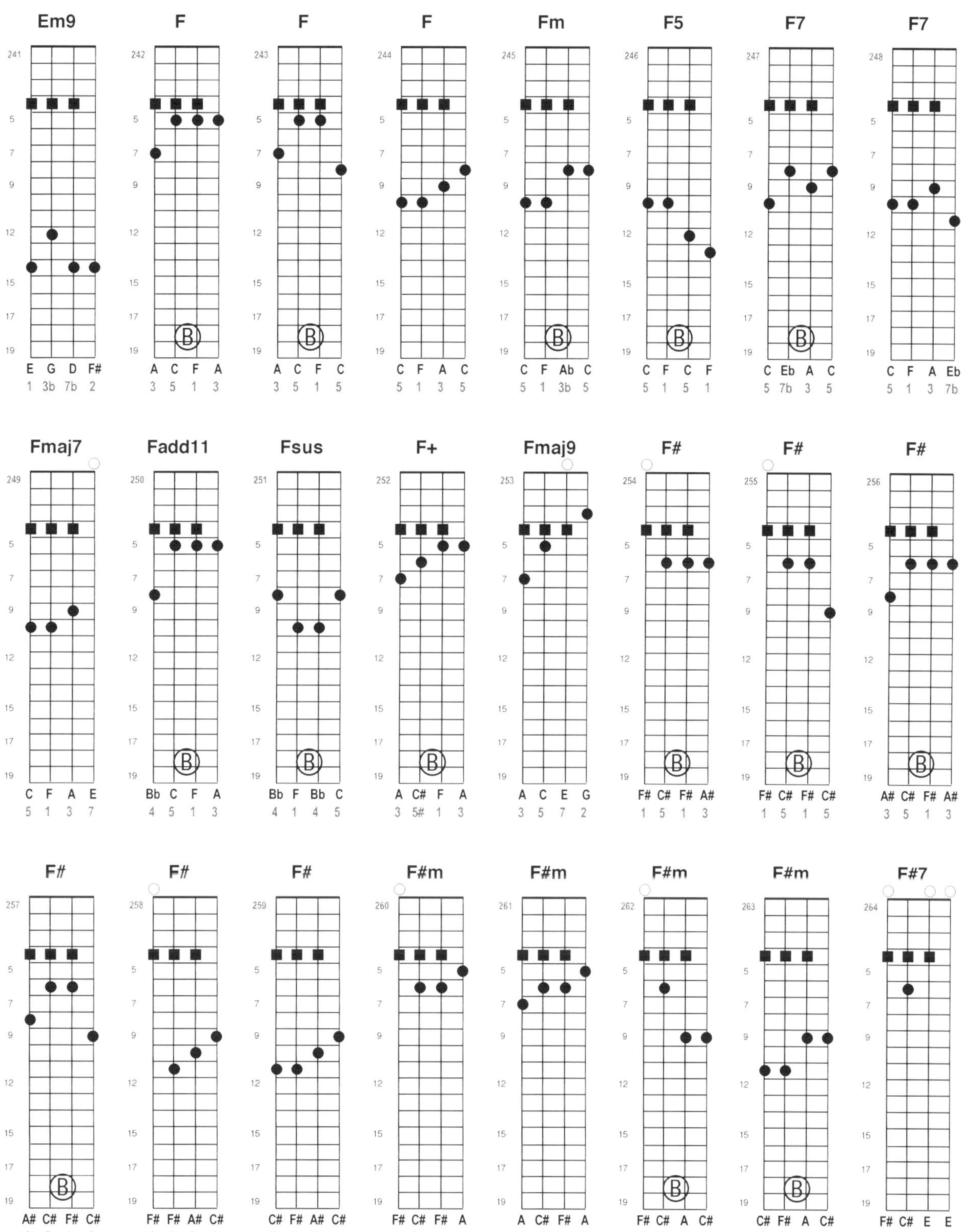

"Liberty Tuning" Chords p.12 (D G C E)

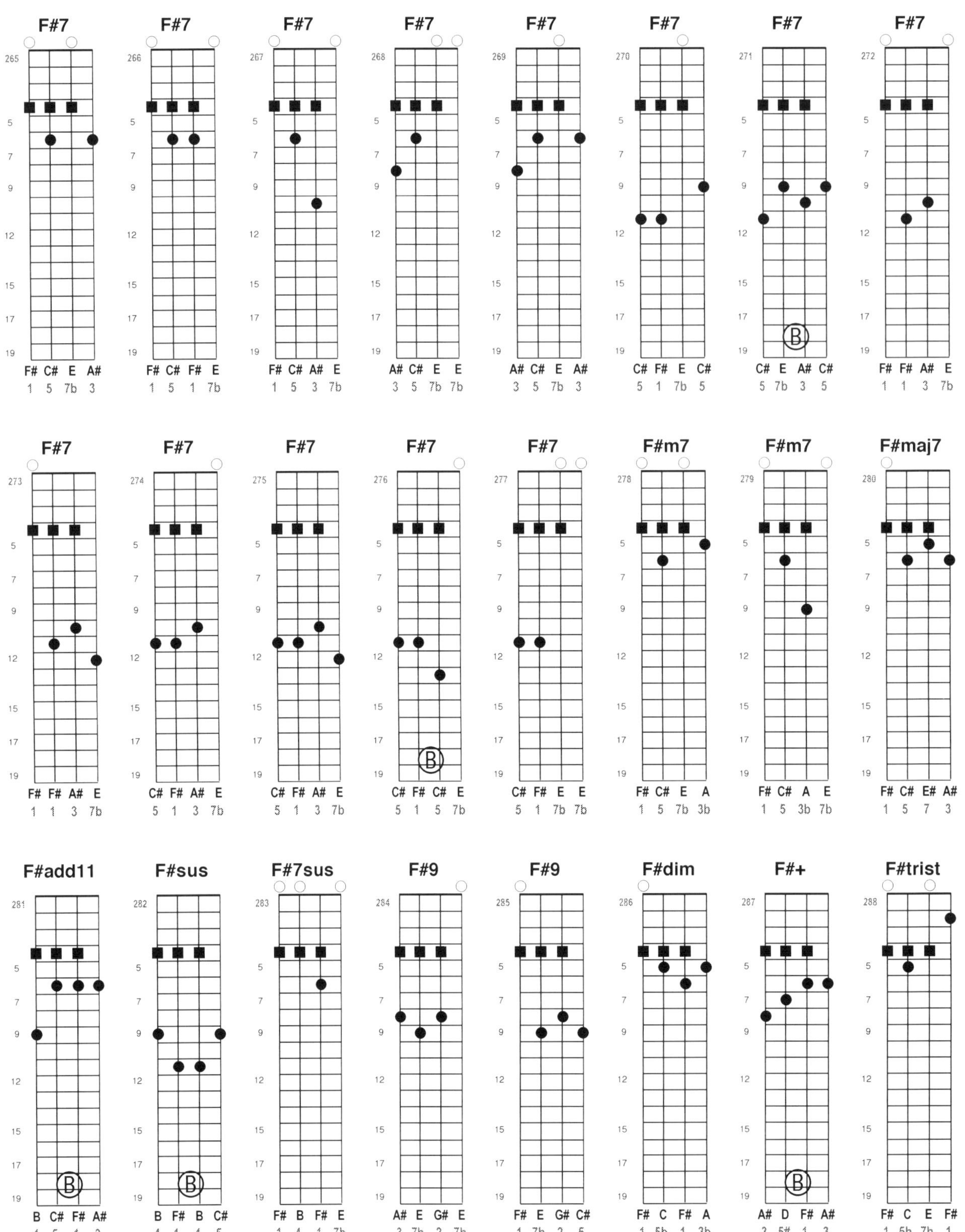

"Liberty Tuning" Chords p.13 (D G C E)

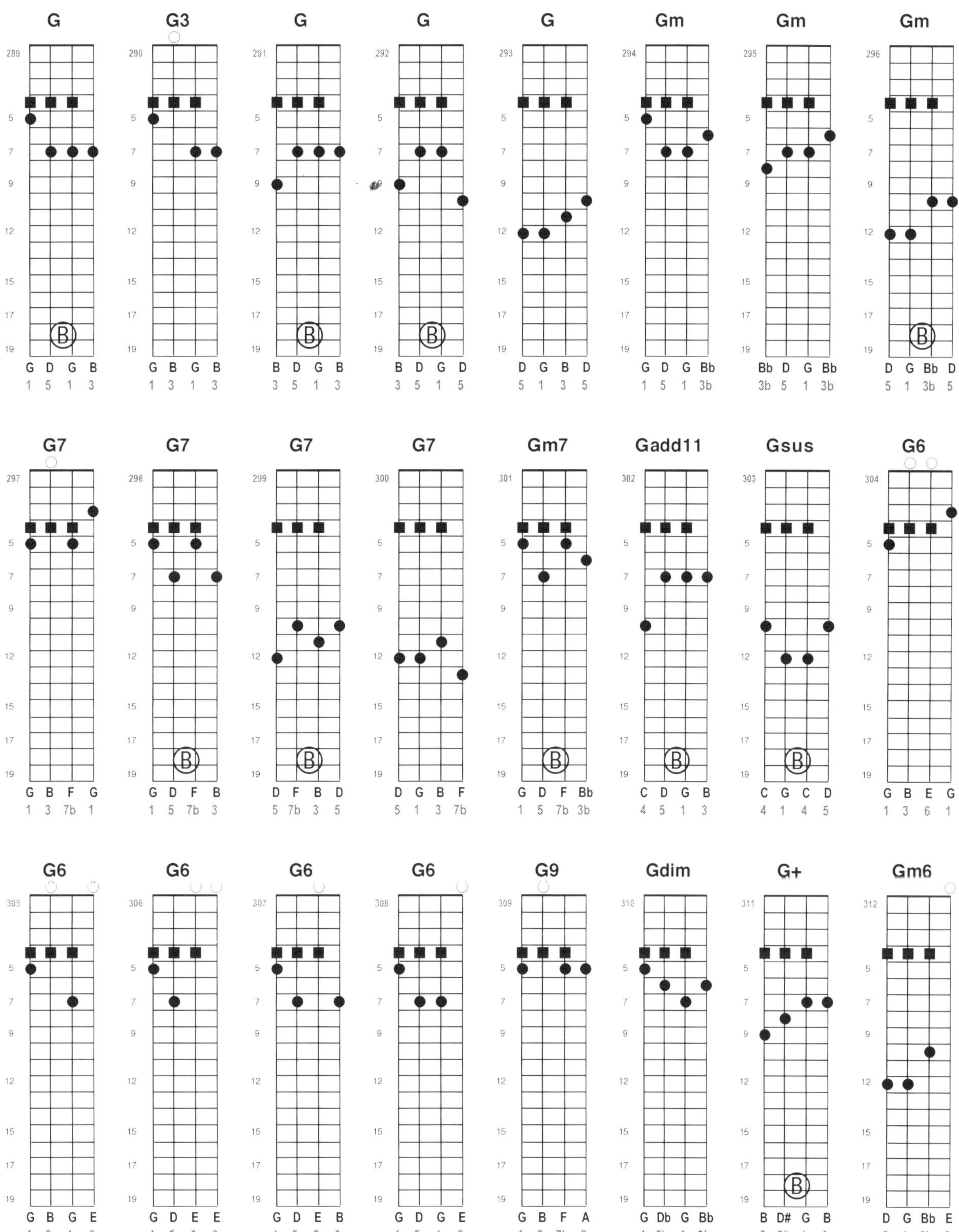

"Liberty Tuning" Chords p.14 (D G C E)

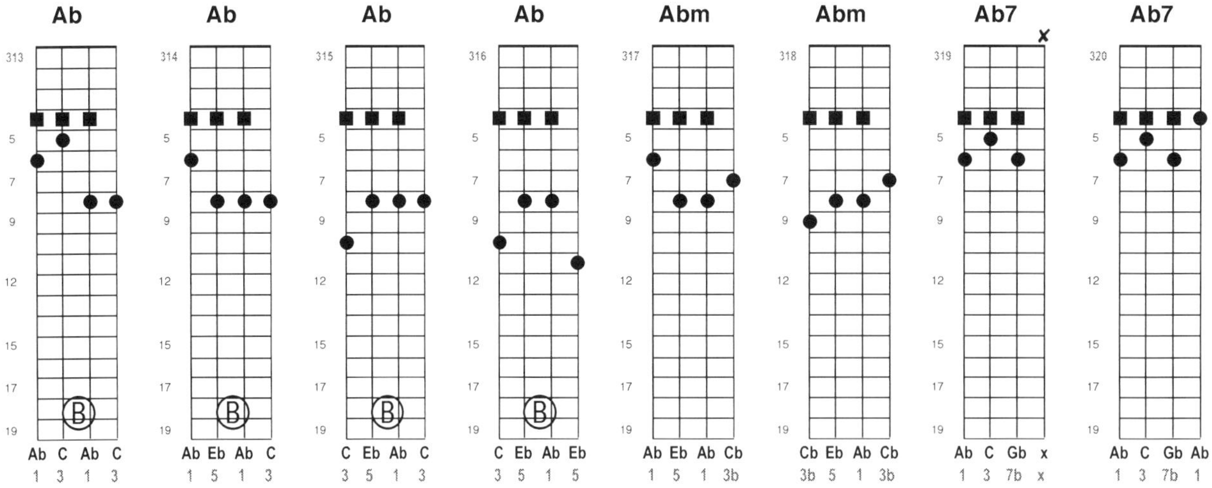

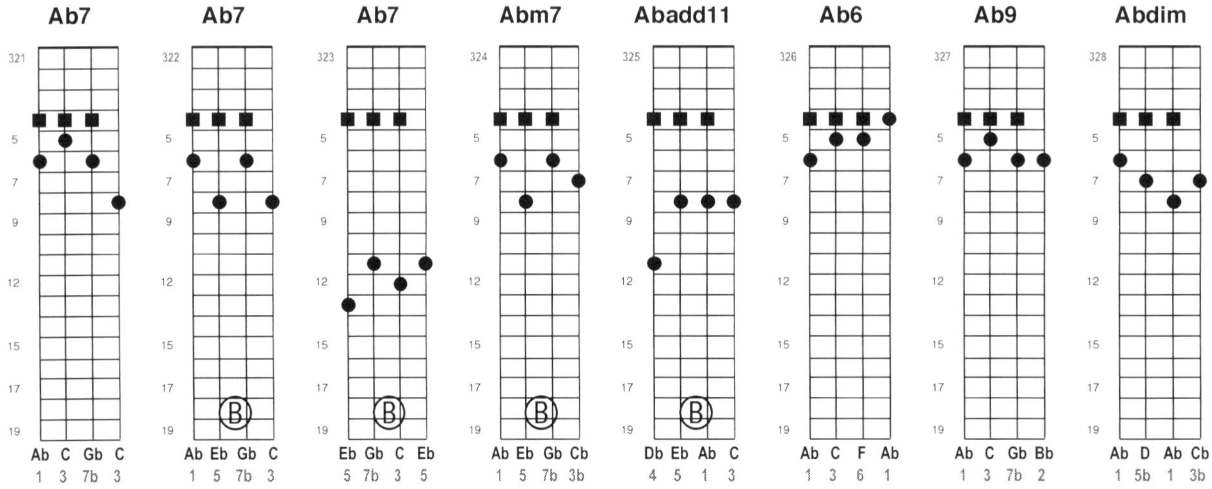

Chord	No.	Notes	Intervals
Ab	313	Ab C Ab C	1 3 1 3
Ab	314	Ab Eb Ab C	1 5 1 3
Ab	315	C Eb Ab C	3 5 1 3
Ab	316	C Eb Ab Eb	3 5 1 5
Abm	317	Ab Eb Ab Cb	1 5 1 3b
Abm	318	Cb Eb Ab Cb	3b 5 1 3b
Ab7	319	Ab C Gb x	1 3 7b x
Ab7	320	Ab C Gb Ab	1 3 7b 1
Ab7	321	Ab C Gb C	1 3 7b 3
Ab7	322	Ab Eb Gb C	1 5 7b 3
Ab7	323	Eb Gb C Eb	5 7b 3 5
Abm7	324	Ab Eb Gb Cb	1 5 7b 3b
Abadd11	325	Db Eb Ab C	4 5 1 3
Ab6	326	Ab C F Ab	1 3 6 1
Ab9	327	Ab C Gb Bb	1 3 7b 2
Abdim	328	Ab D Ab Cb	1 5b 1 3b

(Fret markers on each diagram: 5, 7, 9, 12, 15, 17, 19. Diagrams 313, 314, 315, 316, 322, 323, 324 and 325 are marked with Ⓑ.)

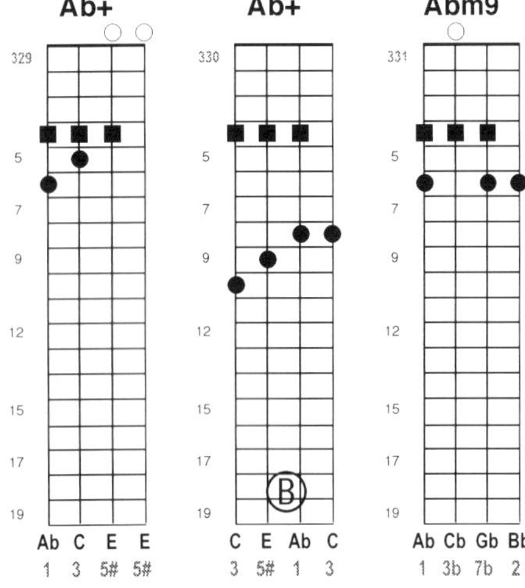

In my book "Baritone Ukulele Tunings" I map out several other new tunings of the fingerboard in detail. Some of them are closely related to Liberty Tuning.

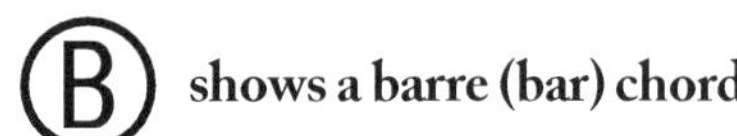

Appendix: About Chord Structure

About Sharps and Flats

Most of us know that D# (D-*sharp*) and Eb (E-*flat*) are two different names for the same musical note that lies between D and E. There is even a fancy term for it: they are called "*enharmonic equivalents*." On the piano, sharps and flats are black keys with 2 names, while white keys have simple letter names. The naming system makes sense to a pianist who reads music, but is quite confusing to a fretted instrument player, whose frets are the same color and who likely plays by ear.

Unfortunately, the musical notation system is most confusing to "campfire" players, who happen to be the largest group of people playing musical instruments, so it is worth taking a little time to explain things.

When the word *sharp* or *flat* is used as a verb, it means to move up or down in pitch, and usually refers to an upward move of a single increment, which would be the next key on the piano or the next fret up the neck. "*Sharp that note, please*" would tell you to move to the next higher note. A singer or violin player might also produce a note that is *flat*, which means it's too low in pitch by any amount. An instrument that is tuned *sharp* would mean that all the strings are tighter than normal. In a chord situation we might mention the sharp fifth (#5) note of a C scale, which means that the normal 5th (G) is sharped up to G#. If we sharp a Bb it becomes a B.

It takes some study of music to understand why this dual-naming is done. The choice of whether to call a note A# or Bb is really determined in the musical context of a particular piece of music. In a chord book, there is no context, so it is a little arbitrary what to name things. I called the section after C in this book C#, while others, especially those who are used to playing jazz with horns (who generally play in flat keys like F, Bb, Eb etc.) would have called it Db.

There are situations in music where a note is written as a double-sharp or double-flat, and there is such as thing as a G##, or even a B# and a Cb, though it would seem that a B# would just be a C natural. (The 7th scale position in the key of G# is an F##.) There isn't a good reason to use double accidentals in this book. There is even a third symbol (these three symbols are collectively called accidentals) known as the "natural." A natural symbol (♮) indicates that the musician is to ignore the flat or sharp symbol on that staff line temporarily. So a piece of music in G, that usually had all F's sharped to F#, might have an F natural note in it, which is the flat 7th note of the G scale, because the F# is the usual 7th note. Understanding that "flatting an F sharp note yields an F natural" is precisely the kind of thing that happens all the time in music, but this language is confusing to a campfire musician. Naturals are used commonly in sheet music because of the parameters imposed by the key signature at the beginning of each line of music, but they are not used in chord diagrams, and don't appear in this book.

♭ ♮ #

It is painfully clumsy to call a note "D-sharp or E-flat" every time you mention it, and what is usually done is determined by a hierarchy of the so-called order of sharps and order of flats. F is the key that uses only one flatted note (black key) in its major scale, so to ensure that the F scale includes each of the 7 letters once and only once, its scale is written F-G-A-Bb-C-D-E-F. So "A-sharp" is much less commonly used for the note between A and B, and it is usually called "B flat." The key of Bb is the next most complex "flat key" and it has both a Bb and an Eb in its scale. For the same reason, we hear people talk about Eb much more than D#.

Among stringed-instrument players, and especially among guitarists, who dominate that population of players, F# and C# are used much more often than their enharmonic equivalents Gb or Db, and stringed-instrument musicians in conversation, instruction books or chord books, tend to use the more common of the 2 names. The order of flats is B-E-A-D-G-C and the order of sharps is F-C-G-D-A-E-B. This works reasonably well, until you go to the "farther" keys like C# and you will always reach some confusion about what to call some things. Choosing between the key name C# or Db can be fuzzy. In this book I used C#, because most string players think in sharps and not flats. This means that the musical 3rd of that scale is an E#. My system does not handle the augmented chord, where the #5 note should be a G## and my charts call it an A. If I called the key Db then the flat 7 note in a lot of chords would be a Cb, and the 5b in a diminished chord would be an Abb. There are similar problems in the keys of F# and G#.

Rather than calling every accidental by 2 names, or doing something radical like calling every accidental a sharp, which makes logical but not musical sense, I chose to use the more common names for each chord and for the notes in the chord. The point of this book is to show you where your fingers go on the fretboard, and to help you understand the musical value of each note in the chord. If you are a novice player, and are using this book, be aware that there is such a thing a D# chord, though you are generally fine just calling it an Eb.

There are also special typographic symbols for sharp ♯ and flat ♭, but I have chosen for the sake of simplicity in typesetting this book to just use a pound sign (#) and lower case B (b) for the flat symbol, even though I know there is a slightly different symbol. The flat and sharp symbols don't occur in normal typefaces, and it is very awkward to typeset them, especially in sentences like this, and the fonts used in e-books sometimes don't even allow them. They also disturb the line spacing in the paragraphs that use them.

Bear in mind that not all chord have common names, there are different names, symbols, abbreviations and nicknames for chords, and not all chords will actually contain every one of the notes in their "spelling." There are dozens of ways to rearrange the notes in every type of chord. Knowing which notes can be doubled or omitted, and how to use the chords in musical situations is something that takes a lifetime to learn.

About Naming Chords

Professors of music probably cringe when guitar or banjo players start talking chord theory, since a lot of what we do is a little contrary to the way Western music has been taught for centuries. It is only because of the proliferation and dominance of guitars in recent decades that there has been a push to use and name chords. Composers and pianists got by for centuries without doing what we all do now, which is to analyze the structure of all our chords, and to catalog and categorize them. They thought more in terms of "lines" and harmony, and not really "chords."

Only some chords have names, and people don't agree on the names, the need for assigning names to chords, or the notation systems used for chords that have been named. **Chords often have more than one name**, which is also confusing when you are compiling a book of chords, and everyone who makes chord books makes up names and uses all sorts of different symbols and terminology. It seems to be all organized, but it is in many ways a lawless jungle.

First We Name The Notes

The naming system for musical notes makes more sense once you have used it for a while, but it is confusing to a beginner, especially if you never studied piano and are a recreational musician. The piano and the notation system evolved together, and the whole notation system really doesn't make sense on just a fretboard. The idea that some of the notes have 2 names is both useful and hard to swallow at first. The note between F and G is sometimes called F# and sometimes Gb.

In Western music, the octave is divided into 12 equal pieces called half-steps or semi-tones, or on fretted instruments, frets. The 12th fret of a stringed instrument has the same name as the open string, and it is 1/2 the string length exactly. (The ratio of the length of each fret of a fretted instruments to the adjacent fret is the 12th root of 2, a thoroughly irrational number.) There is a certain amount of numerological mystery to all this, and most people who have studied either math or music know about the mysterious relationship of integers to music. The harmonic series: 1/2, 1/3, 1/4, 1/5, 1/6 etc has a lot to do with music, and represents the overtones of vibrating objects. The numbers 5, 7 and 12 appear a lot in musical ideas.

There are only 7 note names in most scales, and they are given the 7 letter names from A to G, with the accidentals (sharps & flats) sprinkled in. The only thing you really have to memorize is that there are no sharps or flats between B and C, and between E and F. Remember the piano keyboard layout, where some white keys are adjacent but most aren't. The rest of chord theory you can figure out from some simple rules.

Next We Look At The Intervals

The system for describing how each chord is built used to be based on what are called intervals, which is the musical distance between 2 notes. On a one-dimensional instrument like the piano it makes total sense to think this way. Traditional music theory talks of combining 2 intervals to make a 3-note chord, and stacking up larger groups of intervals, triads and even *tetrachords* (4-note chords) to build the more complex and extended chords. **We don't really need to know about intervals to use this**

book, and fretted instrument players really don't think in terms of them, so I'll be brief here.

Intervals are given names according to how many consecutive letters they span, which can be confusing. Any interval that spans the letter names C to D is a second, though it might be C-D (also a major 2nd) Cb-Db (major 2nd), C-Db (minor 2nd), C#-D (minor 2nd), C#-D# (major 2nd). Intervals get names: unison, 2nd, 3rd, 4th etc, and there are modifiers: *perfect*, *augmented*, and *diminished* for unisons, octaves, 4ths and 5ths, and *major* or *minor* for 2nd, 3rd, 6th or 7ths. All intervals can be augmented. All intervals but the unison can be diminished. Only seconds, thirds, sixths, and sevenths can be major or minor. Got it? Maybe there is a reason this system for describing chord structure isn't universal.

INTERVAL	Steps	Example
perfect unison	0	C-C
augmented unison	1	C-C#
minor 2nd	1	C-Db
major 2nd	2	C-D
augmented 2nd	3	C-D#
minor 3rd	3	C-Eb
major 3rd	4	C-E
augmented 3rd	5	C-E#
diminished 4th	4	C-Fb
perfect 4th	5	C-F
augmented 4th	6	C-F#
diminished 5th	6	C-Gb
perfect 5th	7	C-G
augmented 5th	8	C-G#
minor 6th	8	C-Ab
major 6th	9	C-A
augmented 6th	10	C-A#
minor 7th	10	C-Bb
major seventh	11	C-Bb
octave	12	C-C

Every chord can be described as a series of intervals. A *major triad* (3 notes) is made by stacking up 2 intervals of 4 and then 3 half steps (frets), known as a major 3rd plus a minor 3rd. Reversing the order of these two intervals builds a *minor triad*. Two minor 3rds stacked up makes a *diminished triad*, and two major 3rds create an *augmented triad*. Intervals make sense and are quite visual on the piano keyboard, where letter names are white keys and accidentals are black keys and on paper, since a staff is a linear representation of pitch.

Trouble is, when we play a ninth chord on a fretted instrument, we are not playing the notes in numerical order– we play them the way we can. Our 9th chord might not have a 5th and it might have 2 of them (on guitar, not ukulele), and it might have the 5th on the bottom and it might not.

Describing 4-string fretted instrument chords with intervals is extremely messy, and not that helpful to a player in explaining what is going on musically, because the fretboard is not linear like a piano keyboard. Look at the different D chords in this book. They all have a different sequence of intervals that make them up. But they all are made up of the same 3 notes: D-F#-A.

The interval-based system of describing chords is too clumsy to describe thousands of chords, so a simpler but also slightly illogical numerical system was employed by guitarists that uses the major scale numbers 1 through 7 combined with sharps and flats to mark the position of each note. I use this system in this book, and so do most fretted-instrument chord publications.

The 12 Major Scales

Even if you play music that never uses a major scale, you'll still use the major scale numbers to describe the notes in the chords. That's how it is usually done, and it is what all the numbers in chord names and underneath each chord in this book are about. You need to at least understand what a *major scale* is.

A scale is nothing more than a group of notes arranged in order of pitch. There are dozens, possibly hundreds of kinds of scales that are associated with the various kinds of music in the world, and an exhaustive discussion of them is beyond the scope of this book.

In a so-called major scale, which is just one type of scale, the 7 notes are separated by half-steps (frets) in the pattern 2-2-1-2-2-2-1. Start on any string, and climb up frets in this order, you'll finish at fret 12, and you'll hear a *do-re-mi* major scale. Remember this pattern.

There is a major scale built on each of the 12 note names, and since 5 of the 12 note names have dual names, we could map out 17 major scales instead of just 12. Because Eb is less clumsy than D#, and Bb is much more manageable than A#, we rarely hear about the key or the scale of A# or D#. The notes D# and A# appear in some of chords we play but we don't play in those keys. This is confusing. The B major 7th chord has an A# note in it, and the F#m chord has a D# note in it.

Guitars normally play best in the keys of C, G, D, A and E, which are all "sharp keys." Jazz evolved with horns, which play in "flat keys" like Bb and Eb. Jazz theory uses a lot more flats, and in guitar chord theory where it is not part of a jazz curriculum, we have a tendency to just use sharps and kind of ignore flats. This is why I use C# instead of Db. It's easier to play ukulele family instruments in F or Bb than it is guitar, so a case could be made to use Db or Gb instead of C# and F#.So I put the Db scale next to the C# scale. Let's have a look at the major scales, since these generate all the chord spellings in the book.

Each letter name appears once and only once in each scale. This is a big part of the reason why the sharps and flats are used.

Now We Can Map the Chord Structures

The major chord (which we previously described as an interval of a major 3rd plus a minor 3rd stacked on a note...) can also be defined as the 1st, 3rd and 5th notes of a major scale. The C major chord is the 1-3-5 notes of the first row in the scales chart (previous page), which is the notes C-E-G. Likewise, a D chord has the 1-3-5 notes of the D scale (see chart) which means D-F#-A. Each other type of chord also has a numeric spelling, as shown in the big chart.

The Basic Major Scales (both C# and Db are shown)

Root 1	2	3	4	5	6	7	sharps/ flats
C	D	E	F	G	A	B	none
C#	D#	E#	F#	G#	A#	B#	7#
Db	Eb	F	Gb	Ab	Bb	C	5b
D	E	F#	G	A	B	C#	2#
Eb	F	G	Ab	Bb	C	D	3b
E	F#	G#	A	B	C#	D#	4#
F	G	A	Bb	C	D	E	1b
F#	G#	A#	B	C#	D#	E#	6#
G	A	B	C	D	E	F#	1#
Ab	Bb	C	Db	Eb	F	G	4b
A	B	C#	D	E	F#	G#	3#
Bb	C	D	Eb	F	G	A	2b
B	C#	D#	E	F#	G#	A#	5#

What comes next is a little confusing... When we play in the key of G, our three most common chords are G-C-D, referred to as the *tonic* (1or I) the *sub-dominant* (4 or IV) and the *dominant* (5 or V.) The names of those chords come from the G scale, since we are playing in the key of G. The 1-4-5 positions of the G scale are G-C-D.

But each of those 3 chords is made up of 3 notes. The G chord itself is made up of the 1-3-5 notes (not the 1-4-5-- that was for chords, not notes) of the G scale, which are G-B-D. Look at all the G chords in this book-- they are all made up of various combinations of those 3 notes only. The C chord is the 1-3-5 notes (C-E-G) of the C scale and the D chord is likewise made up of the 1-3-5 (D-F#-A) notes of the D scale. This is confusing at first, to name the notes in every chord according to the major scale built on its root note name, regardless of what key the song is in.

There are of course lots of other types of chords in the world that are not in this book, and there are fuzzy and gray areas within certain types of chords.

An 11th chord, for example, technically has the 1-3-5-7-9-11 scale notes in it, and it usually has only some of them. It's hard to know when to call it an 11th or when it is an "add11," since the ukulele only has 4 strings.

There will always be some chords where it is unclear what to call them, and ambiguous chords are often musically interesting and useful. When you get a chord with 5 or 6 notes in it, and you start scrambling the order and omitting notes, those same notes can often be understood as another kind of chord entirely. What the chord is named has everything to do with how it is used in a piece of music, and in a book like this they are not being used in specific songs, and are just "laboratory specimens."

The Order of Notes in a Chord

The real workings of chord theory are determined by how a chord is used in a piece of music, and studying them too closely out of context can be pointless. There are also a lot of examples of unusual voicings of chords that sound great in certain songs or as part of a progression of chords, but that might sound odd when played by themselves.

On fretted instruments, we take what we can get, and we don't have the same choices of notes that pianists have for the order of notes. We may use a chord whose voicing is not ideal because it is all we can reach, and we may also push ourselves to play a hard fingering because it has a better or different sound.

The note names and scale degrees are shown for all the chords in this book. It offers a formula for the inner workings of all the chords.

Chord Name	Scale Degrees	*Example : C Scale*	Symbol or Abbrev.
major	1 - 3 - 5	C-E-G	C, Cmaj CΔ
minor	1 - 3b - 5	C-Eb-G	Cm C-
modal	1 - 5	C-G	C5
diminished (dim7)	1 - 3b - 5b or 1-3b-5b-7bb (6)	C-Eb-Gb Bbb (A)	Cdim or C°
augmented	1 - 3# - 5#	C-F-G#	C+, Caug
suspended fourth	1 - 4 - 5	C-F-G	Csus, Csus4
sixth (added sixth)	1 - 3 - 5 - 6	C-E-G-A	C6
(dominant) seventh	1 - 3 - 5 - 7b	C-E-G-Bb	C7 Cdom7
major seventh	1 - 3 - 5 - 7	C-E-G-B	Cmaj7 Cma7 CM7 CMa7 C j7 CΔ7 CΔ
minor seventh	1 - 3b - 5 -7b	C-Eb-G-Bb	Cm7 C-7
seventh suspended	1 - 4 - 5 - 7b	C-F-G-Bb	C7sus, C7sus4
add nine	1 - 3 - 5 - 2	C-E-G-D	Cadd9 , Csus2
minor add nine	1 - 3b - 5 - 2	C-Eb-G-D	Cmadd9
add eleven	1 - 3 - 5 - 4	C-E-G-F	Cadd11, Cadd4
minor add eleven	1 - 3b - 5 - 4	C-Eb-G-F	Cmadd11
(dominant) ninth	1 - 3 - 5 - 7b - 2	C-E-G-Bb-D	C9
major ninth	1 - 3 - 5 - 7 - 2	C-E-G-B-D	Cmaj9, Cma9, CM9 C j9 CΔ9
minor ninth	1 - 3b - 5 - 7b - 2	C-Eb-G-Bb-D	Cm9
major sixth	1 - 3 - 5 - 6 - 7	C-E-G-B-A	Cmaj6, Cma6, CM6 C j6 CΔ6
minor sixth	1 - 3b - 5 - 6	C-Eb-G-A	Cm6
6/7 (dominant sixth)	1 - 3 - 5 - 6 - 7b	C-E-G-Bb-A	C6/7
6/9	1 - 3 - 5 - 6 - 2	C-E-G-A-D	C6/9
eleventh	1 - 3 - 5 - 7b- 2- 4	C-E-G-Bb-D-F	C11
major eleventh	1 - 3 - 5 - 7- 2- 4	C-E-G-B-D-F	Cmaj11, Cma11, CM11 C j11 CΔ11
9/11	1 - 3 - 5 - 2- 4	C-E-G-D-F	C9/11
minor eleventh	1 - 3b - 5 - 7b- 2- 4	C-Eb-G-Bb-D-F	Cm11
thirteenth	1 - 3 - 5 - 6 - 7b- 2	C-E-G-Bb-D-A	C13
minor thirteenth	1 - 3b - 5 - 6 -7b- 2	C-Eb-G-Bb-D-A	Cm13
major thirteenth	1 - 3 - 5 - 6 - 7- 2	C-E-G-B-D-A	Cmaj13, Cma13, CM13 C j13 CΔ13
6/11	1 - 3 - 5 - 6 - 4	C-E-G-A-F	C6/11

The Root / Bass Note

When we compare two or more notes, our ear usually uses the lower pitched note as a reference and compares the higher notes to it. (This is why if just our lowest string is out of tune, it often makes us want to tune the others to it.) **The lowest note of a chord is the most important in shaping the flavor and sound of a chord.** Pay attention and keep track of your low notes. The banjo, ukulele and mandolin don't really have any bass, and chord inversions might work on them that don't work on guitar.

About Dissonance and Pitch

Play an A and an A^{b} simultaneously, or any musical interval of a "minor 2nd," which means 2 adjacent keys on the piano. They are quite dissonant. Play the 6th fret of the 4th string [Ab] and the open 3rd string (G) at the same time. It's quite dissonant. Now separate the notes G-A^{b} by an octave and play them again. (This time play the open 3rd string [G] and the 4th fret of the 1st string [A^{b}]. The result is much less dissonant. If you play the open 3rd string [G] and the 16th fret of the 1st string [A^{b}] simultaneously and separate the G from the A^{b} by another octave, the interval is even less dissonant.

Sometimes chords and inversions of chords sound fine if they are spread across several octaves, even though the same letter-named notes would not sound as good if they were closer together in overall pitch.

The location of the notes in the chord has a big effect on the sound. If you find a chord you like or don't like in this book, study the structure more carefully.

About Numbers like 9^{ths} and 11^{ths}

You've probably noticed that the numerals 1-7 mark the musical function of the chords in this book, yet some chords have names like 9th and there are a few I have labeled 11th or 13th chords. This is one of those "gray areas" where things are not totally logical, but it is standard practice to use these numbers. To be rigorous, when you add a D note to a C chord, you should call it a 2nd if it is in a lower octave and a 9th if it is higher, and you might wonder why we don't call adding a D note another octave higher a 16th. The answer is that we don't. The language used, like a lot of linguistic things, evolves and changes as it is passed through the people that use it. Musicians tend to use the term "9th chord" when there is a 1-3-5 chord with both a 7th and a 2nd added, but if there is no 7th, and it is just 1-3-5-2 it is called an "*add9,*" "*add2*" or "*sus2.*" I use the term *add9* in this book, though just as many people call it an add2, and some people use both. Likewise, musicians have adopted the terms 11th and 13th, but you just don't hear talk of 18th or 20th chords, and the distinctions and definitions are often blurred.

There is no legislation or regulation, and not much in the way of organized attempts to standardize things. After decades of independent teachers and publishers inventing notation and terminology, there is quite a lot of diversity in the way music theory is written and discussed. The *Berklee College of Music* in Boston is doing a lot to make the study of contemporary music theory more uniform.

Inversions, Voicings and Doubling

What is also not clear, and something for which there is no terminology, is what happens when there are notes "missing," and one of the grayest areas involves when to reject a voicing because the inversion doesn't sound musical. Here are an A9 chord and an Em7 I rejected, because the bottom 2 notes are the 5, 3b and the 7b, and the chord to my ears does not sound like those chords:

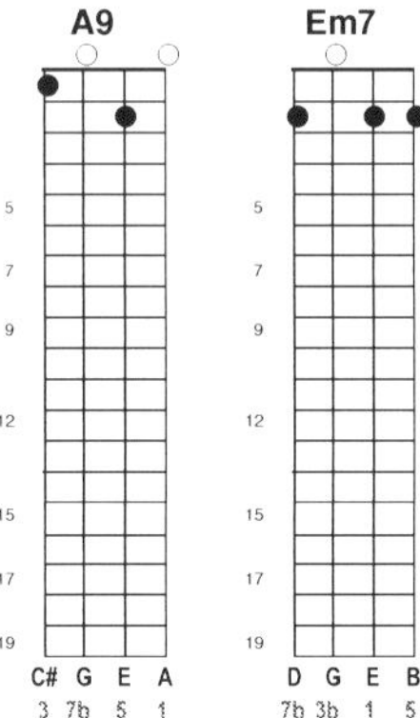

Another "issue" arises when notes are added to a triad in different ways. The popular rock band *Steely Dan* made extensive use of what they called "*mu*" chords, where there is an add9 that does not remove the 3rd of the chord. They are a bit rare but useful on ukulele, and though the effect also happens with added 11ths if you keep the 3rd and the 4th scale notes sounding. I have not flagged the *mu* chords with a symbol. Here are Gadd9 chords where # 1 and #3 are just 1-2-5 and #2, #4 and #5 are 1-2-3-5. The *mu* chord (with both 2 and 3 scale degrees) has a strikingly different sound, especially when you arpeggiate it:

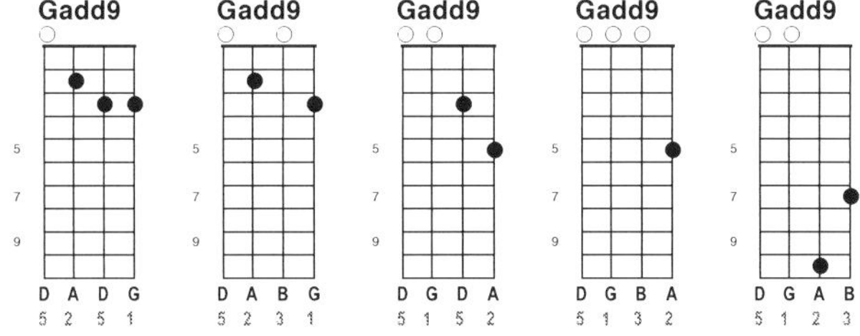

Music theory books teach that an "uninverted" or root position C triad has the notes C-E-G, while a 1st inversion C chord has the spelling E-G-C and a 2nd inversion is G-C-E. These concepts work beautifully on the piano, and you can clearly see the inversions working, though on a fretboard you really can't. The term "inversion" is sometimes used to mean the order of notes or voicing, though technically it refers to which is the lowest note in the group.

Identifying a Chord

It's one thing to look for ways to play a particular chord on the fingerboard, but it's another task entirely to find a chord, and then wonder what it might be called or how it might be used. Our ears are a big part of this, and we can learn to hear the telltale sound of each type of chords. Many chords are "cut and dried" and everyone agrees what they are called. Others can be ambiguous. You may object to the names I have given to some chords, especially if you are used to using an enharmonic equivalent. The point at which a Em7 chord becomes a G6 can be very unclear. If it has an E note on the bottom that will tilt the balance toward calling it an Em7, and if there is a G on the bottom, it is probably a G6. It really doesn't matter what the name is unless you are discussing it with someone.

Try to just enjoy the sounds of chords, and use them in your music, and keep an open mind about what to call them. And whatever you do, don't let chord theory get in the way of enjoying your instrument.

More Musical Resources By Harvey Reid

THE SONG TRAIN (2007) is a landmark resource for beginning guitarists by Harvey Reid & Joyce Andersen. 4-CD boxed set with 80-page color hardback book, contains 56 one & two chord songs. Half the songs are copyrighted, by the likes of Bob Dylan, Hank Williams, Chuck Berry etc, so it offers beginners easy but great songs they can play. Folk, blues, gospel, rock, celtic, country and gospel songs, and an amazing cross-section of American music. **www.songtrain.net**

THE TROUBADOUR GUITAR CHORD BOOK (2013) The best, most complete and readable standard-tuning chord encyclopedia, and an essential new reference tool. A monumental and important new work that may never go back on your shelf. Unlike other large chord books that are tailored for jazz guitarists, the *Troubadour Guitar Chord Book* features over 2900 open and closed-string voicings, optimized and selected for solo acoustic and troubadour-style guitarists.

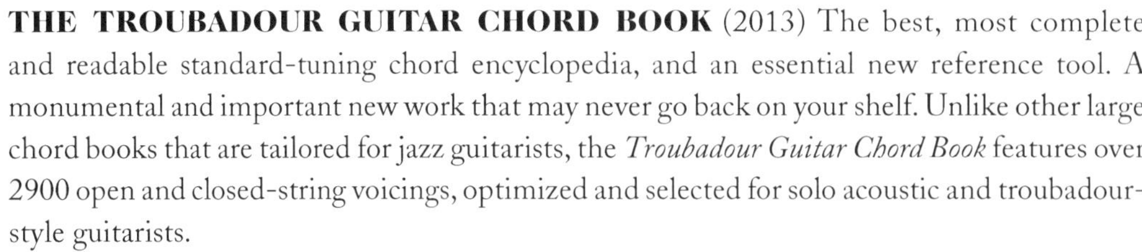

THE BIG DADGAD CHORD BOOK (2014) The best, most complete and readable chord encyclopedia in DADGAD tuning, with 2500 chords mapped out. Another indispensable reference book for anyone who plays in this popular tuning. Also features full-fingerboard diagrams, with every note and scale degree shown for every chord.

THE BIG BOOK OF BANJO CHORDS (2015) The most complete, detailed and versatile book of chords for standard banjo G tuning. The fingerboard shown like never before, with 5th string notes shown.

THE BIG BOOK OF MANDOCELLO CHORDS (2015) The most complete, detailed and versatile book of chords for standard C-G-A-D tuning. Also includes 11 of the first ideas ever published for partial capos on mandocello.

THE BIG BOOK OF BARITONE UKULELE CHORDS (2015) The most complete, detailed and versatile book of chords for standard D-G-B-E tuning.

BARITONE UKULELE SIMPLIFIED (2015) Explores 9 different new tunings and partial capo ideas that reveal for the first time how to play instant music with great-sounding but simpler chord shapes.

SLEIGHT OF HAND (1983) The first book of partial capo guitar arrangements, still in print. 16 solo guitar arrangements using a universal partial capo. Intermediate to advanced level, mostly for fingerstyle guitar, but has 2 flatpicked fiddle tune arrangements (*Sally Goodin'* and *Devil's Dream*) In TAB and standard notation. *Suite: For the Duchess, Für Elise, Scarborough Fair, Minuet in Dm, Flowers of Edinburgh, Simple Gifts, Sally Goodin', Irish Washerwoman, Pavanne, Minuet in Dm, Red-Haired Boy, June Apple, Jesu Joy of Man's Desiring, Devil's Dream, Sally Goodin', Scherzo, Shenandoah, Greensleeves, Sailor's Hornpipe, Fisher's Hornpipe*

CAPO INVENTIONS (2006) 14 intermediate to advanced arrangements from Reid's catalog of guitar recordings. Precisely transcribed for solo guitar, these pieces all use a 3-string *Esus* type partial capo. In TAB and standard notation. *Skye Boat Song, Highwire Hornpipe, Windy Grave, Hard Times, The Unknown Soldier, Suite: For the Duchess, The Arkansas Traveler, The Minstrel Boy, Red in the Sky, Prelude to the Minstrel's Dream, Norway Suite: Parts 1 &2, Star Island Jig, Macallan's Jig.*

THE LIBERTY "FLIP" CAPO IDEA BOOKS (2014-15) Two volumes, totaling almost 400 pages, with over 113 ideas of partial capo configurations that can be done with a pair of *Model 43* and *Model 65 Liberty* partial capos. These were developed by Harvey Reid, and are the new generation of sleek and versatile partial capos that clamp 6, 5, 4 or 3 strings on most guitars, banjos, ukes and mandolins. Volume I shows 72 ideas, mostly in standard tuning, and with a taste of combining capos with altered tunings. Volume 2 combines capos with altered tunings.

SECRETS OF THE 3-STRING PARTIAL CAPO (2010) 24 mind-bending ways to use the popular 3-string *Esus* (*E-suspended*) type partial capo. ***This book may no longer be available after the arrival of the Liberty Capos.*** **18 of these ideas are now in the *Liberty Capo IDEA BOOK* , and the other 6 appear in the *Liberty "FLIP" Capo IDEA BOOK Vol.2.***

MORE SECRETS OF THE 3-STRING PARTIAL CAPO (2013) 27 more ways to use 3-string *Esus* (*E-suspended*) type partial capos. **12 of these ideas are now in the *Liberty Capo IDEA BOOK* , and the others are in the *Liberty Capo IDEA BOOK Vol.2.***

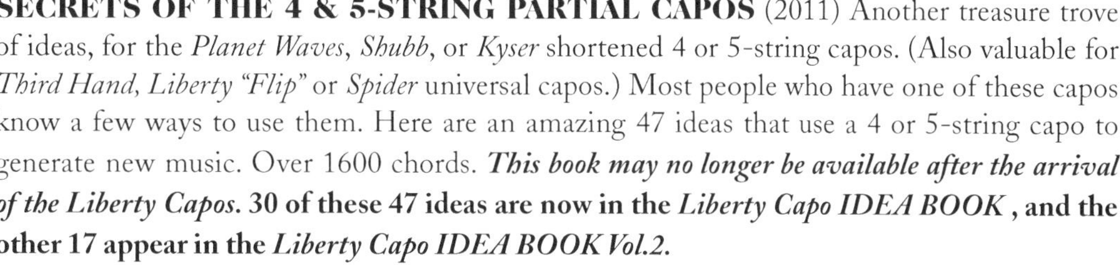

SECRETS OF THE 4 & 5-STRING PARTIAL CAPOS (2011) Another treasure trove of ideas, for the *Planet Waves, Shubb,* or *Kyser* shortened 4 or 5-string capos. (Also valuable for *Third Hand, Liberty "Flip"* or *Spider* universal capos.) Most people who have one of these capos know a few ways to use them. Here are an amazing 47 ideas that use a 4 or 5-string capo to generate new music. Over 1600 chords. ***This book may no longer be available after the arrival of the Liberty Capos.*** **30 of these 47 ideas are now in the *Liberty Capo IDEA BOOK* , and the other 17 appear in the *Liberty Capo IDEA BOOK Vol.2.***

SECRETS OF THE 1 & 2-STRING PARTIAL CAPOS (2012) How to use the unique ***Woodie's G-Band*** 1 and 2-string partial capos. 33 clever ways to use these capos in a number of tunings and in combination with other partial capos, with over 1100 chords. 98 pages are packed with photos, ideas and capo knowledge that is only available here. Even the makers of the capos don't know about these ideas.

SECRETS OF PARTIAL CAPOS IN DADGAD TUNING (2012) Most people think of partial capos as a substitute for open tunings, and don't realize that they can be combined. Harvey Reid shows you over 25 ingenious ways to use partial capos to expand the musical possibilities of DADGAD tuning (4 of them use the similar CGDGAD tuning.) Get new chords, fingerings, voicings, resonances and unlock a new, mysterious world of new music hiding in your fingerboard. **17 of these ideas are now in the *Liberty Capo IDEA BOOK Vol.2.***

SECRETS OF UNIVERSAL PARTIAL CAPOS (2012) 45 ways to get new music from your guitar that can only be done with universal partial capos. This hidden world of music in your fingerboard includes a number of tunings and combinations with other partial capos. Over 1500 chords. Packed with photos, clear explanations and capo strategy will save you years of searching. **Because the *Model 43 Liberty* capo clamps 4 middle strings, 13 of these ideas are now duplicated in the *Liberty Capo IDEA BOOKS, Vol. 1-2.***

SECRETS OF PARTIAL CAPOS IN DROP D TUNING (2014) The most common tuning is *Drop D*: D A D G B E, and like any tuning, it can be combined with partial capos to add another dimension to the guitar. This book presents 24 ways to use one or more partial capos of all types to generate more new music. **9 of these ideas are now in the *Liberty Capo IDEA BOOK*, and 7 more appear in *Vol.2.*** The others use a universal or *G-Band* capo.

THE LIBERTY GUITAR BEGINNER'S BOOK (2015) Play 30 classic folk songs instantly with super-simple, great-sounding chords. For children or adults, this book carefully explains how to use *Liberty Tuning* to play chords and sing songs in 6 different major and minor keys. You need a guitar, a full capo, and a *Liberty FLIP Model 43* capo.

THE LIBERTY TUNING CHORD BOOK (2013) In his partial capo research, Harvey Reid discovered a simple new guitar tuning that introduces a remarkable geometrical symmetry and simplicity to the guitar fingerboard that no one ever dreamed existed. Here is a thorough examination of what this amazing tuning can do, with over 1200 chords, sorted, mapped out and organized to help you find your way in *Liberty Tuning*. Lots of tips, advice & clear explanations. For guitar teachers, beginners and anyone who already plays guitar and wants to learn about this important discovery.

THE LIBERTY GUITAR METHOD (2013) Total beginners can play music like never before. It's easy to do and sounds great. Learn to use *Liberty Tuning* to play great-sounding, simple 2-finger chords to songs by Bob Dylan, Hank Williams, John Prine, Johnny Cash, Chuck Berry, The Beatles, Adele, and more. You won't believe it 'til you try it. *Hush Little Baby, This Land is Your Land, Your Cheating Heart, A Hard Rain's A Gonna Fall, Amazing Grace, The Cuckoo, Folsom Prison Blues, Angel From Montgomery, Maybellene, Let It Be, Imagine, Someone Like You, The Wedding Song, House of the Rising Sun*

THE LIBERTY SONG TRAIN (2013) Learn how to use *Liberty Tuning* to play all 56 two-chord songs in the epic *Song Train* collection with just 2-finger chords, in the same keys as they were done on the *Song Train* recordings. Beginning guitar has never been easier. Careful explanations, with lots of helpful tips, strategy and advice. If you have the *Song Train* 4-CD collection, you need this companion book.

LIBERTY GUITAR FOR KIDS (2013) It's a huge breakthrough in children's guitar. Children as young as 4 can learn to strum simple 2-finger *Liberty Tuning* chords and play guitar like never before. Classic traditional plus modern children's songs arranged in keys young voices can sing in. No need to wait until the children grow bigger or waste your money on crummy small children's guitars. Learn how even small children can instantly start strumming songs on adult guitars. It's really amazing. *London Bridge, Row Row Row Your Boat, Farmer in the Dell, Hush Little Baby, This Land is Your Land, Oh Susannah, Standing in the Need of Prayer, Hey Lolly Lolly, Comin' Round the Mountain* and more.

THE 2-FINGER GUITAR GUIDE (2013) A careful study of simplified guitar chords, this book takes you through each of the common tunings and partial capo configurations that can be used to play simplified guitar chords. Learn the advantages and disadvantages of each of 28 different guitar environments, including the amazing *Liberty Tuning* and related hybrid tunings. If you have a shortage of fingers on the fretting hand, or if you work with hand injuries, special music education or music therapy, this is the definitive guide to showing what can be done musically with just 2 finger chords.

Support Harvey Reid's ground-breaking work in guitar. Buy his books, music, videos, and capos.

www.PartialCapo.com www.LibertyGuitar.com

Available from Amazon.com and other retail outlets

About the Author

Harvey Reid has been a full-time acoustic guitar player since 1974, and has performed over 6000 concerts throughout the US and in Europe. He won the 1981 *National Fingerpicking Guitar Competition* and the 1982 *International Autoharp* contest, and has released 32 highly-acclaimed recordings of original, traditional and contemporary acoustic music.

He is best known for his solo fingerstyle guitar work, but he is also a solid flatpicker (he won Bill Monroe's *Beanblossom* bluegrass guitar contest in 1976), a versatile singer, lyricist, prolific composer, arranger and songwriter. He also plays mandolin, ukulele, mandocello and bouzouki. Reid recorded the first album ever of 6 & 12-string banjo music, and his CD ***Solo Guitar Sketchbook*** made Guitar Player Magazine's Top 20 essential acoustic guitar CD's list. His CD ***Steel Drivin' Man*** was chosen by Acoustic Guitar Magazine as one of **Top 10 Folk CD's** of all time, along with Woody Guthrie, Ry Cooder and other hallowed names. His music was included in the blockbuster BBC TV show *A Musical Tour of Scotland*, and Reid was featured in the Rhino Records **Acoustic Music of the 90's** collection, along with a "who's who" line-up of other artists including Richard Thompson, Jerry Garcia & Leo Kottke.

In 1980 Reid published ***A New Frontier in Guitar***, the first book about the partial capo, and in 1984 he wrote ***Modern Folk Guitar***, the first college textbook for folk guitar. Quite possibly the first modern person to publish and record with the partial capo, he is almost certainly the most prolific arranger and composer of partial capo guitar music, and is responsible for most of what is known about the device. He lives in southern Maine with his family.

Made in the USA
San Bernardino, CA
25 August 2016